Human Rights

in Canada

pq Laurier
Studies in
Political
Philosophy

Laurier Studies in Political Philosophy Series

Global migration, MTV, transnational capital, and colonialism have given birth to a new and smaller world. To a greater degree than at any other time in remembered history, different cultures are brought together to live side by side. This close proximity has brought new mixtures and exciting possibilities—and also new struggles and conflicts. From many quarters comes an urgent call to build a sense of political belonging and unity in a diversity of voices. The call to unity is not, however, for uniformity or hegemony in one particular way of life. The unity to which we refer requires a rethinking and reconceptualization of existing philosophical paradigms that guide our relationships with others. In the spirit of intercultural dialogue, our Laurier Studies in Political Philosophy series is dedicated to exploring key challenges to our changing world and its needs. We are particularly interested in submissions that challenge dominant existing frameworks and approaches. We invite submissions in areas including Multicultural Theory, Aboriginal Studies and Philosophy, Post-colonialism, Globalization, Critical Race Theory, Feminism, and Human Rights Philosophy.

Editorial Committee:

James Tully, Political Science, University of Victoria
Rhoda E. Howard-Hassmann, Canada Research Chair in International Human
    Rights, Wilfrid Laurier University
Frank Cunningham, Philosophy, University of Toronto
Lynda Lange, Philosophy, University of Toronto
Audra Simpson, Anthropology, Columbia University
Sonia Sikka, Philosophy, Ottawa
Bidyut Chakrabarty, Political Science, University of Delhi
Allison Weir, Philosophy, Wilfrid Laurier University
Chandrakala Padia, Political Science, and Director of Women's Studies,
    Banaras Hindu University
Dale Turner, Native American Studies, Dartmouth
Michael Murphy, Political Science, University of Northern British Columbia
Kimberly Rygiel, Political Science, Wilfrid Laurier University
Ashwani K. Peetush, Series Editor, Philosophy, Wilfrid Laurier University

For more information, please contact the **Series Editors:**

Ashwani K. Peetush
Associate Professor of Philosophy
Wilfrid Laurier University
75 University Avenue West
Waterloo, ON N2L 3C5
Phone: (519) 884-0710 ext. 3874
Fax: (519) 883-0991
Email: apeetush@wlu.ca

Lisa Quinn
Associate Director
Wilfrid Laurier University Press
75 University Avenue West
Waterloo, ON N2L 3C5
Phone: (519) 884-0710 ext. 2034
Fax: (519) 725-1399
Email: lquinn@wlu.ca

DOMINIQUE CLÉMENT

Human Rights

in Canada

A History

Wilfrid Laurier University Press acknowledges the financial support of the Government of Canada through the Canada Book Fund for our publishing activities. This work was supported by the Research Support Fund.

Library and Archives Canada Cataloguing in Publication

Clément, Dominique, 1975–, author
  Human rights in Canada : a history / Dominique Clément.

(Laurier studies in political philosophy)
Includes bibliographical references and index.
Issued in print and electronic formats.

ISBN 978-1-77112-163-7 (paperback).—ISBN 978-1-77112-165-1 (epub). — ISBN 978-1-77112-164-4 (pdf)

  1. Human rights—Canada—History. 2. Human rights—Social aspects—Canada. I. Title. II. Series: Laurier studies in political philosophy series

JC599.C3C542 2015   323.0971   C2015-905237-8
                                             C2015-905238-6

Front-cover image: Shutterstock image 80134582. Cover design by David Drummond. Text design by Angela Booth Malleau.

This book is printed on FSC® certified paper and is certified Ecologo. It contains post-consumer fibre, is processed chlorine free, and is manufactured using biogas energy.

Printed in Canada

Dedicated to Jill

Contents

Additional Resources

Canada's Human Rights History
www.HistoryOfRights.ca

Canada's Human Rights History is a site dedicated to exploring every aspect of Canada's rights revolution. It is a research and teaching portal for the study of social movements, state policy, and law. In addition to providing information on critical human rights moments and controversies throughout Canadian history, the site provides access to an extensive collection of archival materials. It also contains detailed reading lists, links to other resources, and information on conferences, publications, research funding, and recent events. Unlike most historical websites, this site is not static but, rather, new content is added as the author's scholarship evolves.

Acknowledgements

THIS BOOK IS THE PRODUCT of almost twenty years of study. It began with an honours thesis in 1997 on the Gouzenko Affair. Since then, my passion has been the study of human rights history in Canada. The writing of this book was ultimately precipitated by two fortuitous opportunities in 2012. In that year I was hired to consult for the Canadian Human Rights Commission. The commission wanted a brief history of the (to use their word) "evolution" of human rights in Canada. For many years now, human rights commissions have been struggling to fulfill their mandate. Not only are they facing extensive cuts to their budgets while the number of complaints is growing, but they are facing a much more diverse array of complaints than was originally envisioned when the legislation was written. I was asked to facilitate a discussion around the origins and evolution of human rights law to help plan a more viable future. It was a welcome opportunity to engage professionals outside academe. That experience inspired me to write this book. I want to thank the commission and its staff for their comments and ideas, some of which have become an important part of this book.

In that same year, I was invited to be a member of the Canadian Museum for Human Rights' National Advisory Council. It is telling that the first national museum built in over a generation, and the first one outside Ottawa, is committed to human rights. In the two years preceding the inaugural opening in 2014, I was privileged to participate in regular meetings where we discussed and debated content for the museum. These encounters were some of the most exciting of my career. They were an opportunity to engage with many of the leading human rights practitioners in Canada. It was a wonderful opportunity to contribute to the creation of a national institution. It was also during these meetings that I developed the central arguments in this book.

This book is based on a wide array of secondary and primary sources. I would, however, like to highlight three texts in particular: Michel Ducharme's *Le concept de liberté au Canada à l'époque des révolutions atlantiques,* Ross Lambertson's *Repression and Resistance*, and the Osgoode Society for Canadian Legal History's series on state trials. Historians are still new to the study of human rights, and these studies have helped shape some of my ideas. I also wish to thank the peer reviewers for their comments. I am especially grateful to Michael Carroll (MacEwan University) and Lucie Lamarche (Université du Québec à Montréal), who took the time to review drafts of this manuscript. Their feedback has improved this book immeasurably.

Preface

IS THERE SUCH A THING as a Canadian rights culture? Rights talk in Canada has evolved dramatically in recent history. In the past, Canadians largely defined rights as civil liberties, which meant the rights to free speech, association, assembly, religion, press, due process, and voting. Rhetoric surrounding discrimination as late as the 1950s was largely confined to race, religion, and ethnicity. Today, the language of rights has been appropriated to apply to a remarkable range of issues. Discrimination is banned in human rights law on the basis of race or colour, religion, ethnicity, or national origin, place of origin, sex (including pregnancy), sexual harassment, age, physical and mental disability, marital status, pardoned conviction, sexual orientation, family status, dependence on alcohol or drugs, language, social condition, source of income, seizure of pay, political belief, and gender identity and expression. The rights of Aboriginal peoples and ethnic and linguistic minorities are constitutionally protected. For historians, this is a noteworthy development. Not too long ago, most Canadians would have balked at the idea of criminalizing hate speech or prohibiting sexual harassment at work.

This book is both a history of human rights in Canada and an attempt to better understand our rights culture. I attempt to integrate the experience of Aboriginal peoples, albeit this an imposing challenge given the lack of scholarship as well as Aboriginal peoples' ambivalent relationship to human rights in the past. I also draw on sources in French. In part, this is a response to what I see as a disturbing trend that remains pervasive in Canadian historiography: the tendency to study French and English Canadian history as separate fields. Most Canadian historians do not conduct research in both languages, or have chosen to assume that the experiences of these two communities are so different as to require separate studies. In this way, historians are failing their discipline. Certainly, in the context of Canada's human rights history, French and English Canadians have formed a dialectical relationship that has produced a uniquely Canadian rights culture. Even if we accept the premise that each group's history must be studied independently from the other—which I do not—the influence of the French and English communities on each other is simply too profound for us to study them separately.

The timing for a debate in Canada on our rights culture is propitious. A new national museum dedicated to human rights opened in Winnipeg in 2014. The Canadian Museum for Human Rights is forcing us to think concretely about the nature of our rights culture. In addition to funding national human rights institutions around the world, Canada provides extensive resources to domestic and transnational human rights advocacy organizations. We have, in essence, been exporting our rights culture for years. Yet there seems to be some ambivalence about what constitutes our rights culture. Canadians' ideas of rights have expanded so quickly—and in such a short period of time— that even human rights agencies are struggling to adapt to a host of new grievances. It is essential that we develop a better understanding of our rights culture if we are to adequately confront new rights claims at home while promoting human rights abroad. An essential beginning to such an endeavour is understanding our own human rights history.

Introduction

NO ISSUE HAS PROVEN MORE bitterly controversial over the past generation than the recognition and enforcement of human rights. We have justified going to war in order to protect human rights. We bomb cities in other countries to prevent atrocities or to liberate women denied the right to go to school. Canadians are divided over whether hate speech is free speech or a form of discrimination that should be criminalized. The death penalty violates the right to physical security. Doctors are insisting on the right to refuse to perform abortions, and pharmacists on the right to refuse to dispense birth control, because of their religious views. Marriage officiates have insisted for the same reason on their right to refuse to marry same-sex couples. Environmentalists are claiming that if a government fails to prevent a company from polluting the environment, and as a result some people die, it is a violation of the right to life. Our right to property is violated when property values decline due to toxic waste dumps or water pollution. And so on.

Human rights is the language we use to frame the most profound—and the most commonplace—grievances. Gloria Taylor, a British Columbia woman suffering from a degenerative illness, sparked a national debate around the right to die with dignity that ultimately led the Supreme Court of Canada to strike down the Criminal Code prohibition on assisted suicide in 2015.[1] Homophobic hate-mongers have succeeded in launching a national debate around free speech to enable them to distribute

1

leaflets to people's homes condemning sexual minorities. The 1999 war in Kosovo and the 2001 invasion of Afghanistan are routinely justified as humanitarian interventions intended to protect human rights. The post-9/11 "war on terror" led to a host of rights violations: Guantanamo Bay, the torture of Afghan prisoners, and antiterror laws that included arbitrary search and detention powers. After several weeks of widespread protests in Quebec throughout the summer of 2012, which mobilized hundreds of thousands of people for daily marches in Montreal alone, the Liberal provincial government passed Bill 78. The law, introduced and passed with alacrity, is one of the most draconian laws in Canadian history: it essentially banned public protests and gatherings. The right to privacy is threatened by new technologies—something that was made abundantly clear in 2013 when leaked documents revealed the existence of a massive phone surveillance operations by governments in Britain, Canada, and the United States. Climate change, the effects of which we are only beginning to understand, may very well kill more people than any mass slaughter by a state. We live in the age of rights, and the age of rights violations.

The purpose of this book is to understand how and when human rights became Canadians' primary language for social change. I suggest that Canada has its own unique rights culture and that it is possible to identify those rights that are (and are not) part of our rights culture. To accomplish this task, I explore the history of human rights in Canada. Our rights culture is most easily identifiable in those rights that are codified in law. Human rights statutes and the *Charter of Rights and Freedoms*, in particular, have special status because they are considered foundational and paramount to other laws. But human rights are not simply law; they are a dialogue. This book posits that human rights are a sociological and historical phenomenon as well as a legal fact. Our rights culture is constitutive of those rights that are deeply embedded in the practices of social and political life. To identify those rights that constitute our rights culture, I document how rights have been defined in political debates, the media, social movements, the law, and foreign policy. As we will see, tolerance for religious minorities, a respect for collective rights, and a commitment to equality, for example, are characteristic of Canada's rights culture. Our rights culture is also historically contingent. The idea of human rights has evolved throughout history. "Rights cannot be defined once and for all," insists historian Lynn Hunt, "because their emotional basis continues to shift, in part in reaction to declarations of rights. Rights remain open to question because our sense of who has rights and what those rights are constantly changes. The human rights revolution is by definition unending."[2] I reject the notion that rights somehow stand above politics or exist in the abstract outside our community. To say that we have a rights culture is to argue that rights are always changing and that rights have a "social life" in that they are a product of our society.

Legal scholars and political scientists have long dominated the study of human rights around the world. Over the past decade, however, that has begun to change. There is an emerging scholarship in most disciplines on the nature and impact of rights discourse. A historical-sociological approach to human rights can offer unique insights into what is perhaps the most profound social, political, and legal phenomenon of the past century. Legal scholars are likely to focus on the judiciability of rights. Sociologists, for their part, tend to be skeptical of a legal approach to rights. This is not to say that rights are not intimately tied to the law. Of course they are. Rather, from a sociological point of view, human rights derive from society rather than from an abstracted pre-social individual. Law matters only insofar as it inhibits or facilitates the realization of rights in practice. A proper sociology of human rights goes beyond abstract universalism and recognizes that each society has its own rights culture that is socially constructed. We can identify this rights culture by historicizing the emergence and development of rights claims in Canada through social, political, and legal actors and institutions.

Human rights are not immutable. They are continually adapting as times change. Much of the history of human rights in Canada is about extending recognition to newly recognized classes of people. Different societies can certainly agree on a universal set of abstract principles. But each society determines the nature and implementation of rights in practice. This process, however, is highly contested. The history of human rights is not a linear process of new rights claims but rather a history of defending existing rights. My primary argument is that human rights are always contested but that the nature of human rights is such that they invariably lead to new rights claims that build upon existing recognized rights.

Understanding Canada's rights culture begins with understanding its history. Several years ago, two historians interviewed Kalmen Kaplansky, one of the founders of the Jewish Labour Committee. A war veteran born in Poland and fluent in Yiddish and English, Kaplansky was appointed national director of the committee in 1946. His organization was at the forefront of the campaigns that led to the first antidiscrimination laws in Canada. Curiously, during the interview, Kaplansky struggled to explain why he never campaigned to include sex alongside race, ethnicity, and religion in antidiscrimination legislation. It was not that he and the other members of the Jewish Labour Committee opposed women's equality. They simply took certain gender roles for granted, as common sense. In other words, it did not occur to them at the time.[3] This was not unusual. In 1959, the Vancouver Council of Women—the leading women's rights organization in the province, and one of the largest in Canada at the time—passed a resolution calling for antidiscrimination legislation that would recognize race, colour, religion, and ancestry. The resolution did not include sex discrimination.[4] By the 1970s, however, the Jewish Labour Committee was campaigning alongside the Vancouver Council of Women to include sex discrimination in human rights legislation.

In this way, human rights have a history. Perhaps because human rights are premised on the idea that they are timeless, universal, and inalienable, it is easy to assume that human rights have no history. Yet before the advent of the rights revolution, people were just as likely to articulate grievances using the language of socialism or Christianity.[5] At a meeting of the Victoria School Board in 1922, for instance, trustee Bertha P. Andrews condemned the systemic segregation of Asians in the schools as "a violation of the fundamental principles of British justice and even a greater violation of the basic principles of our Christian religion."[6] Such appeals to shared religious values were not uncommon in the past. Others, such as blacks who faced discrimination at work and in state policy, framed their grievances in the language of dignity or citizenship when appealing to the state for redress.[7] Workers, too, rarely framed their grievances as human rights.[8] Rather, they spoke of economic justice, or in some cases framed their vision for social change by appealing to the principle of industrial democracy (transforming the workplace to operate according to the same standards that guided democratic institutions). In this way, workers challenged the power of employers to dictate employment conditions.[9] And there are numerous instances of activists who have rejected framing their grievances in the language of rights. Mahatma Gandhi and Martin Luther King, for instance, expressed reservations about rights talk. Many feminists and gay liberationists in Canada have rejected rights talk as incompatible with their vision for social change.[10] Rights talk is nonetheless pervasive. It has emerged as the dominant language people use to express their claims against the state and society.

Rights talk has become especially pronounced since the 1970s. To say that Canadians experienced a rights revolution at that time is to argue that rights talk has become a common vernacular for framing grievances. There are innumerable examples of how human rights have had a profound impact on Canada: we have established one of the most sophisticated human rights legal regimes in the world; we have largely abandoned the principle of Parliamentary supremacy; we have produced a unique human rights movement; and we have become an advocate for human rights as a cornerstone of international politics. Human rights have expanded to encompass a wide range of issues that would have surprised even the most ardent rights advocates fifty years ago.

Human rights are the rights one has simply by virtue of being human. They affirm the moral worth of every human being and take priority over all other claims.[11] A right must be recognized by other people to exist and must be secured through human action. A right is an entitlement premised on a widely held set of beliefs about the nature of that entitlement; even when it is not recognized in law, a right emerges from a moral or ideological belief.[12] With every human right comes a correlative duty for the rest of us to respect and help realize those rights. Human rights are an essential element of any democracy committed to protecting the minority from oppression by the majority. Rights protect human agency and are the language we use to adjudicate conflicts between individuals and civil society or the state. They connect citizens to a wider community of humanity that transcends the nation-state. Human rights are grounded on the presumption of the equal worth and dignity of all human beings. In addition to the right to physical security and dignity—which includes the right to be free from torture and degradation—equal treatment and the freedom to determine one's own destiny are elemental human rights principles. These principles are not absolute but they are universal and inalienable and they existed prior to law.[13]

From a legal point of view, human rights derive from an abstract pre-social individual who has rights by simple virtue of her humanity. In theory, there is no limit to how we define human rights, and there is no such thing as a rights culture because rights exist outside of society. So when lawyers and judges debate human rights, they are appealing to abstract principles. In contrast, in the sociological tradition, "any discussion of human rights should be firmly linked to the capacity of the state and society at large to guarantee the enjoyment of those rights."[14] A historical-sociological approach posits that human rights are not an abstract principle. Rather, they are a particular type of social practice. A historical-sociological approach can help us understand how and why human rights have emerged as a powerful social force, as well as those social conditions that made rights significant in a particular historical moment. A proper theory of human rights, I suggest, can only be developed by exploring the intersection of politics, law, and social movements. As Mikael Madsen and Gert Verschraegen explain, human rights become real when there is a broad consensus around the principles the underlay rights: "For human rights to have social meaning, they must become institutionalized socially and become embedded in people's mindset as well as in the day-to-day workings of societal institutions such as the judiciary, the schooling system, healthcare and the family."[15] In other words, a historical-sociological approach helps us understand the societal preconditions for the emergence of human rights.

Rights have, throughout history, been a rallying cry for those committed to equality, inclusivity, and diversity rather than exclusion and privilege. Conflict is at the very heart of human rights: it is a language that the weak appropriate to challenge the powerful. It is an effective language for framing our grievances because human rights—unlike socialism, for instance—represent a vision for social change that is embraced and accepted by the weak and the powerful alike. At the same time, the practice of human rights differs among communities. "Rights culture" refers to the way a community interprets and applies rights in practice. Canada's rights culture is most apparent in those rights that are codified in law. But human rights are not simply law;

in fact, the law is simply a reflection of existing social practices. To have social meaning, human rights must be part of our daily lives and integral to social institutions, from the courts to our schools and our families.[16] Our rights culture is constitutive of those rights that are deeply embedded in the practices of social and political life. To say we have a rights culture is to assert that rights are a product of community and that they evolve in tandem with community. Rights are not above politics, nor do they exist in the abstract outside our community. They do not exist on some higher moral plane akin to religious faith; they are a product of law, society, and politics. There may indeed be universal principles that (should) apply to every human being, but putting rights into practice is contingent on a society's rights culture. Perhaps the only genuinely universal human right, as Hannah Arendt once suggested, is the right to have rights. In other words, the only universal human right is to belong to a community that recognizes and protects rights. A stateless person has no human rights.[17]

In sum, although rights are a moral claim, it is misleading to suggest that they are based on universal truths. In fact, human rights have an instrumental or political function.[18] People frame their grievances and their vision for social change using the language of rights. Human rights have a social life in that they emerge from shared understandings of what rights should be. It follows that every society has its own rights culture. Human rights have universal appeal as abstract principles, but they are not premised on a shared universal understanding. Rather, institutions, social practice, historical context, and resistance shape rights cultures.

It is easy to take the idea of human rights for granted. Who but a dictator could possibly disagree that human rights are a good thing? Actually, the validity of human rights has been contested throughout history. Jeremy Bentham famously described rights as "nonsense upon stilts" because of the social nature of morality and law. He preferred to base laws on a utilitarian calculation of objective pleasure/pain and happiness rather than an abstract ideal. Karl Marx saw rights as emerging alongside capitalist modes of production to protect property, which served the interests of the bourgeois class. Both men saw rights as individualistic and egoistic.[19] Rights encourage individuals to focus on their self-interest rather than the collective good. In other words, rights subsume the needs or values of the community to those of the individual. Many of the notable philosophers we associate with popularizing the rights of man—Hugo Grotius, Thomas Hobbes, John Locke, Thomas Paine, Jean-Jacques Rousseau—did not mean human rights in the way we do today. None of them, for instance, seriously considered extending equal rights to all human beings irrespective of gender, race, and religion. Thomas Jefferson had no difficulty writing about the rights of men in the American constitution while possessing his own slaves. Also, none of these men struggled over the inherent conflict between individual rights and the public good.

Debates surrounding the validity of rights continue today. Some argue that human rights are a Western concept and that they are culturally relative. Also, linking culture to rights has led to clashes between individual rights and collective cultural rights. For example, should religious tribunals (e.g., *sharia* courts) be given the force of law in divorce proceedings? Should the Quebec government be allowed to impose French-language requirements on schools and businesses? Others disagree over periodization: Is the idea of human rights rooted in ancient civilizations (the Code of Hammurabi, for instance, or the philosophy of Aristotle), or in religious tradition? Did the principle gain popular acceptance because of the Holocaust? Did the United Nations and the Universal Declaration of Human Rights spur the rights revolution? Or did the rights revolution emerge in the 1970s as the Cold War began to decline? For others, the debate is about competing ideologies. Some labour historians lament that the labour movement has abandoned the principles of industrial democracy in favour of advocating for human rights. Feminists have questioned whether a gender-neutral language of rights has undermined the law's capacity to address rights violations that are unique to women. Another debate is over whether economic, social, and cultural rights are as legitimate as political and civil rights. More fundamentally, are human rights derived from a moral imperative or are they a product of state formation and politics? Without a doubt, this is an exciting and controversial field of study.

My purpose with this book is far more modest: to demonstrate the malleability of human rights discourse by showing how our society has produced a unique rights culture. As historian E.J. Hobsbawn suggests, human rights discourse is the natural language of politics because "it provides a built-in moral backing for any demand or action."[20] Or, to quote philosopher Jürgen Habermas, human rights "constitute the only language in which the opponents and victims of murderous regimes and civil wars can raise their voices against violence, repression and persecution, again injuries to their human dignity."[21] Martha Minow, an American legal scholar, believes that rights discourse has the potential to constrain those with power by exposing and challenging hierarchies of power.[22] According to Canadian political scientist Miriam Smith, people outside the hegemonic classes can politicize their grievances and gain recognition from mainstream members of society by framing their demands in the language of rights. Of course, rights discourse is not the sole preserve of the marginalized. All citizens use the rhetoric of rights to advance claims against public and private institutions. Yet as sociologist Evelyn Kallen has surmised, human rights have the greatest potential for those who lack power: "For minority populations, by definition, lacking the power to vastly change their disadvantaged status, the human rights approach provides a positive avenue through which to seek redress against past human rights violations and through which to seek new protections for their fundamental human rights in law and public policy."[23]

I also intend this book to demonstrate how rights are histor-ically contingent. In other words, we can identify the boundaries and limits of Canada's rights culture at different moments in our history. The term human rights had very different connotations in the past than it does today. Until the mid-twentieth century, Canada's rights culture was constitutive of only those most fun-damental of freedoms: speech, association, assembly, religion, press, voting, and due process. Traditions inherited from Britain and France, as well as nineteenth-century struggles over represen-tative democracy, emphasized political and civil rights. Canada's rights culture began to undergo a profound transformation in twentieth century, when formal legal equality for women and minorities, social and cultural rights, and a humanitarian foreign policy entered Canadians' human rights vernacular. Canada's rights culture evolved from simply prohibiting abusive acts by the state and overt forms of discrimination to embracing the principle of substantive equality. A commitment to multicultur-alism has shaped our rights culture; so has the impact of having English, French, and Aboriginal peoples bound within a single nation-state. However flawed the Canadian state's policies may be towards Aboriginal peoples, French Canadians, and ethnic minorities, their presence has resulted in a rights culture that is attentive to collective rights. We have also created the most sophisticated human rights legal regime in the world. Human rights may be a universal language, but rights cultures differ.

When documenting the history of Canada's rights culture, we must distinguish between civil liberties and human rights. Unlike Americans, for example, we do not frame rights as "civil rights," which in Canada is a constitutional term referring nar-rowly to property rights.[24] The distinction between civil liberties and human rights reflects ideological disagreements surround-ing the validity of rights claims. Thus, when a federation of social movement organizations was formed in 1972 to defend rights, its members believed that the conceptual distinction was significant enough to burden the organization with a cumbersome title: the

Canadian Federation of Civil Liberties and Human Rights Associations.[25] Canadians have long associated the term civil liberties with a narrow conception of rights as limited to civil and political rights. *Civil liberties* are rights that date back to the early stages of state formation and that are necessary to the functioning of a liberal capitalist democratic state: due process, voting, speech, religion, association, assembly, and a free press. Over time, civil liberties have also become associated with the principle of equal treatment and non-discrimination. *Human rights* is a more expansive conception of rights: it refers to civil liberties as well as to a host of economic, social, and cultural rights that have become popularized in the twentieth century. The Universal Declaration for Human Rights, for instance, includes such rights as education, social security, and employment.

For some, this distinction is based on profound philosophical distinctions. Civil libertarians abhor unnecessary restrictions on individuals in their pursuit of the good life. They believe that people must be free from restraint as they carry out their desires. Equality is based in procedural law, not in substantive conditions; in other words, liberal democracies promise one law for all citizens but do not guarantee that the law will not produce inequalities among citizens. In contrast, human rights advocates have sought to ensure individuals' capacity to formulate their desires and goals. This definition of rights considers lack of education, food, health care, or training as equally restrictive on an individual's freedom. Human rights, from this point of view, are those rights that guarantee an individual's capacity (rather than simply the opportunity) to bring about what he or she desires.

Many human rights scholars reject this crude dichotomy between what is often referred to as negative and positive freedom. In theory, the latter requires state action whereas the former only requires state inaction. Many experts believe that because of limited resources, it would be dangerous to define housing or education as human rights.[26] Their argument is a paper tiger. It is hardly impractical to impose economic obligations on the state;

after all, consider the enormous costs involved in maintaining a justice system to ensure the right to due process. We choose not to provide adequate housing to all Canadians, not because we lack the resources but for political and economic reasons.[27] Isaiah Berlin, a renowned liberal philosopher who rejected positive rights, nonetheless acknowledged that "to offer political rights, or safeguards against intervention by the state, to men who are half-naked, illiterate, underfed, and diseased is to mock their condition; they need medical help or education before they can understand, or make use of, an increase in their freedom."[28] Yet although the dichotomy between negative and positive rights may lack a convincing philosophical basis, it has nonetheless historically shaped how many Canadians think about rights. The history of Canada's rights culture is, therefore, a history of abstract and sometimes contradictory claims. This conflict lies at the heart of our rights culture.

A society with a strong rights culture allows individuals to make rights claims even though, at the time, they are not recognized by the state or civil society. Rights discourse enables people to frame their grievances in abstract principles that are already widely accepted. Gays and lesbians—and, more recently, the transgendered—have successfully appropriated rights discourse to challenge the power of the sexual majority to define what is "normal."[29] Canada was one of the first countries to recognize same-sex marriage and to prohibit discrimination on the basis of gender identity. In this way, social movements have been essential to the rights revolution.[30] Still, human rights are only tangibly realized through law.[31] Human rights are, by their very nature, statist. Social movements must seek out the state to have their rights claims recognized. Throughout history the law has been the only tool that can enforce human rights. Does this mean that human rights are limited to legal rights or that they are derived from the state? Not at all. In fact, rights claims have a powerful moral force. Determining the meaning of human rights at any point in history has been a social process that engages political, legal, and social actors.

Even so, where rights are the dominant vernacular, legal institutions play a central role in facilitating the emergence of new rights claims. The law shapes grievances and claim-making by requiring people to frame their grievances in the language of rights. The law, therefore, is a useful barometer for beginning to understand the boundaries of Canada's rights culture. After all, defining our rights culture is meaningless unless we also determine what it is *not*.[32] South Africa's constitution has incorporated social rights—to housing, health care, food, water, social security, and education—as well as the right to a healthy environment and to join a trade union. Canada's has not. Education, health care, food, and housing are not human rights in Canadian law. There is no human right to a safe and clean environment: few Canadians would frame Alberta's oil sands as a human rights violation. Our constitution recognizes no right to bear arms. Until 2012, discrimination towards transgendered people was not prohibited by any law. No law guarantees a human right to peace or against war—at best, this is an aspiration. Canada is a signatory to human rights treaties that include a host of civil, political, social, economic, and cultural rights that have not been incorporated into domestic law. Among these rights are the right to rest and leisure and to a standard of living that includes sufficient food, clothing, housing, and medical and social services. Abortion may no longer be illegal, but it is not a human right.[33] The Supreme Court of Canada ruled in 1988 that the law regulating abortions violated the *Charter of Rights and Freedoms* because the implementation of the law was flawed. Unlike the United States, the Canadian Court did not place constraints against future governments from introducing legislation restricting abortions (until 2015, for instance, New Brunswick required the approval of two doctors for any abortion performed in a public hospital). A right that exists only in the voluntary absence of a legal restriction is not a true human right.

To understand the boundaries of Canada's rights culture we must also explore the nuances of rights that are entrenched in law. South Africa explicitly guarantees the right to privacy in its Bill of Rights, whereas Canadian law only recognizes the right to privacy in statute. We have a right of access to government information in Canada, but the statutes relating to that right are filled with loopholes and have become notorious in recent years for *restricting* public access.[34] Although human rights law in this country is largely uniform, there are notable distinctions: political opinion, pardoned criminal conviction, social condition, gender identity, and addictions are prohibited grounds for discrimination in some jurisdictions but not in others. Canadian law recognizes that women should be treated equally, but not that they should be equal. Systemic inequality for women in Canada is evident in much lower rates of pay, the feminization of poverty, and weak representation in business and politics. There is a right to *attempt* to create a labour union, and to belong to one, but no human right to have a union.[35] A right to property has not prevented resource extraction on Indigenous lands. Religious minorities cannot claim a collective right that overrides individual rights, as we have seen with recent controversies in Quebec.[36] Multiculturalism has engendered a powerful backlash while doing little to address the social and economic inequality faced by minorities.

This is our rights culture as it exists today. As we will see, this is a dramatically different vision of rights than what existed for most of the twentieth century. And by no means is this definition static or comprehensive—our rights culture is always evolving. That the law has failed to recognize some human rights does not prevent people from making rights claims. Over time, these claims might gain public support and be incorporated into law. Understanding the full scope of Canada's rights culture begins with an understanding of history. Historians are ideally positioned to demonstrate how human rights have been put into practice.

Historians have been late to the study of human rights. Until recently, most of the literature on human rights was in philosophy or law, which tended to ignore the social practice of rights.[37] Ahistorical claims are pervasive in the scholarship on human rights. Part of the problem is that the first historians who sought to document a history of human rights began with such a broad definition that any reference to *rights* became part of the history of *human rights*. That is why the two most popular textbooks on the history of human rights begin with the founding of the world's major religions, or with the ancient Greeks.[38] Yet there is something disingenuous about attributing the origins of human rights to religion. Religious intolerance, as we will see, was commonplace in Canadian history. The Catholic Church, for example, initially opposed the principle of human rights, going so far as to explicitly condemn the French *Declaration of the Rights of Man and of the Citizen* in 1791 as blasphemous and heretical. It was only in the twentieth century that the Catholic Church repudiated its earlier rejection of the doctrine of human rights.[39] Only in the twentieth century did the world's major religions appropriate human rights, as a way to reframe long-held beliefs and values. As historians, we should be cautious in how we frame our human rights history, especially when the historical actors themselves would never have conceived of their beliefs in the way we understand human rights today.[40]

Revisiting our history is essential if we are to better understand our rights culture. The justification for human rights, as Michael Ignatieff suggests, is based not on a foundational philosophy but rather "on human history, on what we know is likely to happen when human beings do not have the protection of rights."[41] Besides, there is no true "origin" in the history of human rights. Instead, there are moments in history that shock and unsettle communities. When rights abuses are especially egregious—including during moments of extreme brutality and violence—they can lead to profound change, but such abuses can continue afterwards in other forms. Challengers invariably emerge who question our beliefs about rights, introduce new interpretations, and seek to undermine past accomplishments. Human rights history is as much a story of defending against the forces of retrenchment as it is about progress. Historians must avoid presenting the history of humanity as linear progress. We should also be careful not to assume that the mere existence of an international human rights declaration, whether it is the League of Nations treaty (1920) or the Universal Declaration of Human Rights (1948), reflects the popularization of human rights values. Focusing on treaties or famous thinkers can lead historians to produce false generalizations about the pervasiveness and nature of rights rhetoric. Canada's rights culture could easily be written as a product of European intellectuals, particularly British, but that would ignore our distinctive history.

The most important lesson that our history teaches us about Canada's rights culture is that it is liberal and individualistic. It ranks civil and political rights above economic, social, or cultural rights. New rights claims have emerged within a particular framework, one that acts as a type of filter in determining which claims become rights. A liberal structure has provided the dominant ideology of rights, and that structure has been deeply embedded in Canadian life since the early stages of state formation. Ian Mckay calls this the "liberal order framework." "A liberal order," according to Mckay,

> is one that encourages and seeks to extend across time and space a belief in the epistemological and ontological primary of the category "individual" ... Canada as a project can be defined as an attempt to plant and nurture, in somewhat unlikely soil, the philosophical assumptions, and the related political and economic practices, of a liberal order ... Liberalism begins when one accords a prior ontological and epistemological status to "the individual"—the human being who is the "proprietor" of him- or herself, and whose freedom should be limited only by voluntary obligations to others or to God, and by the rules necessary to obtain the equal freedom of other individuals.[42]

Such a framework is apparent in the types of rights claims that have become part of Canada's rights culture. Those moments in history when the boundaries of our rights culture expanded have followed a similar trajectory as mutations in the liberal framework. The rebellions, Confederation, the crises of war, the patriation of the constitution, and other moments in Canada's human rights history have reinforced the primacy of the liberal order and a particular conception of rights. The classical liberal model, which remained dominant until the mid-twentieth century, was based on an exaggerated notion of the individual, who was self-reliant and independent. Rights, as we will see, reflected this context: they were limited to basic civil and political rights to protect individual autonomy. Threats to the dominant liberal framework, as Mckay notes, were met with oppression and marginalization. Although it may seem contradictory to limit rights while at the same time proclaiming their primacy, these practices were in fact entirely consistent with refusing rights to those who challenged the dominant liberal order.

To understand Canada's rights culture, I will be focusing on moments in history when human rights transformed law, politics, social movements, and foreign policy. Sometimes this involved the institutionalization of rights; other times, the public assertion of new rights claims. The book is divided into five periods. Chapter 1 covers a long period from the rebellions to the First World War. Those decades were defined by state formation. Canada was a nation ostensibly born from an empire already founded on principles of justice and liberty after centuries of struggles against despotic monarchs. British justice was integral to the founding of the Canadian state. Yet the process of state formation in Canada was awash with vicious attacks on even the most sacred British liberties. Whether it was the rebellions or Confederation in 1867, it was evident that although rights did exist, they were subject to severe and sometimes arbitrary restrictions. This state of affairs was widely accepted, and it would continue throughout most of the early twentieth century. Chapter 2 ends in the early 1960s, a period defined by the first attempts to entrench as state policy the principle of non-discrimination. Not until 1944 was the first antidiscrimination law introduced in Canada, and even that was a weak and hollow piece of legislation designed to ban only the most obvious forms of discrimination. Several other antidiscrimination laws were passed over the next two decades, and they were similarly ineffective. Chapter 3, which covers the period from the 1960s to mid-1970s, sets the stage for the rights revolution. In 1962, Ontario passed the first human rights legislation, which eventually led to similar statutes being adopted in other jurisdictions in Canada. Meanwhile, several notable events, including the October Crisis of 1970, brought to light citizens' vulnerability to state imperatives. By this time, Canadians were increasingly using the language of human rights to articulate their grievances. In the decade to follow, which is the period addressed in Chapter 4, Canada experienced a genuine rights revolution. Its achievements, however, were highly contested. Chapter 5 covers more recent moments in Canadian history, when the contested nature of human rights became especially salient in public debate. In 1984, British Columbia became the first province to eviscerate its human rights programs and statute. Nonetheless, minorities continued to appropriate rights discourse to assert new claims. Their demands were bitterly resisted, especially around the divisive issue of sexual orientation.

Readers will note that 1948 does not figure prominently in the periodization for this book. Many historians attribute the beginnings of the international rights revolution to the Universal Declaration of Human Rights (UDHR), which the UN General Assembly passed in 1948 (a vote, as we will see, that Canada supported only grudgingly). In truth, this focus on 1948 simply reflects a common bias among scholars of international law and institutions, who largely neglect domestic developments.[43] The UDHR was a powerful symbol to be sure, but it was largely irrelevant in Canada at the time. This is not to say there were no important developments in the postwar period. Among other things, the UN symbolized the dominance of states in the international system and the dissociation of human rights from the theory of natural law.[44] Human rights were intimately associated with the modern state. But the significance of the postwar period is easily exaggerated. It was only beginning in the 1970s that the rights revolution became a reality.

Another way this book differs from recent historical accounts of human rights, most notably by Samuel Moyn and Lynn Hunt, is that it focuses on the local.[45] Too much of the new historical literature has focused on human rights as a global phenomenon. While the history of human rights in Canada has certainly been influenced by developments abroad, the global human rights revolution is largely a history apart. On the one hand, I agree with Moyn's assertion that "historians of locales, jealous of the specificities of their geographical domain, risk losing the integrative view that the larger view tends to afford."[46] It is essential to contextualize a nation's rights revolution within world history. On the other hand, documenting local responses is essential in understanding how abstract principles are translated into social practice. Human rights history may be global, but rights cultures are local. Human rights have evolved in Canada, not because of the existence of some abstract principle or in response to global developments, but because of circumstances specific to this country.

To explore the boundaries of Canada's rights culture, and how it has evolved historically, I focus on law, social movements, political culture, and Canadians' engagements abroad. No single study could possibly provide a comprehensive history of human rights violations or campaigns. Whether historians have been writing about class, race, gender, or sexuality, they have in effect documented the history of rights abuses and campaigns for redress. I focus instead on critical moments that facilitated the emergence and recognition of new rights claims. The central argument in this book is that there is a uniquely Canadian rights culture. Those rights that constitute our rights culture are derived not from an abstract principle but rather from a consensus in politics, law, and society that has evolved throughout history. For instance, as we will see, there was a clear consensus in the nineteenth century around such principles as free speech and freedom of religion. The nature of the principle was, of course, highly contested, but its legitimacy was unquestionable. Similarly, by the 1970s, a comparable consensus had emerged around the principle of non-discrimination. Central to this argument, however, is that our rights culture evolved within a liberal framework. Human rights have not been, and cannot be, transformative because past and future rights claims live within this framework.

In addition, I advance several arguments about history. First, since the founding of the nation-state, Canadians have spoken of rights largely in terms of "British justice" or "civil liberties." We can identify a moment in history beginning in the 1970s when human rights replaced civil liberties as the primary language of rights in Canada (and, therefore, the primary language of social change). What this means is that, unlike in the past, when people like Kaplansky spoke of rights but at the same time did not campaign for sex discrimination, by the 1970s campaigns for human rights were far less likely to contain such an inherent contradiction. This is not to say that all minorities' rights were recognized by the state. Rather, rights talk by this period in history was no longer founded on the principle of differential rights among citizens, and movements were already under way to seek equal rights for unrecognized minorities. Second, although there have been events in history when rights violations have shocked the nation and stimulated public debate, progress most often occurs when people—usually those who are targets of rights violations—act on the belief that something is unfair. Change begins when someone believes they are being treated unfairly and decides to take action. Non-state actors have been responsible for the most significant advances in human rights. Third, no study of human rights is possible without understanding the law. Rights may be framed as a moral imperative, but they do not exist in practice until they are recognized in law. Moreover—and this is a theme that informs some of the subtext throughout this book—the state can violate human rights through inaction or through fear of punishment. Some of the most egregious restrictions on, for instance, free speech, were laws that never resulted in a trial and conviction. We should never underestimate the chilling effect that the *threat* of prosecution can have on human rights.

CHAPTER 1

Liberty and State Formation

[Equality is that] monstrous fiction, which, by inspiring false ideas and vain expectations into men destined to travel in the obscure walks of laborious life, serves only to aggravate and imbitter that real inequality, which it can never remove; and which the order of civil life established as much as for the benefit of those whom it must leave in humbled state, as those whom it is able to exalt to a condition more splendid, but not more happy.

Men have a right to live by that rule; they have a right to justice, as between their fellows, whether their fellows are in public function or in ordinary occupation. They have a right to the fruits of their industry; and to the means of making their industry fruitful. They have a right to the acquisitions of their parents; to the nourishment and improvement of their offspring; to instruction in life, and to consolation in death. Whatever each man can separately do, without trespassing upon others, he has a right to do for himself; and he has the right to a fair portion of all which society, with all its combinations of skill and force, can do in his favour. In this partnership all men have equal rights; but not to equal things.

—Edmund Burke, *Reflections on the Revolution in France*

THERE IS COMMON MISCONCEPTION THAT, unlike the American or the French, the Canadian state was a product of a peaceable compromise rather than violence. In truth, the rights Canadians enjoyed at Confederation were the result of people fighting—and dying—for those rights. Thousands took up arms (or pens) to defend a more expansive conception of freedom. The history of human rights in Canada, therefore, begins with the process of state formation following the European conquest. This is not to say that Aboriginal peoples did not express beliefs that we might today associate with human rights. But they did not frame their grievances in the language of rights, and as we will see, they rarely did so until the late twentieth century. As historian J.R. Miller explains, human rights were

> culturally inappropriate for their societies. In their communities, rights were recognized and respected by an elaborate system of kin and clan requirements, and individual rights were subordinate to those of the collectivity. One owed obligations to kinfolk, including fellow clan members and those who were kin by marriage or ascription, that constrained one from acting in ways that violated the kinfolk or clan person's rights or interests ... Protecting rights was a matter of kinship obligation, not state action.[1]

European colonists brought their own traditions of rights when they conquered Aboriginal lands, and these traditions were imposed through the process of state formation. The state became the primary vehicle for institutionalizing rights and was often a site of contestation over the meaning of rights.

If there was a rights culture emerging in the colonies and most of the Western world in the eighteenth century, it was largely in response to state action. This was a transformative period. An emergent bourgeoisie was challenging aristocratic privilege and asserting a right to property irrespective of birthright, and this was commonly framed in terms of natural rights. The potential for social and physical mobility created by the Industrial Revolution and capitalism slowly undermined religious and aristocratic elites' monopoly over political and economic power. For the first time in history, the world's leading philosophers were committed to the idea of individual rights. John Locke (1632–1704), Jean-Jacques Rousseau (1712–1778), Thomas Paine (1737–1809), Mary Wollstonecraft (1759–1797), Thomas Jefferson (1743–1826), and others were engaging in fierce debates that would reshape the Western world. But they articulated a narrow conception of rights compared to today. Locke, for instance, defined rights as life, liberty, and estates. Jefferson asserted the right to life, liberty, and the pursuit of happiness. Paine, however, was driven from England for publishing a pamphlet critical of the government, while Jefferson was prosecuted under federal law for his writings. If there was a right to a free press, it was highly circumscribed. It would be another century before freedom of association was extended to workers.[2]

Rights talk in the colonies concerned a combination of basic liberties, which included due process, religion, speech, assembly, association, and a free press. These rights were often vulnerable to the dictates of authoritarian generals. Even by the standards of the time, governments in New France and (later) British North America engaged in repressive practices.[3] In 1677, for example, Governor General Buade de Frontenac of New France decreed that "no one could circulate collective petitions or hold 'any assemblies, [or] conventicles' without his expressed permission since unauthorized gatherings were usually a 'pretext for all the monopolies, cabals, and intrigues that evil-minded persons would wish to create.'"[4] Individual petitions were allowed, but only the Royal administration could represent collective interests. France's *lèse-Majesté* laws, which were exported to New France, severely punished all crimes against the state and the church. Acts of disrespect through word or gesture were punishable.[5] Even death was no escape: dead bodies could be prosecuted for offending His Majesty. The law had provisions for putting the memory of a deceased individual, or the corpse itself, on trial.[6] Between 1760, when the French surrendered and the regime ceased to function, and 1763, when the British established a new system of courts, British military courts dispensed justice for civilians. Trial by jury was not introduced until 1764 for criminal cases, and not until 1785 for civil cases. It was unclear for many years whether the right to habeas corpus extended to the colonies.[7]

The British conquest of New France in 1760 brought a particular rights culture to the colonies. This included the Magna Carta (1215), which limited the monarch's arbitrary power and promised certain basic freedoms of religion and due process. The constitutional crises in England in the seventeenth century, most notably the English Civil War (1642–51), produced a series of laws that became foundational to the British—and, later, Canadian—state. Among these were the Petition of Rights (1628), which restricted taxation, arbitrary imprisonment, and the use of martial law; the Bill of Rights (1689), which delineated the powers of the monarch and guaranteed elections, the freedom of Parliament, and some religious freedom; and the Habeas Corpus Act (1679), which confirmed the right against arbitrary imprisonment. After the Conquest, British governors routinely trampled on rights.[8] Among the most controversial of these governors were Guy Carleton (1768–78, 1785–95), a decorated career soldier who had participated in the attack on Louisburg and who had been wounded at the Battle of the Plains of Abraham; Robert Prescott (1796–99), who was with Carleton at the siege of Louisburg and whose administration so badly alienated French Canadians that he was recalled; and James Craig (1807–11), a distinguished soldier during the American Revolution and the Napoleonic Wars who sought to reduce French Canadians to a minority. These governors were especially hostile to elected officials, demands for reform, and any type of political dissent.[9] Carleton declared martial law during the American Revolution, and the British Parliament suspended the right to bail and a trial in the colonies between 1777 and 1783 for any person charged with abetting the revolutionaries. Frederick Haldimand, the governor of Quebec from 1778 to 1785, used these powers to imprison at least twenty-five men suspected of collaborating with Americans (including a journalist, Fleury Mesplet, who later founded the Montreal *Gazette*).[10] Carleton, who returned to replace Haldimand in 1785, shut down and imprisoned the editors of *Gazette du commerce et littéraire de Montréal* (one of only two journals in the colony) in 1779 for criticizing judges and writing about tolerance.[11] The *Alien Act*, passed in 1794, suspended the right to bail, speedy trial, and habeas corpus for persons accused of (not charged with) high treason; required the registration of all aliens and British subjects (forcing them to carry documents at all times); and empowered officials to deport foreigners at will and to imprison those who refused to cooperate. On 30 October 1794, General Prescott ordered all Frenchmen who had entered Lower Canada since 1 May to leave within twenty days. Almost one hundred men were imprisoned in the year following the law's enactment. The same statute redefined sedition to include any attempt to disturb the happiness of His Majesty's subjects, and the accused were denied the protections of the *Libel Act*.[12] This had the effect of banning any public utterance, no matter how moderate, that could be construed as criticism of the government or as fostering ill will towards the propertied classes.

The French Revolution raised the spectre of discontented French Canadians overthrowing the government. Once again, the government responded by restricting civil liberties, justifying these measures as necessary to the security of British North America.[13] The colonial legislature passed the *Better Preservation Act* in 1797, which suspended habeas corpus in cases of suspected treasonable practices and allowed the authorities to hold suspects indefinitely without charge. Craig—whose tenure as governor has been called the "reign of terror"—used the law to imprison the elected leaders of the *Parti canadien* from the Legislative Assembly without bail or trial.[14] Meanwhile, in Montreal, Chief Justice James Monk was busy addressing the grand jury for the case of David McLane. McLane was on trial for espionage and

for attempting to raise a fifth column to assist French revolutionaries to invade Lower Canada. Monk explained to the grand jury
that any collective violent resistance to law enforcement (e.g., a
riot) might be construed as levying war and, therefore, as high
treason (even if those involved had no treasonable intent).[15] The
trial ended with McLane's brutal execution: he was hanged, then
beheaded and quartered, and his remains burned in front of a
crowd of men, women, and children.

Craig also used the *Better Preservation Act* to shut down the
journal *Le Canadien*, which was a voice for reform in the colonies,
and threw the editors in jail (the printing press was confiscated
and sold at auction).[16] In fact, it was not uncommon during this
period for journalists to be imprisoned for defamation, libel, or
sedition and to use the courts to intimidate editors.[17] In 1810,
Chief Justice Sewell of Lower Canada explained to the grand jury
for *Le Canadien* case that freedom of the press did not mean the
right to criticize the government. Rather, the function of the
press was to aid in the preservation of order: "Any writing, therefore, which was 'detrimental to the public safety or happiness,'
which raised discontents against the ruling authorities, or whose
'effect is prejudicial to the public' could not be tolerated by government 'without a dereliction of its own fundamental principles.'"[18] In Lower Canada, the editor of the *patriote* journal *Le
Minerve*, Ludger Duvernay, was imprisoned three times. William
Lyon Mackenzie was temporarily expelled from the legislature of
Upper Canada for his writings in the *Colonial Advocate*. Between
1818 and 1820, Upper Canada prohibited all meetings of a political nature. Anyone found guilty could be imprisoned for life.

In 1837, after years of brutal repression, Louis-Joseph Papineau, Robert Nelson, and others led a rebellion in Lower Canada
against British power. The British responded to the uprisings
with the predictable spate of emergency legislation. Martial law
was declared in Upper and Lower Canada, which allowed the

governor in Lower Canada to put aside elected legislators and judges who were sympathetic to his political opponents. The British Parliament quickly replaced the legislature of Lower Canada with a Special Council in 1838 that was appointed by the governor.[19] In Upper Canada, the legislature suspended habeas corpus for people accused of treason or having knowledge of treasonous activities. It also passed the *Lawless Aggressions Act*, which facilitated the confiscation of property as well as the prosecution of rebels by providing for the selection of juries outside the jurisdiction, putting individuals on trial in absentia, trying civilians in military courts, and allowing regular courts to hear felony cases.[20] The legislature also passed a law empowering constables and justices of the peace to disperse any unlawful meeting or assembly and to arrest or detain the participants. Yet those who engaged in illegal acts to protect the Crown were given special immunities from prosecution.[21] In Lower Canada, the Special Council passed thirty ordinances to deal with the security threat; these, among other things, granted the governor special powers to search private dwellings and declared secret societies illegal and participation in such societies as treason.[22] The council implemented the highly unorthodox practice of putting civilians on trial in courts martial during peacetime.[23] The Court Martial Ordinance imposed the unusual provision of retroactive guilt; it also restricted access to defence counsel. Guilt was punishable by death. All told, the trials following the rebellions led to the execution of 32 men, the exile of 144 more, and 248 convictions for a host of crimes.[24] The newspapers *La Minerve*, *Vindicator*, and *The Constitution* were all shut down.[25]

The rebellions were a defining moment in the history of state formation in Canada. Although the *Quebec Act* (1774) and the *Constitutional Act* (1791) recognized certain basic rights for French Canadians, such as the right to exercise their religion and maintain civil law, in practice "imperial rule in the colony was intolerant."[26] The rebellions were, in part, a response to the brutal practices of British governors and their attempts to suppress the French minority. As historian Michel Ducharme explains in his seminal work on the concept of liberty during the rebellions, liberty was the rallying cry of colonial reformers in the nineteenth century. In an era of divine right of kings and aristocratic privilege, there was nothing more revolutionary than principles that challenged the legitimacy of the state and the social order.[27] *Modern liberty*, the philosophy undergirding the constitutionalists who opposed the rebellions, was rooted in the belief that liberty was founded on the assurance of individual rights (especially religion, speech, political participation, due process, and security). A monarchical political system was legitimate if it was founded on the guarantee of these freedoms through a Parliament and independent judiciary. In contrast, *republican liberty* was premised on the idea that all rights flowed from a free political system wherein political institutions represented the people. In other words, individual rights could change over time depending on the political system, and rights were protected so long as the political system was constitutive of the people.[28]

Within these political conflicts, which had their most tragic manifestation in the rebellions, we can discern a rights culture. Rights talk in nineteenth-century British North America encompassed only basic civil and political rights: to participate in the political system; to exercise one's religion; to express critical viewpoints (within certain limits); to organize and associate openly; and to be free from arbitrary detention or abuse.[29] There was a widespread belief that liberty, albeit often poorly defined even among its most vocal proponents, was essential to the legitimacy of the state.[30] Modernists argued that republicanism would place rights at the mercy of a minority of elected officials. Political legitimacy, according to the modernists, flowed from the recognition of certain inviolable rights: physical security, due process (including jury trial), religion, speech, and a free press, as well as the right to vote and own property.[31]

The republicans who drafted Lower Canada's 92 Resolutions, which became a manifesto for the *Patriotes*, made reference to similar rights including religion, physical security, and due process of law. Robert Nelson, one of the *Patriote* leaders, issued a Declaration of Independence in 1838 that made explicit reference to religious freedom, free speech, and trial by jury as well as the right to vote and to speak in French or English in all public matters.[32] William Lyon Mackenzie, the leader of Upper Canada's abortive insurrection, drafted a constitution in 1837 that recognized "civil and religious liberty" and provided guarantees against excessive bail and cruel and unusual punishment.[33] Republicans, though, were convinced that rights could be ensured only through participation in the political system, whereas modernists were equally convinced that such a system would put rights in jeopardy. The Sons of Liberty, a secret militant association of French Canadians led by Louis-Joseph Papineau, had been founded on the belief that "governments are instituted for the advantage of, and can justly exist only with the consent of those governed ... A government by choice is no less an inherent right of the people." The Sons of Liberty sought "strict equality before the law for all classes regardless of origin, language or religion."[34] Those beliefs, and British leaders' repressive tendencies towards French Canadians, made civil war inevitable. In his famous report to investigate the grievances that led to the rebellions, Lord Durham recommended the complete assimilation of the French population.[35]

The rebellions were a microcosm of a much broader ideological conflict dividing the Atlantic world in the eighteenth and nineteenth centuries. The idea of rights inspired campaigns against torture, slavery, and the death penalty in Europe and the Americas in the eighteenth century.[36] Liberals, drawing on ideas espoused by Locke, Rousseau, and Paine among others, rallied around the principle of natural (universal) rights and led revolutions against monarchical power. Conservatives, most notably Edmund Burke, reacted with a defence of traditional rights rooted in history and custom rather than abstract universal principles.[37] Historian Elizabeth Heaman describes these rights as the "rule of law, the right to a jury, the right to bear arms (if Protestant), a prohibition on excessive or cruel fines or punishments, and a series of parliamentary privileges and powers (such as free speech and control of taxation and armies)."[38] The inevitable consequence, however, was to deny rights to those who were not British in custom and practice, most notably Aboriginal peoples: "They did have contractual rights and they might also maintain some form of bodily human rights—protection against murder for example and perhaps starvation as well—but they weren't outfitted with the specifically British rights that other ethnic groups could claim."[39]

By the end of the eighteenth century, the nature and function of rights preoccupied some of the great philosophers of the age. Debates surrounding rights gained momentum throughout Europe and North America. Rights talk had entered mainstream political discourse for the first time in history. It is worth pointing out, however, that the expression and practice of rights in the nineteenth century was premised on a hierarchy among citizens. Slavery existed in the colonies until the 1793 Upper Canada antislavery law, but it lasted throughout the empire until an Imperial statute eliminated slavery in 1833. Declarations of rights, which were often part of the process of state formation in the nineteenth century—most notably France's *Declaration of the Rights of Man and of the Citizen* (1789) and the United States' *Bill of Rights* (1791)—presumed that not all people had the moral autonomy to exercise rights. Slaves, children, the poor, the insane, and women were deemed not to have this requisite autonomy. Declarations of liberal-democratic rights drew on a language of universality, yet they denied women and minorities basic political rights. Equality was based on procedural law, not in substantive conditions; in other words, liberal democracies promised one law for citizens, but they did not guarantee that the law would not discriminate among those citizens. In 1832, for instance, the Legislative Assembly of Lower Canada, which was dominated by the Patriotes, who were agitating for greater political freedom, passed laws prohibiting women from voting.[40]

Confederation in 1867 was another pivotal moment in the history of state formation in Canada. The lack of a bill of rights, however, raises the question of whether protecting individual rights was part of the original compact that led to the creation of the Canadian state. We should first acknowledge that the *British North America Act* did contain some rights. The constitution guaranteed French-language rights in Parliament and in Quebec's Legislative Assembly (including that statutes would be published in English and French), as well as the right to operate Catholic or Protestant schools. It also required periodic elections. True, the constitution contained no listing of rights similar to the American Bill of Rights. But as Janet Ajzenstat has shown in her study of Confederation, the founders were profoundly committed to rights.[41] They placed their faith in Parliament to protect liberty: Parliament's primary purpose was the protection and preservation of rights. A bill of rights was, therefore, unnecessary. This system of government, like its British counterpart, was premised on the idea of Parliamentary supremacy. Parliament could make or unmake any law, and no institution could override those laws. This philosophy, as one historian has noted, informed Canada's rights culture: "Rights are secure because Parliament is supreme and only when Parliament is supreme."[42] Human equality was closely linked to the principle of popular sovereignty. But whereas the Americans protected rights through a written constitution, Canadians articulated rights with reference to British liberties that were protected through customary law, historical precedents, and the supremacy of Parliament.

The founders' speeches were filled with assertions of liberty and rights. However, they did not speak of *human* rights. Rather, rights discourse was rooted in references to being British subjects and the rights derived from that tradition. For some historians, the fact that the Fathers of Confederation did not employ the language of human rights is irrelevant.[43] Those founders adhered

to the principles of human rights even when they did not frame
their grievances in that language. But did they? There remained
inherent contradictions in the supposed universality of rights
in the nineteenth century. Many advocates of rights sanctioned
slavery and were silent on women's rights. Rights, including the
right to vote and to practise religion, did not extend equally
to a significant proportion of the population because of their
race, ethnicity, religion, or gender. It was, at the very least, a
conception of rights restricted to only the most fundamental
liberties.[44] Moreover, this conception of rights was linked to citizenship. The principle that rights should belong to all irrespective of inherent qualities such as race or gender was not widely
accepted in the nineteenth century. It would be more accurate to
say that Confederation was founded on a particular conception
of rights expressed as British liberties. These liberties derived
from British history rather than abstract universal principles,
and they belonged to British subjects. This conception of rights
had remained largely unchanged since the rebellions with one
notable exception: the religious and linguistic rights of French
and English Canadians had become an integral component of the
compact that was at the heart of Canada's founding.

State formation involved the systemic exclusion of identifiable
classes of people—most notably non-Europeans and women—
from positions of influence in politics, business, and social life.
Education, as Timothy J. Stanley explains, was one way that governments inculcated minorities to accept exclusionary practices
in their daily lives: "If someone is being excluded, someone else is
concomitantly included. If someone is being oppressed, someone
else is being privileged. If someone is being exploited, someone
else is profiting."[45] This process included the construction of
people of British descent as native to the region and of Asians as
foreigners or outsiders: "Chinese/Canadian difference was one of
the key notions that regulated who had political rights and who

did not, determined economic opportunities, and shaped where and with whom people could live and even where they could be buried ... Racialized exclusions were integral to the governmental, economic, and social arrangements that had invented the territories of British Columbia and Canada and their institutions."[46] These and other exclusions shaped Canadians' relationship with the state and in turn influenced relationships within civil society.

Discrimination was a fact of life in Canada by the twentieth century: barbers refused to serve blacks, taverns posted signs banning Jews or Aboriginals, golf courses prohibited racial and religious minorities, hotels did not admit Aboriginal people, university fraternities and sororities and tennis and ski clubs excluded Jews, trade unions barred racial minorities, police and building inspectors harassed minority business owners, and landlords refused to rent apartments to minorities. Blacks in Canada routinely experienced discrimination. They might be refused service in bars and restaurants, restricted to the back of theatres, refused service in hospitals, and barred from hockey rinks, dance halls, and sporting arenas. There are numerous stories of segregation in Canada: a black veteran denied service in a Windsor restaurant, an Edmonton ordinance banning blacks from all public swimming pools, a Halifax cemetery segregating whites and blacks, an orphanage in Nova Scotia called the Home for Coloured Children (founded and staffed by whites), a Calgary municipal policy restricting blacks from buying homes away from the railway yard, and a Montreal opera house requiring blacks to sit in the upper balcony, which was referred to as the "Monkey Cages."[47] Segregated schools for blacks existed in Ontario and Nova Scotia until the 1960s.[48]

Most visible minorities were denied the right to vote and licences to operate businesses. They were barred from holding public office or serving on a jury. In British Columbia, Asians and Aboriginals were segregated in public schools.[49] Restrictive covenants—contracts stipulating the ethnic, racial, or religious mix of a neighbourhood—were common. At a time in history when lepers were quarantined, the federal government left "Chinese lepers" to die on D'Arcy Island off the coast of British Columbia while "white lepers" were given food and basic care on Sheldrake Island near New Brunswick.[50] British Columbia, Saskatchewan, and Ontario prohibited white women from working for Orientals.[51] Ontario also banned Chinese and non-English speakers in 1877 from working in coal mines, which was only one of numerous regulations in that province that denied some minorities the right to access public services or to work in some professions.[52] By the 1920s, the Ku Klux Klan had found its way into Canada, and was especially active in Saskatchewan.[53] Besides burning crosses, the KKK's activities included at least one incident in Ontario in 1930 where a group of Klansmen dressed in white robes and hoods kidnapped and threatened a black man who was dating a white woman (the kidnappers were caught, charged, and found not guilty).[54]

Immigration policies were explicitly racist and targeted specific classes of people. Immigrants from China had to pay a "head tax" and were later banned almost entirely under the 1923 *Chinese Immigration Act*. One inventive MP tried to introduce legislation that would have made it illegal for people with hair longer than 5.5 inches to work on railway construction.[55] The federal government also implemented policies to discourage immigration from India and Japan.[56] When 376 Indians aboard the *Komagata Maru* attempted to defy these policies, their ship was forced to remain at anchor for two months until the navy escorted it out to sea. Even the migration of African Americans to Canada became a political issue in the early twentieth century despite the absurdly low number of blacks who sought to move north. There were numerous informal practices: government officials paid medical examiners an extra $5 as a bonus for rejecting black immigrants at the border or for denying standard reduced railway rates for black settlers.[57] At one point, in response to an outpouring of antiblack protests in Alberta, the federal cabinet passed an order-in-council banning African Americans and residents of the West

Indies from immigrating to Canada.[58] This was the first state policy prohibiting a specific racial group from entering the country.

Anti-Semitism was ubiquitous in Canada.[59] Many Canadians genuinely believed that Jews were an inferior race, and even among the educated elite, it was thought that Jewish people threatened Christian civilization. Abbé Groulx, Quebec's famous historian and an influential intellectual figure in the interwar years, believed that Jews were "the very essence of all that was despicable in religion, politics, and morals."[60] In the 1920s, an economic campaign in Quebec, *Achat chez nous*, encouraged French Canadians to boycott Jewish businesses.[61] In 1933, Toronto's Pit Gang, which had a history of violence against minorities in Toronto, provoked a riot at Christie Pits when they displayed a huge banner featuring a swastika during a baseball game involving a Jewish team. People poured into the park from shops and homes around the neighbourhood while police on horses and motorcycles charged repeatedly into a crowd of more than 8,000 people in what was largest riot in the city's history at that time. A Gallup poll conducted at the height of the Second World War asked people what nationalities they would ban from Canada; 43 percent said they would ban Jews along with Germans and Japanese.[62] Pierre Berton perfectly captured the temperament of the time in his now famous article for *Maclean's* published in 1948 titled "No Jews Need Apply." In it, he recounted the story of Norman Lyons, a young accountant seeking employment during the war. Lyons visited numerous businesses that were desperate for workers, but every time he applied they insisted there were no openings. One accounting firm manager was blunt and told Lyons when they met in his office: "There's no use beating around the bush. We don't employ Jews here."[63] So pervasive was anti-Semitism at the time that even Jewish businesses sometimes refused to hire Jews.[64]

Religious persecution was not limited to Jewish people. Hutterites, Doukhobors, and Mennonites were banned from immigrating to Canada after the First World War. Hutterites, an

Anabaptist Christian sect that rejected personal ownership and that owned land communally, were strict pacifists who refused to vote or hold public office. The province of Alberta passed the *Land Sales Prohibition Act* (1942–47) to restrict Hutterites from owning land on the premise that their collective farms created an unfair advantage for other farmers.[65] This was a blatant piece of discriminatory legislation directed at an unpopular religious minority. Doukhobors and Mennonites were disenfranchised during the First World War and again between 1934 and 1955, ostensibly because they were pacifists.[66] But no religious group was more vilified and persecuted than Jehovah's Witnesses. They were pacifists who lived a strict reading of the Bible and who rejected any displays of patriotism. Jehovah's Witnesses believed that the world was ending (first in 1925, then 1975, and now within the lifetime of people born in 1914). They saw it as their duty to save other Christians by showing them to truth of the world so that they could survive Armageddon and live in paradise. Their mortal enemy was the Catholic Church, which they perceived as the tool of Satan. It is easy to understand why Jehovah's Witnesses were bitterly disliked in the vastly Catholic province of Quebec. They distributed pamphlets on the streets and made unsolicited visits to people's homes, where they described the Catholic Church as the "whore of Babylon."[67] For this, they faced severe repression: banned as an illegal organization, derided publicly for refusing to enlist, prosecuted for subversion because of their lack of patriotism, interned for opposing the war, and jailed for proselytizing (between 1946 and 1953, Quebec authorities instigated 1,665 prosecutions against Jehovah's Witnesses). A school in Hamilton, Ontario sent a group of children home in September 1940 for refusing to sing the national anthem because they were Jehovah's Witnesses. They were not permitted to return.[68]

Thus, the process of state formation in Canada involved exclusion and marginalization for many. The most salient example is Aboriginal peoples, who after Confederation were systematically stripped of any semblance of equal rights under a legal regime designed to assimilate them. They were denied the right to vote in provincial, territorial, and federal elections.[69] To become citizens they had to surrender their status and demonstrate that they were literate, debt-free, and of good moral character (by 1876, only one man had chosen enfranchisement).[70] Aboriginal people living on reserves had no property rights; the federal government held their property in trust, which restricted economic development because it was impossible to mortgage the property for credit. The 1876 *Indian Act* extended an 1869 policy that required elections for band chiefs (the government later gave itself the power to depose chiefs) and restricted the powers of band councils by requiring federal Cabinet approval on some issues. It also required Aboriginal people to secure permission from the Indian Agent to sell their harvest to non-Aboriginals or to have the minister validate their will. Later iterations of the law banned Aboriginal people from being intoxicated off reserve, forced women to abandon their status if they married a non-Aboriginal (the same did not apply to men), banned women from running for band leadership, and required widows to prove they were of "moral character" to inherit property.[71] In 1884 the federal government outlawed the potlatch, a ceremony that involved feasting and sharing goods to promote conciliation and cooperation among Aboriginal peoples. In 1885, the band was extended to the Sun Dance and Thirst Dance.[72] A federal ban on Aboriginal political organizing and land claims was instituted in 1927. Together, these policies amounted to a coordinated attempt to undermine Aboriginal peoples' cultures and ways of life. In the 1880s, the federal government required Aboriginal children to attend schools. These residential schools, often operated by Christian missionaries, were designed to further their assimilation. Tens of thousands of Aboriginals were profoundly traumatized and alienated from their families and communities as a result of their treatment in those schools.[73]

There are so many examples in the period following Confederation of violations of what we consider today to be basic rights that it is impossible to list them all. The principle of equality before the law, as articulated by the famous British legal writer A.V. Dicey, was procedural and not substantive: everyone had a right to due process and equal application of the law (one law for all), but not all people enjoyed protection against discrimination in the content of the law.[74] There was no law limiting the power of governments to restrict civil liberties. As a result, in both state policy and social practice, individuals did not enjoy the same rights.

Yet amidst these developments, Canada's rights culture did not remain static. People demanded equal protection under the law, and to that end they appealed not to human rights but to the principle of British justice. For example, when the Chinese Consolidated Benevolent Association mobilized a campaign against segregated schools in 1923, it argued that "segregation is contrary to all British Ideals of Justice [and] Fair Play."[75] Saskatchewan Premier James Gardiner denounced the Ku Klux Klan in his province as un-British and condemned that organization's blatant racism as inconsistent with British tradition.[76] At the same time, such rights claims were strongly contested. These debates reshaped Canada's rights culture.

No issue better highlights the contested and changing nature of rights than religion. Religion was fundamental to social and political life in the colonies. There was also greater religious tolerance.[77] Catholics' right to practise their religion and serve in public office was guaranteed under the *Quebec Act* of 1791 and was later reaffirmed in the 1858 *Freedom of Worship Act* (in England, Catholics could not vote or be elected to Parliament until 1829).[78] Still, there were profound religious divisions in Canada, particularly when it came to education. The *British North America Act* confirmed the right of Catholics and Protestants to operate their own schools, although it provided no guarantee of public funding of denominational education. The issue became especially acute in Manitoba.[79] Manitoba was founded as a bilingual province, but it abolished public funding for Catholic schools in 1890.[80] This action generated a national debate, which was only partly resolved when Prime Minister Wilfrid Laurier negotiated an agreement with the premier of Manitoba to reinstate limited rights for Catholic education in the province. The issue, however, continued to divide the country. Laurier failed to secure guarantees for Catholic education in the new provinces of Saskatchewan and Alberta in 1905, and Manitoba abrogated the compromise in 1916. In 1912, the Ontario government issued Regulation 17, which restricted French-language education in public schools to the first two years of primary school.[81] Long before this, Newfoundland had handed a monopoly over education to the province's Christian churches. Quebec had been dividing public education between Catholic and Protestant school boards since 1870.

Debates surrounding religious education during this period were infused with references to "minority rights." As Prime Minister John Thompson explained to the House of Commons in 1893: "The province of Manitoba commenced existence in 1870, and the first question which arises in connection with the rights of the minority in that province depends for its solution on the condition of education in that province at that time."[82] Saskatchewan premier Walter Scott (1905–16) defended separate schools as a "moral obligation to protect minority rights."[83] The right to be educated in a Catholic (or Protestant) school became part of Canadians' rights vernacular, and this idea shaped post-Confederation debates surrounding education.[84] Consider, for example, Prime Minister Laurier's comments to Parliament in 1896 on the Manitoba Schools Question: "So long as I have a seat in this House, so long as I occupy the position I do now, whenever it shall become my duty to take a stand upon any question whatever, that stand I will take not upon the grounds of Roman Catholicism, not upon the grounds of Protestantism, but upon grounds which can appeal to the conscience of all men, irrespective of their particular faith, upon grounds which can be occupied by other men who love justice, freedom and toleration."[85]

The campaign for women's rights also exemplifies the changing and contested nature of rights. [86] The process of state formation included the unequal treatment of the nation's female citizens, which was pervasive and entrenched in law. Women were denied the right to vote and were unable to become legislators, coroners, magistrates, or judges; they were also unable to sit on juries. They lost more than their last name when they married: they lost all status in civil law and could not own property or keep their own wages. In 1905 a Supreme Court judge in New Brunswick, reflecting on the role of women in society, explained that "the paramount destiny and mission of women are to fulfil the noble and benign offices of wife and mother. This is the law of the Creator."[87] Yet women were denied custodial rights over children. Also, criminal law was rife with double standards. In the case of divorce, for instance, men had only to prove adultery whereas women had to prove adultery as well as desertion without reason, extreme cruelty, incest, or bigamy. Marital rape was unknown, not because it never happened but because it was not against the law. Discriminatory laws touched on almost every aspect of women's lives: birth (infanticide), childhood (maintenance, child custody), work (labour laws, professions), courtship (seduction, marriage), sexual relations (rape, prostitution), marriage (property, citizenship, naming), parenting (maternity leave, abortion, adoption, legitimacy), divorce or separation (maintenance, child custody, pensions, desertion), and death (inheritance).[88]

There were currents of liberal rights discourse within first-wave feminism. Many reformers framed their demands for women's rights—most notably the right to vote—with reference to British liberties and secured new rights for women. In the early twentieth century, the first women were elected to public office, appointed as judges, and joined professions such as law. They participated in the workforce in greater numbers. Legislative reforms allowed married women to keep their wages and own some property separate from their husbands. Minimum wage laws were passed, and the law recognized some minor custodial rights for mothers. By the 1920s, after a campaign that mobilized masses of people across the country, women had secured the right to vote in most jurisdictions. In 1929 a group of women led a successful challenge to the Judicial Committee of the Privy Council in London against the presumption that references to "persons" in the constitution included only men (an interpretation that was used to ban women from sitting in the Senate). Throughout these campaigns, reformers insisted that the laws and practices that discriminated against women were aberrations of British justice. These precedents were necessary first steps before women could begin to mobilize around demands for women's equality.

State formation in Canada during this period was further premised on restricting the rights of workers and political radicals. Throughout the nineteenth century, workers who sought to organize had to contend with "master and servants" legislation (which required employees to be loyal), conspiracy laws, and the state's use of violence to quell strikes. Even the legality of trade unions remained uncertain until 1872. During the First World War, to suppress political opposition, the federal secretary of state was empowered to arbitrarily deny naturalization to anyone deemed a threat to the public good. Also, the entire foreign press in Canada was suppressed, enemy aliens were required to surrender firearms and explosives and (later) to register with the government, and radical organizations were banned.[89] By far the most controversial federal policy following the war involved Section 98 of the Criminal Code. Less than a year after the war, when workers in Winnipeg launched the largest general strike in the country's history, the federal government reacted once again with extraordinary measures. Section 98 of the Criminal Code was amended to make it a crime to belong to an organization that sought the overthrow of the state or economic change through violence.

Section 98 was an unusual law: it did not criminalize an action; rather, it made it illegal simply to belong to a political party. The penalty was up to twenty years in jail. Furthermore, individuals who rented space to members of such an organization were liable for imprisonment or a fine of $5,000. The RCMP could seize without warrant all property suspected of belonging to an illegal organization. The government also removed Section 133 from the Criminal Code, which had provided that a person could not be charged with seditious intent for merely pointing out defects in government or the constitution.[90] In addition, complementary amendments to the *Immigration Act* created new powers to deport anyone who was not a citizen and to deport individuals advocating the destruction of property or belonging to an organization promoting the overthrow of the government (other amendments dramatically expanded the classes of foreigners who could be excluded).[91] Not to be outdone, the federal government also amended the *Naturalization Act* so that it had the power to revoke an individual's citizenship. These powers were used to suppress political dissent. There had been an average of 1,000 deportations each year from Canada between 1902 and 1928; soon after the amendments, the number of deportations skyrocketed, to 4,025 in 1930 and to nearly 7,000 the following year.[92] In 1931 the leaders of the Communist Party of Canada were placed on trial under Section 98. The trial was a farce. As one historian has suggested,

> Assuming that the underlying purpose of the legislation was to prevent revolutionary dogma from developing into revolutionary fact, this particular prosecution was itself unusual, in that there was no evidence to suggest that the particular accused were in the slightest degree capable of accomplishing their Party's stated goals; nor was there evidence to suggest that they had ever tried. The accused, however criminal their associations and their rhetoric, had by time of trial done rather more violence to the English language than to the Government.[93]

Nonetheless, general secretary Tim Buck and his Communist Party of Canada colleagues were found guilty and spent several years in jail. The decision effectively banned the party in

Canada—the only country in the Commonwealth to do so.[94] Within a year, another 1,500 people had been prosecuted, and 355 convicted, for political crimes.[95]

These are only a few examples of how state formation was premised on the exclusion of political radicals. There were myriad ways that the state suppressed political activity. In Toronto, for instance, the police commission issued an edict in 1929 banning all political meetings held in any language other than English and promised that any public places that rented space for "communist or Bolshevik" meetings would lose their licence. The edict went so far as to declare that "no disorderly or seditious reflections on our form of government or the King, or any constituted authority will be allowed."[96] Over the next few years, the Toronto police harassed and physically abused anyone who violated these edicts. When the Canadian Labour Defense League sponsored a theatre production that was critical of the government for imprisoning the leader of the Communist Party of Canada, the Toronto police shut it down.[97] Meanwhile, the fledgling Canadian Radio Broadcasting Commission routinely denied communists airtime with the national broadcaster.[98] One MP, speaking before the House of Commons, offered an explanation for these types of policies that echoed the justifications favoured by autocratic British governors: "Sedition must be stamped out. It is all very well to talk of free speech, but to talk of Bolshevism and riots and overthrowing the Government is a different thing."[99]

Still, a great deal had changed since the days of James Craig and his reign of terror. In Parliament, critics insisted that Section 98 "was contrary to British custom and British institutions, and what we ordinarily term British liberty."[100] One of the country's foremost constitutional experts suggested that the "permanent restriction on the right of association, freedom of discussion, printing and distribution of literature, and fear of severity of punishment, is unequalled in the history of Canada and probably any British country for centuries past."[101] When Prime Minister William Lyon Mackenzie King stood before the House of Commons to denounce Section 98, he framed his criticism of the law as a

violation of the "British principle of Free Speech and Free Association" and promised to repeal the section if he was elected.[102]
It was a promise that he honoured in 1936. As it became increasingly difficult to suppress political dissent, Canada's political
landscape began to change. Socialist political parties, in particular, played a key role in shaping Canadians' rights culture. The
Co-operative Commonwealth Federation (CCF) emerged as a
vocal advocate against limits on the freedoms of speech, association, and assembly as well as discrimination against minorities.
With the Regina Manifesto, its landmark founding document,
the CCF became the first major political party in Canada to call
for the recognition of racial and religious minority rights as well
as a bill of rights. The political left was soon at the forefront of
the campaign for antidiscrimination laws.

Canada's rights culture had progressed dramatically since
the mid-nineteenth century, when dissent was rarely tolerated.
There was, as a result, the beginning of a subtle change in law.
True, as of 1944 the Supreme Court of Canada and the Judicial
Committee of the Privy Council had never ruled a law invalid
because it violated civil liberties. Still, the courts could at times
be creative. In 1937, the newly elected Social Credit government
in Alberta passed an *Act to Ensure the Publication of Accurate News
and Information*, which required newspapers to publish "correc-
tions" from the government of any critical coverage, to disclose
sources, and to identify writers. It was, unquestionably, the most
blatant peacetime attempt to censor the press. The Supreme
Court of Canada ruled the legislation *ultra vires* the powers of
the Alberta legislature; in other words, the law was seeking to
regulate activities that fell under federal jurisdiction. This has
since been viewed as the first legal decision in Canadian history to
address the issue of civil liberties and legislative authority. Justice
Lawrence Cannon accused the provincial government of imposing a doctrine that "must become, for the people of Alberta, a
sort of religious dogma of which a free and uncontrolled discussion is not permissible."[103] Justice Lyman Duff argued that "even

within its legal limits, it [public discussion] is liable to abuse and grave abuse, and such abuse is constantly exemplified before our eyes; but it is axiomatic that the practice of this right to free public discussion of public affairs, notwithstanding its incidental mischiefs, is the breath of life for parliamentary institutions."[104] The Supreme Court of Canada, as we will see, would draw heavily on this precedent in several key civil liberties cases in the 1950s.

State formation involved the systematic exclusion of classes of people from full and equal participation in public life. Sometimes this exclusion took the form of restricting access to material goods, putting perceived dissidents in jail, or denying individuals a voice in government. Exclusion could also be symbolic: all minorities were constructed as foreigners. In response, people appropriated the language of British justice to frame discrimination or attacks on civil liberties as violations of British tradition and history. In other words, rights were intimately tied to citizenship and national identity.[105] It is not surprising, given the nature of state formation, that Canada's rights culture had evolved largely in response to state action. Each small victory provided the foundation for making additional rights claims. The period from the rebellions to the beginning of the twentieth century produced greater recognition of the rights to religion, assembly, association, speech, and press as well as due process of law. Conflict was at the heart of our rights culture. This conflict would become apparent again in the wake of the First World War and another critical moment in Canada's human rights history.

CHAPTER 2

Civil Liberties in Canada

THERE ARE SO MANY INSTANCES in the mid-twentieth century of what we would today consider human rights violations that it seems trivial to focus on a single one. Yet even by the standards of mid-twentieth-century Canada, Maurice Duplessis stands out. His tenure as premier of Quebec (1936–39, 1944–59) is referred to as *Le Grande Noirceur* (The Great Darkness). Duplessis was born in Trois-Rivières in 1890, obtained a law degree at Université Laval in Quebec City, and worked as a lawyer in his hometown until he entered politics in 1927. Duplessis used a combination of patronage and repression to remain in power for nearly two decades. He introduced *An Act Respecting Communist Propaganda* (the Padlock Act) in 1936, which prohibited printing or publishing any document (including newspapers or pamphlets) propagating communism.[1] The Attorney General—Duplessis was both premier and Attorney General—could order the closing of any premises suspected of producing subversive material, and there was no process for appealing to the courts. Since the law did not define communism, Duplessis was able to use the law against anyone who criticized him. Jehovah's Witnesses, whose attempts to proselytize (often on people's doorsteps) earned them the enmity of most Quebeckers, were routinely prosecuted and jailed, often for seditious or blasphemous libel.[2] After Frank Roncarelli provided bail to dozens of Jehovah's Witnesses, Duplessis charged him with sedition and later had his liquor licence revoked (the Supreme Court of Canada fined Duplessis for abuse of power).

A bachelor who never had children, Duplessis ensured the church's tight grip on education and social services throughout the province; he also used violence and intimidation to undermine organized labour.[3] One of his most notorious acts involved transferring orphans to psychiatric hospitals to exploit federal policies that provided greater funding to hospitals. Healthy orphans were diagnosed as mentally unfit, and in some cases, entire orphanages were reclassified as psychiatric institutions. His audacity knew no bounds. When a 600-metre bridge in Trois-Rivières collapsed during –26-degree weather in February 1951, killing eight people, the premier, who had commissioned the bridge amidst charges of corruption and named it after himself, blamed the collapse on communists.[4]

Duplessis was responsible for some of the most infamous acts of state abuse of civil liberties in Canada's history. His actions generated intense criticism and contributed to the creation of the first civil liberties groups in the country. The postwar period was a significant moment in Canadian human rights history to be sure, but the rights revolution would come later. Instead, it was during this period that we see the first attempts to codify human rights in Canadian law. There were also new social movements dedicated to rights. Racial, ethnic, and religious minorities appropriated the language of rights to frame their opposition to discrimination in public policy and private practice. And their opposition bore fruit. Civil liberties—a concept historically associated with state abuse of rights—was slowly redefined during this period to include the principle of non-discrimination in the public and private spheres.

There was a long history in Canada, as we have seen, of using extraordinary powers during emergencies.[5] Habeas corpus had been suspended in Lower Canada almost every year between 1793 and 1812. It was suspended again in 1866–67 in response to Fenian raids from the United States (the Fenians were Irish nationalists who hoped to use violence against Canada to pressure Britain to free Ireland). Meanwhile, the Legislative Assembly dusted off the post-rebellions *Lawless Aggression Act*, which was extended to Lower Canada and made retroactive. Fifty-seven men suspected of Fenian sympathies were arrested and tried; twenty-two of them were eventually convicted and hanged.[6] A year later, police arrested and detained twenty-five men without charge during their investigation into the assassination of a former Fenian turned Canadian nationalist, Thomas D'Arcy McGee.[7] These arrests were an effective tool for undermining the Fenian movement in Canada (the same tactic would be used again a century later to deal with Quebec nationalists). When civil war erupted between the Métis in the North-West Territories and the expansionist Canadian state, the federal government sent an army to pacify the region and arrest the leaders. The Métis leader, Louis Riel, was ultimately tried for treason and hanged.[8] In the aftermath, a pass system was introduced that required residents of Aboriginal reserves to have a pass signed by the Indian Agent to travel off reserve.[9]

The tendency to enact ambiguous legislation that has the potential to severely limit civil liberties during emergencies is part of Canada's rights culture. One of the most notorious examples of state excess during a period of emergency was the *War Measures Act* enacted in 1914 at the onset of the First World War. The statute, barely two pages long, gave the federal government the power to suspend all rights.[10] It transferred power from Parliament to Cabinet, which effectively ruled the entire country by decree for four years. The range of orders that flowed from the legislation was stunning. The government suspended habeas corpus, imposed widespread censorship, declared numerous associations to be unlawful, broke strikes and banned newspapers from reporting on their actions (and later banned striking), limited due process to facilitate prosecutions, interned thousands of enemy aliens, and created agencies to regulate prices and control the production or distribution of goods. Parliament imposed conscription, which led to the jailing of thousands of men for desertion, and the government threatened to conscript anyone who incited or participated in labour unrest.[11] Citizens were encouraged to spy on their neighbours to discourage hoarding or waste in the midst of food shortages. Any individual expressing "objectionable speech"—including unfavourable comments about the government or the war—was liable for a fine of $5,000 and imprisonment for five years.[12] Government officials were authorized to seize and destroy any materials they judged prejudicial to the war effort. The onus of proof was reversed for prosecutions: rather than being innocent until proven guilty, the accused were required to prove they were not guilty. The government also gave itself the power to deem any organization to be unlawful, seize its property, break into and search any premises without a warrant, and prosecute any member or individual affiliated with the group.[13] Any utterance might be construed as supporting an unlawful organization, which the order-in-council defined as (among other things) any comment that was profane, scurrilous, or abusive towards the government. People who rented or provided space to the unlawful organization were equally guilty. The accused were presumed guilty, and guilt was retroactive: if they had supported the organization in any way at the beginning of the war they were guilty even if there was no proof of affiliation for years.

These were only the most blatant examples of restrictions on civil liberties during the war.[14] Such power inevitably led to abuses, such as an absurd order-in-council that criminalized loafers and a policy that banned dog shows.[15] Following a conscription riot in Quebec City in 1918, the government passed an order-in-council allowing the military to prosecute individuals by court martial, a policy that was disturbingly reminiscent of the post-rebellion *Lawless Aggression Act*. Another order-in-council made it a crime for women with a venereal disease to have sexual intercourse (or to solicit) with any member of the armed forces. Any woman who violated this order could be forcibly detained for at minimum one week for a medical examination.[16] And the government's penchant for excessive measures did not end with the war. Even for a nation traumatized by war, the federal government's decision to expand the regulations governing internment—months after the war was over—was clearly unwarranted. The policy allowed any county or district court to intern an individual for no better reason than "a feeling of public apprehension entertained by the community."[17] The accused was barred from having legal counsel and did not even need to be at the hearing to be convicted. At least thirty-three men would be interned following the Winnipeg General Strike in 1919, and the internment camps remained open until 1920.

It turns out that the use of emergency powers between 1914 and 1919 was only a dress rehearsal. The state's true capacity for repression was fully realized during the Second World War. The federal government reimposed the *War Measures Act* in 1939 and, under its authority, passed the Defence of Canada Regulations. These powers were quickly put to use. The government censored 325 newspapers and periodicals (compared to 184 during the First World War), banned more than thirty religious, social, ethnic, and political organizations, interned 2,423 Canadians (compared to 1,800 in England), arrested and summarily tried hundreds of people for speaking out against the war or distributing literature on behalf of banned organizations, and granted police the authority to arrest and detain individuals without charge or trial.[18] Although the RCMP failed to secure approval for the power to arrest British citizens "likely" to incite unrest, the cabinet did pass an order authorizing RCMP officers to issue search warrants against illegal organizations.[19] This was a remarkable departure from due process: RCMP officers could simply write their own warrants without seeking judicial approval.

Meanwhile, hundreds of German Canadians were arrested and detained on the grounds that they were probably Nazi sympathizers. Jehovah's Witnesses were declared an illegal organization. Municipal and provincial governments "purged" suspected subversives by removing politicians from office or firing civil servants. The mayor of Montreal, Camille Houde, was interned without trial for four years because he refused to cooperate with a national manpower registry and criticized the government (the censors initially prohibited newspapers from publishing his statements, but the Montreal *Gazette* evaded the censors by having an MP read Houde's speech into the minutes of the House of Commons).[20] The Cabinet repeatedly passed orders-in-council banning any appeal to the courts. Police intimidation was also common: authorities could threaten people with warrantless searches or charge them under the regulations. Everyone was vulnerable: in one case, a doctor was interned because one of his patients was a Communist.[21] War hysteria severely restricted free speech: universities discouraged criticism of the war effort, and even legislators feared they would be arrested if they criticized war policies.[22] There were several cases involving imprisonment for public comments—for example, one man was sentenced to three months in jail for uttering "Chamberlain is as bad as Hitler" while drinking in a tavern. Another man, Samuel Levine, was jailed and then interned for renting a room to a man in possession of Communist literature.[23] There was also a wide range of blatantly discriminatory practices. Jewish refugees were largely banned from entering the country. Only white men were allowed to join the air force until 1943 and the navy until 1944, and even after some racial minorities were permitted to enlist in the armed forces, all Chinese and Japanese men were banned from serving in the air force and navy.

The government's wartime policies did generate some small opposition. The Canadian Jewish Congress and African Canadian groups in Toronto, for instance, found common cause in 1942. They formed a successful alliance to have the National Selective Service eliminate a provision on a wartime registration form that required the unemployed to indicate their race. A few civil liberties groups were established in the late 1930s, largely in response to Duplessis's *Padlock Act*, and a several more were formed during the war. These were the first civil liberties groups in Canadian history. Two incidents in particular, both in 1946, further energized the civil liberties movement. The first was the treatment of Japanese Canadians. Thousands of Japanese Canadians living on the west coast were forcibly removed from their homes, pushed onto crowded trains, and sent hundreds of miles away to live in remote parts of the country. Yet the government's actions were largely accepted even by many social progressives. Curiously, it was the federal government's decision in 1946 to disenfranchise British citizens of Japanese descent, and to forcibly deport thousands of them to Japan, that generated intense opposition. Many Canadians were appalled that the government would go so far as to deny its own citizens so fundamental a right as the vote. For many, this was going too far. Frank Scott, the celebrated constitutional lawyer, opined at the time that the deportation "makes a farce of citizenship ... Every Canadian is attacked in his fundamental civil liberties by this policy."[24] These incidents generated one of the first organized rights campaigns in Canadian history.[25] Opponents of these policies—including organized labour, churches, youth groups, ethnic minorities, and Japanese Canadians themselves—formed an alliance to campaign against them.

Equally shocking was the Gouzenko Affair. Igor Gouzenko, a cipher clerk at the Soviet Union's Ottawa embassy, made a momentous decision in September 1945: he stole documents from the embassy and defected. Leaving the embassy one evening clutching a handful of classified documents under his coat, he first approached the *Ottawa Journal* and then the Department of Justice. Amazingly, not realizing the significance of what was happening, both turned him away. After a frantic night of scurrying around the streets of Ottawa, with Soviet agents desperately trying to track him down, Gouzenko finally managed to contact the RCMP. Within hours, Prime Minister Mackenzie King learned to his chagrin that, in the midst of critical postwar multi-nation negotiations with the Russians, he had a defector on his hands. But Gouzenko was bringing evidence of something that the prime minister simply could not ignore: a Soviet espionage network in Canada that, among other things, was intent on securing information on the atom bomb. Mackenzie King reluctantly offered Gouzenko sanctuary. In a top-secret meeting with three cabinet ministers, the government passed an order-in-council under the War Measures Act to provide the RCMP with special powers to investigate Gouzenko's allegations.

King and the RCMP's response was, to say the least, excessive. The investigation continued until February 1946, long after the war was over. The secret order-in-council, passed under a wartime statute, remained in force. King appointed two Supreme Court of Canada justices to lead a Royal Commission on allegations of a spy ring. The RCMP used the order-in-council to detain dozens of *suspected* spies and hold them incommunicado in tiny cells under suicide watch, then subjected them to repeated interrogations by the police and the commissioners. They were denied access to lawyers and any knowledge of their rights. In effect, the government was using its wartime powers in peacetime to authorize a Royal Commission that circumscribed accused criminals their right to due process. The suspects' "testimony" was later used in court to convict them. One of the detainees, Emma Woikin, was so traumatized by her incarceration that when she was finally brought before a judge, all she could do was repeat over and over again, in a flat and unnatural tone, "I did it." In the end, very few were convicted and the commissioners uncovered no evidence that the "spies" had provided classified information to the Soviets.[26]

The treatment of Japanese Canadians and the Gouzenko Affair launched a national debate in Canada that led to the formation of a half-dozen civil liberties associations. Yet in retrospect, it is far more noteworthy that the federal government lost little electoral support despite such extensive attacks on Canadians' civil liberties. Only a small minority spoke out against the government's draconian regulations during the war. Even among lawyers, as one legal scholar notes, "what is remarkable about constitutional thought during the war is the pronounced absence of civil liberties concerns."[27] There were profound divisions within the ranks of civil liberties activists. Many accepted the government's wretched treatment of Japanese Canadians during the war, and it took the extreme act of disenfranchising British citizens to mobilize widespread opposition. Ideological divisions also contributed to a muted response from civil libertarians to the Gouzenko Affair. Many liberals and social democrats were, frankly, unwilling to come to the defence of communists.

There was, however, a critical moment near the end of the war that signalled a momentous change: in 1944, Ontario introduced Canada's first antidiscrimination law—the *Racial Discrimination Act.*[28] At the time, people walking along Toronto's Yonge Street might observe signs on doorways such as "No Jews or Dogs Allowed."[29] The purpose of the legislation was to prohibit the display of discriminatory signs and advertisements. Three years later, Saskatchewan passed a provincial Bill of Rights. That statute recognized several civil liberties, such as free speech and religion, while at the same time banning discrimination in employment on the basis of race, ethnicity, or religion.[30] Neither statute, however, included an enforcement mechanism or clear penalties. They were never applied, but they did symbolize changing ideas about rights.

Around the same time, the federal government initiated Parliamentary hearings into the possibility of a national bill of rights. The hearings—committees were appointed in 1947, 1948, and 1950—offer some insight into how Canadians conceived of rights at the time. The co-chairmen of the 1947 committee, for instance, distinguished between *rights* and *freedoms*: they defined rights as requiring state action (right to work, property, education, and social security) and freedom as the absence of state interference (press, speech, religion, association, and assembly).[31]

During the 1950 hearings there was an unspoken consensus in favour of civil and political rights. Irving Himel of the Association for Civil Liberties as well as representatives from the Department of External Affairs were skeptical about placing economic and social rights in the constitution. Even organized labour was divided. Eugene Forsey, speaking for the 350,000 workers of the Canadian Congress of Labour, believed that a bill of rights was only capable of defending traditional liberal rights. The rights to work and to education, Forsey insisted, required positive action by the state, which was best left to governments rather than the courts.[32] In contrast, the Trades and Labour Congress called for the entrenchment of economic rights, such as the right to employment, in the constitution. But their views were not shared by most of the people who participated in these debates.[33]

It is no surprise that labour organizations played a leading role during the Parliamentary hearings. Organized labour—often working alongside minorities who were victims of discrimination—was at the forefront of campaigns for antidiscrimination legislation. This had not always been the case. Labour leaders had, for many years, portrayed immigrants and racial/ethnic minorities, most notably the Chinese in British Columbia, as low-wage strikebreakers who threatened to undermine organized labour.[34] At the inaugural meeting of the Canadian Brotherhood of Railway Employees, the most powerful labour union at the time, the membership agreed that they would only allow white men to join the union.[35] Changes in the labour force and the need for working-class unity had a profound impact on the labour movement.[36] This was evident in the Co-operative Commonwealth Federation's founding program, which called for a bill of rights.[37] Racial minorities were also active agents in challenging their own marginalization. In 1946, for instance, a group of Chinese Canadians formed the Committee for the Repeal of the Chinese Immigration Act to lobby for the removal of a ban on Chinese immigration to Canada.[38] The Jewish Labour Committee, though, was especially prominent. The JLC established several offices across Canada to lobby for antidiscrimination legislation. They campaigned alongside civil liberties groups in Vancouver, Montreal, Toronto, and a few other cities in the 1950s.[39] Their efforts would prove remarkably successful in raising awareness and changing the law.

Discriminatory state policies and business practices were perfectly legal in this period. In 1936, Fred Christie and two friends, Emile King and Steven St. Jean, entered the Montreal Forum's York Tavern for a beer. As they sat down to order a drink, a waiter quietly approached the three men and informed them that they had to leave. The tavern was under new management, he said, and the owners did not want blacks in the bar. Christie, a chauffeur and avid Montreal Canadiens fan who had been to the tavern many times in the past, was indignant and refused to leave. Eventually the police arrived and escorted Christie and his friends from the tavern. Christie sued York Tavern in court. The case pitted the merchant's freedom of commerce against Christie's right to equal treatment. Ten years later the Supreme Court of Canada ruled in favour of the merchant's right to choose, not Christie's right to be served. Such was the prevailing attitude towards racial minorities that Christie's own lawyer did not even bother to question the assumption that whites did not want to eat and drink alongside blacks.[40] A decade later a court in Alberta reaffirmed the same principle. Ted King attempted to rent a room at Barclay's Hotel in Calgary on 13 May 1959, but when he arrived at the hotel, the proprietor informed him that "we don't take coloured people here." A year later the Alberta District Court ruled that the hotel was within its rights to refuse service despite provisions in the *Hotelkeeper's Act* prohibiting innkeepers from refusing to serve travellers. The court, which based its decision on a technicality surrounding the definition of an inn, acknowledged that King had been discriminated against.[41] The effect of this decision was to sanction discrimination.

Canadian law was, nonetheless, becoming another site of contestation in shaping the nation's rights culture. There was no bill of rights in the Canadian constitution, and Parliament was supreme. The judiciary was constitutionally subordinate to the legislatures and Parliament, although it was responsible for adjudicating disputes between the federal government and the provinces over the proper exercise of their authority as outlined by the division of powers in the constitution. As a result, when confronted with legislation that restricted civil liberties, judges' only recourse was to determine whether the law had been properly applied/interpreted or whether it fell under the appropriate jurisdiction. If, for example, a province passed a law criminalizing trade unions, no judge could strike down the law on the grounds that it violated freedom of association. But the judge could rule the law *ultra vires* because criminal law fell under the constitutional jurisdiction of the federal government. Still, the courts were not completely ineffective. The 1950s was one of those moments in Canadian history when civil liberties were an especially prominent issue for the Supreme Court of Canada. Several cases reached the court that raised questions regarding the state of civil liberties in Canada. Frank Scott, who argued the *Roncarelli* case before the Supreme Court, described the 1950s as "predominantly the decade of human rights."[42]

Unsurprisingly, the four most prominent cases arose from policies implemented under the Duplessis regime. Aimé Boucher, a farmer in St-Germain Parish and a Jehovah's Witness, was arrested for sedition in 1946 because he had distributed copies of a flyer titled "Quebec's Burning Hate." Sedition was a common charge used to harass Jehovah's Witnesses. Boucher decided to challenge the government's definition of sedition in court. Two years later, John Switzman, a prominent Marxist in Montreal, rented an apartment from Freda Elbling. It was not long before the police raided and barricaded the apartment. Duplessis's *Padlock Act* permitted the police to close buildings without warrant, charge, or trial for promoting communism. In a direct reversal of legal tradition, the accused was assumed guilty and had the burden of proving his or her innocence. Elbling sued Switzman for loss of rent, and Switzman used the opportunity to challenge the law's constitutionality. In another case, Laurier Saumur was arrested under a municipal ordinance in Quebec City that prohibited the distribution of any book, pamphlet, circular, or tract without permission of the chief of police (with no procedure for appealing the decision).[43] He also challenged the law in court.

Meanwhile, Frank Roncarelli, the owner of Quaff Café in Montreal, was busy providing hundreds of jailed Jehovah's Witnesses with bail in defiance of Duplessis's campaign against the unpopular sect. Duplessis was outraged and publicly admonished Roncarelli about posting bail. Speaking to a reporter from the Montreal *Gazette*, Duplessis explained that "the communists, Nazis as well as those who are the propagandists for the Witnesses of Jehovah, have been treated and will continue to be treated by the Union Nationale government as they deserve for trying to infiltrate themselves and their seditious ideas in the Province of Quebec."[44] When Roncarelli refused to stop, Duplessis used his influence to have the restaurant owner's licence revoked, and the restaurant soon went bankrupt. Roncarelli sued the premier for $100,000. The case ignited what one historian described as "the most extensive campaign of state-sponsored religious persecution ever undertaken in Canada."[45] Jehovah's Witnesses were dragged from their homes at night and arrested, police stood by as violent mobs attacked them, hundreds were imprisoned, prayer meetings were raided, and their literature was burned on the streets.

The Supreme Court of Canada sided with the defendants in each case. In *Boucher v the King* (1949), the Court narrowed the definition of sedition. In putting aside the guilty verdict, it concluded that an individual was not guilty of sedition for simply fomenting ill will or hostility. The accused also had to be guilty of inciting violence against the state. *Saumur v. City of Quebec and Attorney-General* (1953) was a confusing mix of contradictory judicial findings: the justices were divided over whether the case constituted a violation of freedom of religion and whether the power to legislate on civil liberties was provincial or federal (one justice decided that the ordinance violated the *Freedom to Worship Act*). Fortunately for Saumur, the collective result was to rule that the arrest was illegal. In *Switzman v. Elbling* (1957) the Court struck down the *Padlock Act* as *ultra vires* the province's jurisdiction because it functioned as criminal law. And Duplessis was fined $8,000 in *Roncarelli v. Duplessis* (1959) for abusing his powers.[46]

These were victories, to be sure, but hardly transformative. Each case was decided on the grounds of technicalities and the division of powers, not civil liberties.[47] The same approach explains the results of another famous Supreme Court of Canada case in the 1950s. Bernard Wolf challenged the validity of a restrictive covenant that barred him from buying Annie Noble's cottage in the Beach O'Pines neighbourhood on Lake Huron. The covenant—a contract among neighbours—prohibited anyone from selling to someone who was Jewish. He won his case in 1951, albeit on a technicality involving the use of land.[48] Ivan Rand, one of the most respected Supreme Court of Canada judges in the 1950s, used these cases to formulate an argument for an *implied* bill of rights in the Canadian constitution. The idea, however, did not gain widespread support among the Court's justices. The Court never engaged in serious discussion about human rights during this period. Instead, it produced a series of dissenting but nonetheless inspiring opinions on the broader scope of civil liberties in Canadian law.

Despite having himself introduced the *Racial Discrimination Act*, Ontario premier George Drew insisted in 1944 that "the best way to avoid racial and religious strife is not by imposing a method of thinking, but by teaching our children that we are all members of a great human family."[49] Within a decade there was a sustained campaign, led primarily by the Jewish Labour Committee, for more effective legislation to ban discrimination in employment and accommodation. As a result, in 1951, the Conservative government in Ontario introduced the country's first *Fair Employment Practices Act* and, in 1954, the *Fair Accommodation Practices Act*. Both statutes applied only to racial, ethnic, and religious discrimination in employment and accommodation (the government also passed, in 1951, a *Female Employees Fair Remuneration Act*). Similar laws were later enacted in five other provinces.

In addition to the *threat* of sanctions, the law provided a powerful symbolic affirmation of new rights claims. Rights were manifest in social practice as well. Organizations such as the Jewish Labour Committee were able assert new rights claims and effect social change without the state. The JLC's leaders, including Kalman Kaplansky, Sid Blum, and Alan Borovoy, developed several strategies in the 1950s to pressure private businesses to recognize the right to non-discrimination. For instance, in Vancouver in 1959, the local JLC convinced the Downtown Hotel to stop refusing service to blacks after the committee secured a promise from the British Columbia Automobile Association to remove the hotel from its "approved" ranking.[50] Another case, in St. Catharines, Ontario, involved a black family that had rented an apartment only to have the landlady serve them with a notice of eviction soon after they moved in. The landlady insisted that neighbours were complaining about having blacks in the building. Borovoy drove to St. Catharines and knocked on the door of each tenant; the vast majority eagerly signed a petition indicating that they had no objection to black tenants. The petition was presented to the landlady; she agreed to stop discriminating. In another case, Borovoy convinced the United Auto Workers Union to cancel plans to rent facilities at a golf club that banned blacks, which ultimately led the club to rescind its practices. These and similar practices demonstrated how new rights claims could be asserted without having to resort to the law.[51]

But even limited legislation faced intense opposition.[52] Canada's rights culture remained rooted in traditional British liberties, and political opposition drew on this tradition. Premier Ernest Manning of Alberta rejected demands for antidiscrimination legislation on the grounds that the "government prefers to rely upon those individual rights and privileges as established by the Common Law of England and the British Commonwealth."[53] Unsurprisingly, Duplessis dismissed outright the idea of antidiscrimination legislation; Quebeckers, he insisted, need only to read the Bible. Others simply felt that these laws were unnecessary or would prove ineffective. In British Columbia, during the debates surrounding the 1956 *Fair Employment Practices Act*, one member of the Legislative Assembly insisted that "discrimination on any grounds contemplated by this bill is virtually non-existent ... Besides, you simply cannot legislate people into the Kingdom of Heaven."[54] In the end, these laws failed to achieve even their own limited mandate. Only one complaint, for example, was prosecuted in Ontario between 1955 and 1962 under that province's *Fair Accommodation Practices Act* (a restaurant owner, determined to refuse to serve blacks, was fined $25 in damages and $155 for legal costs in 1955).[55] Fair employment and practices laws and equal pay laws were rarely enforced. The legislation had been poorly drafted, and few people were aware the laws even existed.[56]

Canada's rights culture had not changed dramatically since the nineteenth century. For example, none of the antidiscrimination statutes included gender. Male activists were often blind to discrimination against women. As historians Ruth Frager and Carmela Patrias explain, "most human rights activists apparently believed that women were so fundamentally different from men that issues of sex discrimination could be dismissed on that basis. Many activists held deep convictions concerning the injustice of racist, ethnic and religious discrimination, while remaining blind to sex discrimination. In short, they reflected the sexism that was so widespread in Canadian society at that time."[57] That such a limited conception of rights had broad appeal during this period is best exemplified in the failure of women's groups to campaign for legislation prohibiting sex discrimination. The Canadian Federation of Business and Professional Women's Clubs, for example, campaigned against low salaries and passed resolutions opposing workplace discrimination based on marital status. Yet "even the federation's president used the language of need rather than rights to justify her organization's defence of employed women. In a similar vein, most spokespersons for the National Council of Women (an umbrella organization for various women's groups) steered clear of the language of rights and argued that only financial need could justify married women's work."[58] In 1959 the Vancouver Council of Women passed a resolution calling for fair accommodation practices legislation to prohibit discrimination *only* on the basis of race, colour, religion, and ancestry. Similarly, when the National Council of Jewish Women's Toronto branch sent a letter to the premier of Ontario to end discrimination in employment, they called for legislation dealing with race, colour, or creed—not sex.

The 1960 federal *Bill of Rights* was another landmark piece of rights legislation. Prime Minister John Diefenbaker's original vision had been for a constitutionally entrenched bill of rights. His opponents, however, citing the principle of Parliamentary supremacy, undermined any attempt to amend the constitution. It was passed simply as a federal statute. Also, the *Bill of Rights* defined rights largely in the same terms as other antidiscrimination laws in Canada, with the sole exception that it banned discrimination on the basis of sex (alongside race, religion, and national origin). It was the first Canadian statute to prohibit sex discrimination, although unlike race, religion, and national origin, sex discrimination was only banned in employment. The *Bill of Rights* was ultimately ineffective in practice. Of the thirty-five claims brought under the legislation between 1960 and 1982, only five were successful and only one led to the striking down of legislation.[59]

A weak *Bill of Rights* was only one indicator of a rights culture that had yet to produce strong guarantees against state violations of civil liberties. The International Woodworkers of America strike in 1959, one of the bitterest labour disputes in Newfoundland history, which left one man dead, provided another vivid reminder of the vulnerability of Canadians' civil liberties. Faced with a crippling strike in a key industry, the Newfoundland government took the extraordinary step of passing emergency legislation that authorized the government to decertify and dissolve any union, prohibit secondary picketing, and impose liability on any union for the activities of their members. Both the Canadian Labour Congress and the International Labour Organization condemned the law, and the prime minister refused Premier Joey Smallwood's appeal for additional RCMP officers to police the strike.[60]

Human rights progress during this period may have been minimal, but these were essential first steps.[61] In the past, the rights to freedom of speech and association were interpreted to mean the right to express prejudicial ideas and to refuse service to certain groups. In contrast, antidiscrimination legislation "represented a fundamental shift, a reversal, of the traditional notion of citizens' rights to enrol the state as the protector of the right of the victim to freedom from discrimination. It was, in fact, a revolutionary change in the definition of individual freedom."[62] That the state should prohibit any form of discrimination was an important milestone in the development of Canada's rights culture.

One area that remained immune to these developments was foreign policy. Human rights were simply not a foreign policy priority during this period. Canada accepted some minor international human rights obligations in the first half of the twentieth century: Canadians attended the Paris Peace Conference in 1919, signed the Treaty of Versailles, and joined the League of Nations. But Canada was hardly committed to advancing human rights abroad. As John Humphrey, the Canadian who helped draft the

Universal Declaration of Human Rights, noted in 1948: "I knew that the international promotion of human rights had no priority in Canadian foreign policy."[63]

It is a historical irony that, in the same year it was denying due process to suspected spies and disenfranchising Japanese Canadians, the federal government received word from San Francisco that the UN was drafting a Universal Declaration of Human Rights (UDHR). The UDHR raised serious concerns in Canada, especially among the Canadian Bar Association and leading members of the federal Cabinet.[64] Pressure from its allies—and the distasteful possibility of voting alongside South Africa, Saudi Arabia, and the Communist Bloc—forced Canada to support the UDHR in the final vote in 1948. However, Canada joined South Africa, Britain, Australia, and the United States in demanding a domestic jurisdiction clause to prevent the UN from intervening in domestic affairs.[65] Officially, the federal government insisted that it was concerned about violating provincial jurisdiction.[66] Privately, the prime minister was far more apprehensive that the declaration could be used "to provoke contentious even if unfair criticism of the Government."[67] History would prove him correct.

As of 1962 the federal government had yet to embrace human rights as a foreign policy priority. Canada had gone so far as to cite the principle of state sovereignty in opposing intervention over gross human rights abuses in South Africa in 1955 (and, later, in Nigeria in 1968).[68] The terms "human rights" and "civil liberties" do not appear once in the publication *Documents in External Relations* for the period between 1946 and 1960. "The early Canadian attitude toward United Nations involvement with rights," explains Cathal Nolan, "was clearly apathetic, and even a little smug. Ottawa considered the US proposal on human rights wrongheaded at best, and at worst as constituting an invalid interference in the internal affairs of states."[69] Canadian foreign policy privileged state sovereignty to the detriment of human rights intervention.[70] The country's support for human rights, especially within the UN, was initially based on a cold calculation

of self-interest: "Ottawa slowly accepted an international dimen-
sion to rights because it came to believe that the popular appeal
of the idea might help keep afloat the UN and thereby the promise of security that multilateral statecraft was thought yet to carry
in its hold."[71]

What is most notable about postwar public discourse in Canada is that the term "human rights" was rarely employed.[72]
The treatment of Japanese Canadians and the Gouzenko Affair
launched national debates that exemplified how the language of
civil liberties guided public discourse surrounding rights. The
Gouzenko Affair, for instance, dominated Canadian newspaper
headlines and editorials between February and April 1946. The
most common theme was the state's abuse of the suspects' civil
liberties. Members of Parliament as well as non-governmental
organizations framed their concerns using the language of civil
liberties—the term "human rights" almost never appeared in the
print media or in Parliament. Popular discourse remained rooted
in references to traditional British liberties. A typical example was
one author, writing for the *Dalhousie Review*, who suggested that
the government "created popular sympathy for the accused and
erred greatly in not taking scrupulous care that the established
practices of British justice were followed."[73]

The first non-partisan associations dedicated to promoting
rights for all citizens were explicitly oriented to civil liberties:
the Canadian Civil Liberties Union and the Association for Civil
Liberties. There were no self-professed "human rights" associations. These organizations' founding documents defined rights
as civil liberties—in particular, as civil and political rights.[74] The
Emergency Committee for the Protection of Civil Liberties, for
instance, was devoted to "the fundamental rights and liberties
of British citizens."[75] Civil liberties organizations campaigned
for freedoms of speech, association, assembly, religion, press,
and due process. To this vernacular they added the principle of

non-discrimination, which had gained support since the 1930s. Similarly, antidiscrimination laws were narrowly construed, and by the late 1950s there was only a scattering of such statutes in Canada. Federal politicians debated a constitutional bill of rights, but to no avail.

If there was little interest in promoting human rights in Canada, then there was none at all for promoting human rights abroad. The United States, Britain, and France shared Canada's misgivings about the UDHR.[76] None of the major powers, in fact, considered human rights as a foreign policy priority.[77] Even the International Labour Organization had never used the language of human rights in its conventions.[78] Human rights simply lacked popular appeal in the postwar period: international lawyers overwhelmingly rejected it as a basis for international law; anticolonial movements embraced human rights not to promote individual freedom but for the purposes of state formation; the UN did little to promote human rights; and social movements had yet to embrace human rights as a vision for social change.[79]

The Cold War further retarded human rights progress. A 1946 Gallup poll asked Canadians if communists had a right to free speech: a majority said no. The result was unsurprising given the emerging Cold War and fears about a looming conflict with the Soviet Union.[80] The Cold War dominated international and domestic politics to the detriment of human rights progress. Governments often dismissed concerns surrounding human rights abuses, including their own brand of McCarthyism and vicious attacks against trade unionists, by accusing critics of being soft on communism.[81] Social movements were largely concerned about civil liberties and discrimination against racial, ethnic, and religious minorities. This did not prevent activists from using Cold War rhetoric to advance human rights claims. Rabbi Abraham Feinberg, a prominent figure in Toronto and a proponent of civil liberties, pointed out to Ontario premier Leslie Frost during one encounter that "it is a sham to attempt to defend western democracy against communism if a man or woman is prevented from getting a job because of discrimination against race, religion or colour."[82] Curiously, although he mentioned women, like so many of his colleagues he did not see any need to include gender in antidiscrimination law. In fact, none of the polls that were produced in Canada between 1946 and 1962 asked questions about sex discrimination. Polling on rights during this period was dominated by questions about civil liberties, due process, race, and religion.

The Cold War, as we will see in the following chapter, also stifled human rights progress in the international arena. One issue, however, transcended these divisions: children's rights. Although an enforceable human rights treaty eluded the UN during this period, in 1959 the member states were able to find sufficient common ground to pass the Declaration of the Rights of Children, which banned discrimination against children and declared that they had a right to social security and a secure family environment as well as a name, nationality, education, decent work, and priority in receiving relief.[83] This was the type of issue around which, despite Cold War tensions, governments on both sides could rally support. There were also, as several historians have demonstrated, notable advances for children at home. Margaret Little has shown how women in British Columbia framed mothers' pensions (introduced in 1920 to support child rearing) as a right, and Dominique Marshall has made a good case for framing compulsory schooling and family allowances as a form of children's rights.[84] These policies became a focal point for framing the state's duties towards children, who were increasingly seen as autonomous individuals with rights. But there was no clear consensus around such programs as anything more than public policy. To be sure, the welfare state constituted a significant advance in codifying minimum standards for social and economic rights. But in law and in the popular imagination, such entitlements did not enjoy the same status as civil liberties.

Still, tentative advances in children's rights, and the recognition of a right against discrimination (even if limited), were noteworthy developments. The emergence of new rights claims was almost inevitable given the potential of rights discourse to empower marginalized people. It was the beginning of a new era in the history of Canada's rights culture. It was also a crucial first step in producing momentum for the rights revolution.

CHAPTER 3

Human Rights Beginnings

THE *WAR MEASURES ACT* HAS BEEN employed only twice during peacetime. The Gouzenko Affair in 1946 was the first, and that event launched widespread debates about civil liberties in Canada. The October Crisis of 1970 was the second and only other time wartime powers have been used during peacetime. As was the case with so many other developments during this period, it was not a decisive moment for advancing human rights, but it did signal the beginnings of a new era.[1]

The Front de libération du Québec (FLQ) spent the better part of the 1960s pursuing their vision for an independent socialist Quebec nation through violence. They exploded a bomb in the Montreal Stock Exchange, injuring twenty-seven people; they stole weapons and bomb-making materials from army barracks; they carried out dozens of armed robberies, including of banks and armoured trucks; they hurled Molotov cocktails through the windows of army recruiting centres and English-language radio stations; they placed bombs around federal institutions, including post office boxes and radio towers; they plastered posters and graffiti throughout Montreal on flagpoles and walls. By 1970, dozens of *felquistes* had been arrested and imprisoned: François Schirm (32 years old) and Edmond Guénette (20 years old) were sentenced to death (later commuted to life in prison), while Pierre-Paul Geoffroy received 124 life sentences. One FLQ cell upped the stakes on 5 October 1970 by kidnapping a British trade consul named James Cross at gunpoint. Five days later, several men from a second FLQ cell, armed with machine guns, found Quebec cabinet minister Pierre Laporte throwing a football on his front lawn with his children. They dragged him into a car and held him captive at a home in suburban Montreal.

The government's response was predictable. As we saw in Chapter 1, there is a long history in Canada of the state using excessive powers during a crisis. Under the powers appropriated by the federal Cabinet through the *War Measures Act*, police conducted over 3,000 searches and detained at least 497 people without charge or judicial warrant. People were denied habeas corpus, and many were held incommunicado (a process reminiscent of the Gouzenko Affair and the investigation into the assassination of Thomas D'Arcy McGee). Many of the detainees spent a month or longer in jail, but in the end only two were convicted under the Public Order Regulations. Widespread censorship was imposed on the media, especially on student newspapers that wanted to publish the FLQ's manifesto. In Toronto, the school board considered a motion to ban teachers from discussing the FLQ in classrooms. The government of British Columbia approved an order-in-council directing school boards to fire teachers who expressed sympathy with the FLQ.

The October Crisis ignited another national debate about civil liberties. Several civil liberties groups emerged amidst the crisis. Students protested on the streets of Montreal. Labour leaders demanded an end to the arrests and searches. Protest meetings were held at universities and libraries. Yet, much like in 1946, Canadians seemed to largely accept the suspension of their civil liberties. A CTV poll released on 15 November 1970 suggested that 87 percent of Canadians approved of the invocation of the War Measures Act (only 5 percent explicitly disapproved). Several other opinion polls released in 1971 reaffirmed support in Quebec and the rest of Canada for the federal government's tactics. The media were divided but largely sympathetic, especially in English Canada. Frank Scott and other notable civil libertarians

publicly endorsed the use of emergency powers. Of the 12,000
letters Prime Minister Trudeau received from the public regarding the crisis, barely 2 percent were critical of his actions. Claude
Ryan, the influential editor of Le Devoir, was dismayed at the
uncritical support Trudeau enjoyed outside Quebec: "One had
the impression that, but for a few voices crying in the wilderness,
all critical reflection had practically ceased in English Canada."[2]
Nonetheless, the debate triggered by the crisis made it clear that
the *War Measures Act* was poorly suited to deal with emergencies
in the age of human rights.

The momentum towards codifying human rights began outside
Canada soon after the Second World War. The UN's founding
charter included a mandate to promote human rights. In 1948
the Organization of American States produced the *American
Declaration of the Rights of Man*, and the UN General Assembly
approved the *Convention on the Prevention and Punishment of the
Crime of Genocide* and the *Universal Declaration of Human Rights*.
But it was the UDHR that became a potent symbol. Anticolonial movements, especially in Africa, drew on the language of
the UDHR.[3] Twelve new African nations incorporated part or
all of the UDHR in their constitutions. The *European Convention
on Human Rights* (1950), inspired in part by the UDHR, created
the first regional enforcement mechanism for human rights: the
European Court of Human Rights. The first global human rights
treaties were also a legacy of the UDHR: the *International Covenant
on Civil and Political Rights* (1967) and the *International Covenant
on Economic, Social and Political Rights* (1967). Meanwhile, a global
human rights movement was taking shape. There was already
the International Labour Organization (1919), Fédération inter-
nationale des ligue des droits de la personne (1922), Freedom
House (1941), and the International League for the Rights of
Man (1942).[4] But it was the founding of Amnesty International
in 1961 that heralded a new era of transnational human rights

activism. In Canada, dozens of human rights and civil liberties groups were founded in the 1960s.[5]

But the Cold War continued to stifle human rights progress.[6] Within the UN, the great powers fought over the meaning of human rights.[7] Treaties became a propaganda tool for nations to attack one another and to secure alliances around the world, most notably in the Third World. The Soviet Union repeatedly highlighted instances of vicious racial discrimination in the United States; meanwhile, the Americans attacked the Soviets for violating civil liberties—for example, by restricting the free movement of peoples. During the worst moments of the Cold War, violations of human rights at home and abroad were justified as necessary to defeat communism. Human rights did eventually transform international politics as the Cold War began to wane.[8] This transformation took the form of action and rhetoric premised on the belief that citizens and governments had a legitimate interest in the human rights of people in other states.[9] Human rights placed the individual beyond the state and legitimized intervention in the internal affairs of states to protect the rights of their citizens. Examples of how human rights informed international politics abound in the literature on human rights: the Carter administration promoted human rights in American foreign policy; the US State Department began compiling annual human rights reports; international human rights organizations began to emerge; international treaties were negotiated such as the UN covenants and the Helsinki Accords; the international humanitarian effort in Biafra set a precedent for future interventions; transnational advocacy networks were mobilized to combat gross human rights abuses in Argentina and Chile; Soviet dissidents began to organize around the regime's international human rights obligations; the Ford Foundation began making forays into human rights abroad; a global campaign against apartheid in South Africa began to take root; and there was a proliferation of human rights policies in foreign aid programs. As a result of these and similar developments, human rights "reached consensual ('prescriptive') status on the international level."[10]

The most obvious sign that a rights revolution was brewing in Canada was widespread legal reform. The federal government introduced a new policy in the early 1960s to remove all references to racial preferences in immigration, and within five years implemented a points system. Meanwhile, the province that introduced the first antidiscrimination law in Canadian history also passed the country's first human rights legislation. Ontario's *Human Rights Code* incorporated existing antidiscrimination laws into a single statute that was enforced through the Human Rights Commission.[11] The Code prohibited discrimination on the basis of religion, race, or ethnicity in accommodation, employment, services, and the display of signs. This was a landmark achievement. First, it contained provisions for an effective enforcement mechanism, human rights investigators, informal conciliation, and administrative tribunals with the power to enforce settlements. Second, it included a mandate for human rights education. Third, the legislation provided for a much broader range of remedies, reflecting the new focus on conciliation rather than punishment: offenders might pay a fine, offer an apology, reinstate an employee, or agree to a negotiated settlement.

The *Human Rights Code* represented a new approach to addressing discrimination. Instead of defining discrimination as the product of prejudiced individuals, human rights laws were premised on the belief that prejudice could be unspoken and systemic.[12] Human rights statutes—unlike antidiscrimination statutes—were designed to eliminate the conditions that produced discriminatory acts. Over time, the legislation was interpreted in such a way as to recognize that intent was not required to prove discrimination and that seemingly neutral practices could have discriminatory effects. In this way, Ontario's *Human Rights Code* addressed substantive as well as formal equality.[13] Over the next fifteen years, every other jurisdiction in Canada would pass similar legislation.

Human rights legislation was only one example of how rights discourse was changing the law. Governments across Canada initiated widespread legal reforms between 1968 and 1971. Two major inquiries in 1968—Ontario's Royal Commission into Civil Rights, and Quebec's Commission of Enquiry into the Administration of Justice on Criminal and Penal Matters—resulted in extensive statutory reforms designed to protect individual rights.[14] These inquiries addressed hundreds of issues, including ombudsmen, legal aid, juvenile and family courts, coroner's inquests, bail, compensation to victims of crime, and the processing of appeals. Meanwhile, most jurisdictions passed privacy legislation to protect individuals from such actions as unnecessary wiretaps, or insurance companies disclosing information about their clients. Linguistic rights were affirmed in 1969 with the passage of the federal *Official Languages Act*, and in 1971 the federal government endorsed a policy of promoting multiculturalism.[15] In 1969 an omnibus bill with 120 amendments to federal statutes partly legalized abortion, decriminalized homosexuality, restricted the scope of material witness orders, and instituted stronger criminal penalties for cruelty against animals.[16] A prohibition on hate speech was added to the Criminal Code in 1970, making it a crime for anyone to promote genocide or incite hatred against an identifiable group.[17] But the most significant developments at the turn of the decade involved emerging social movements and a Parliamentary committee.

One of the most formidable social movements of this period—in an era already famous for its activism—was the Aboriginal rights movement. Aboriginal peoples had rarely articulated their grievances using rights talk. Their hesitancy to embrace human rights was most apparent amidst the controversy over the federal government's 1969 White Paper. The policy recommended, in essence, eliminating Indian status: "The policies proposed recognize the simple reality that the separate legal status of Indians and the policies which have flowed from it have kept the Indian people apart from and behind other Canadians. The

Indian people have not been full citizens of the communities and provinces in which they live and have not enjoyed the equality and benefits that such participation offers."[18] The federal government sought to surrender responsibility for Aboriginal people to the provinces, repeal the *Indian Act,* and transfer control of lands to individual Aboriginals. The language of the proposed policy was deeply mired in rights discourse: "The Government believes in equality. It believes that all men and women have equal rights ... To argue against this right is to argue for discrimination, isolation and separation."[19] But the policy was fundamentally flawed: it ignored more than a century of discrimination and a host of inequities that the state had imposed on Aboriginal peoples. The approach was profoundly assimilationist.[20] Individual ownership of land, for instance, would have undermined collective landownership. The White Paper, which was quickly retracted, galvanized Aboriginal peoples.[21] This was a critical moment in the emergence of the modern Aboriginal rights movement.[22] Central to this activism was "the expansion of the term 'Aboriginal rights," which had often connoted land rights but was increasingly used to frame a host of grievances such as the right to self-government."[23]

Similarly, the federal Royal Commission on the Status of Women reinvigorated the women's rights movement. The commission's groundbreaking report in 1970 identified a host of laws and policies that discriminated against women. By 1977 the federal government had implemented over 80 percent of the report's recommendations. For example, the 1974 federal *Statute Law (Status of Women) Amendment Act* removed discriminatory provisions in immigration, pensions, unemployment insurance, elections, and citizenship.[24] More importantly, the report energized the movement. Throughout the country, social movement organizations proliferated, as did Status of Women Councils. Vancouver Status of Women, for instance, was created in 1970 and quickly became one of the largest and most active social movement organizations in the country. VSW's activism included documenting cases of discrimination and drawing attention to sexism in the media; producing surveys and conducting research on issues such as equal pay (e.g., documenting employers' pay scales); launching letter-writing campaigns at employers who discriminated against female employees; sending volunteers to employers to discuss hiring and management practices; organizing conferences on human rights; creating an ombudswoman position to assist women who were filing human rights complaints; and lobbying government departments and school boards on policy issues such as gender stereotyping in textbooks.[25] There had been only a handful of women's rights organizations by the late 1960s; by the end of the 1970s, there were nearly three hundred organizations in British Columbia dedicated to pursuing gender equality.

These were remarkable years. During this brief period, governments initiated extensive legal reforms and thousands of Canadians mobilized into social movements. The Jewish Labour Committee and the Association for Civil Liberties had spent much of the postwar period advocating for a national bill of rights and antidiscrimination laws. These two groups were largely defunct by the time a new generation of rights associations emerged in the 1960s. The first to appear were the British Columbia Civil Liberties Association (1962), Ligue des droits de l'homme (1963), and the Canadian Civil Liberties Association (1964). In 1968, the federal government provided $1 million in funding to organize local community groups to celebrate the twentieth anniversary of the UDHR. Several human rights associations were formed in each province. The Newfoundland Human Rights Association and the Alberta Human Rights Association, among others, became permanent, independent social movements.[26] Each cited the UDHR in its founding constitution.[27]

Another indication that a rights revolution was on the horizon was the subtle change in political discourse surrounding the constitution. Opponents of a bill of rights had routinely paid homage to the principle of Parliamentary supremacy. The first breakthrough was the 1960 *Bill of Rights*, which, albeit a statute and not a constitutional amendment, demonstrated that codifying rights was not inconsistent with a parliamentary system of government.[28] However, it was a vague and limited statute that contained only the most elementary civil and political rights. Frank Scott disdained the law: "That pretentious piece of legislation has proven as ineffective as many of us predicted."[29] Only a constitutional amendment could overcome the weakness of the *Bill of Rights*. In an attempt to secure an agreement with the provinces to patriate the constitution with an entrenched bill of rights, the federal government appointed a Joint Committee of the Senate and House of Commons in 1970. Although the initiative ultimately failed, it is notable that there was a consensus that Parliamentary supremacy was no longer an obstacle to a bill of rights: "Parliamentary sovereignty is no more sacrosanct a principle than is the respect for human liberty which is reflected in a Bill of Rights. Legislative sovereignty is already limited legally by the distribution of powers under a federal system and, some would say, by natural law or by the common law Bill of Rights."[30]

But the committee did not profoundly challenge Canada's rights culture. The provinces viewed civil liberties (press, speech, association, assembly, and religion), due process, and voting as the only appropriate human rights for the constitution.[31] Manitoba alone defined economic and social welfare as human rights; however, the committee chairmen concluded that "it seems to be generally accepted that it would be unrealistic to think of entrenching such rights in a Constitution."[32] Most of the social movement organizations participating in the process shared this assumption.[33] The National Council of Women was concerned primarily with prohibiting discrimination on the basis of sex, national or ethnic origin, colour, religion, and marital status.[34] The National Indian Brotherhood declined to recommend any specific rights: they were committed to first addressing Aboriginal peoples' land claims.[35] Perhaps the most controversial submission came from the Action League for the Physically

Handicapped Advancement (ALPHA).[36] After presenting a grim picture of the lives of people with disabilities, who were routinely denied jobs and services, ALPHA appealed to the committee to recognize a human right to accessible transportation, housing, and public institutions. Mark MacGuigan, the MP co-chairing the inquiry, was doubtful: "The difficulty with putting something of that kind and of that nature in the constitution is that it is so broad that it would be very hard to bring court cases on the basis of it ... If it is negative in the Bill of Rights, I think it can be handled by the courts, but if it is to be positive, it is so broad that it is very difficult for a court to say the government must do this or the government must do that."[37]

The beginnings of a rights revolution were also evident in foreign policy. Canada had become a major contributor to the Colombo Plan, which, although it had no mandate for human rights, provided foreign aid to support democracy in countries such as India, Sri Lanka, and Pakistan. In fact, Canada's commitment to humanitarian aid expanded dramatically in the 1970s. The Miles for Millions walkathons, begun in 1967, raised millions of dollars in aid for Third World countries. Meanwhile, the federal government was under intense pressure from international institutions, a domestic human rights movement, and a maturing Canadian legal profession to ratify human rights treaties.[38] A White Paper in 1970 called for a more positive approach to human rights at the UN: "There is an expectation that Canada will participate in international efforts in the human rights field on a more extensive and meaningful scale than in the past."[39] It was not much of a commitment. In fact, the federal government had given no indication at all that it planned to promote human rights abroad. Yet this was the first time in history that the Canadian government had come close to endorsing the principle that human rights was a cornerstone of international politics. Soon after, the federal government targeted South Africa for its human rights abuses—withdrawing trade commissioners, cancelling export credits, halting arms sales, and banning that country's athletes from entering Canada. The prime minister, John Diefenbaker, also joined Indian prime minister Jawaharlal Nehru in shaping a resolution on racial discrimination within the Commonwealth, which forced South Africa to withdraw its bid for membership.[40]

Jennifer Smith's case in 1970 exemplified how Canada's rights culture was changing. Smith was a thirty-year-old single mother struggling to raise four children in Toronto after her husband deserted her. She was taking courses to complete her high school degree and had been on welfare since 1966. Smith received an unexpected letter in 1970 informing her that her welfare was being cut off because she was no longer living as a single person. The decision to withdraw her support was based on a surprise inspection a week earlier, which Smith described as follows:

> On October 11 at 10:00am a [welfare official] came to my door, showed me a card indicating that he was from the Department of Social and Family Services, and advised me that this was a routine investigation. He said that he wanted to see the apartment and then began to look around. Upon opening a closet in the living room, he discovered some beer bottles and said 'I don't give a shit what you do with your cheque; what I want to know is whether you're good for those kids.' Then he asked me for a picture of my husband and as I was searching for one in my purse, he went into the bedroom without asking my permission. He opened the closet in the bedroom and found therein my boyfriend ... who had hidden there when he had heard the knock on the front door. He had hidden there in order to avoid trouble between the welfare authorities and myself. He [welfare official] said that he no longer needed a picture of my husband because he had discovered my husband in the bedroom. I advised the [welfare official] that said man in the cupboard was not my husband. The [welfare official] asked my boyfriend a number of questions relating to

our relationship. The [welfare official] said that my "sex life" was my own business and that it had nothing to do with my receiving welfare cheques. Thereupon he left my premises. On October 15, when I telephoned the welfare office to enquire whether I could attend there to collect my cheque my [regular] welfare worker ... advised me that [the welfare official who had visited me] had informed them that because he had found a man in my apartment, I could not collect my cheque until that man attended at the office of the Special Investigation Unit and answered some questions.

Denied any right to challenge the decision and having to wait until a Board of Review was called, Smith was typical of single mothers who were victims of a welfare system eager to cut costs. Single women suspected of having a man in the house were routinely denied access to welfare. The "spouse in the house" rule clearly discriminated against women—it assumed that a sexual relationship implied a financial one, yet that same assumption was not made about men. Welfare officials also applied questionable practices during their inspections. Officials would demand to know about the most intimate aspects of a recipient's relationships, and in some cases they drew conclusions based on flimsy evidence such as the presence of open beer cans or a raised toilet seat. A Deserted Wives Unit was created in 1961 to track down husbands to sue them to reclaim benefits, but most of the department's efforts were directed at monitoring the lives of women on welfare rather than their deadbeat husbands. For this reason, women on welfare—not the men—suffered the bulk of the public's resentment.[41]

Smith brought her case to the Canadian Civil Liberties Association, which embraced the issue on behalf of all single mothers on welfare. Within a decade, rights activists and feminists had successfully framed the spouse-in-the-house policy as a women's rights issue. Although it would take many years, the policy was eventually eliminated.[42] Jennifer Smith's case typifies much of what happened during this period. Single mothers on welfare perceived something to be unfair; emerging social movements provided a vehicle for fighting this abuse of power; activists appropriated the language of rights to frame their grievances. It is worth remembering that, when mothers' allowances were introduced in the 1920s, government officials routinely sought to regulate women's private lives and impose unfair double standards. But at that time, women's organizations framed mothers' allowances as *privileges* and found no contradiction in denying pensions for racial minorities or requiring recipients to abide by a strict moral code. In contrast, women's organizations in the 1970s often framed their grievances in the language of rights.[43] In the same way that racial, religious, and ethnic minorities appropriated rights discourse to articulate their grievances, so did the women's movement.

There were, to be sure, many crucial milestones during this period: a UN declaration of rights followed by a host of international and regional treaties; widespread social movement mobilization, including a robust human rights movement; human rights legislation expanding beyond race, religion, and ethnicity; and serious discussions around codifying rights in the constitution.[44] Perhaps the most fundamental development, however, was the way in which rights talk was changing in Canada. The language of human rights was supplanting civil liberties in public discourse. The scope of rights discussed during the Special Joint Committee on the Constitution, for instance, was far broader than in 1947, 1948, and 1950, when similar hearings were held.[45] In the 1940s, Canada's rights culture could be defined primarily in reference to free speech, association, religion, press, assembly, and due process. By the 1960s, it was clear that a culture of rights was emerging that embraced the principle of non-discrimination.

Nonetheless, the rights revolution was at best an unfilled promise. Sex discrimination, for instance, became the subject of opinion polls beginning in the 1950s. Many Canadians, according to a 1955 poll, were uncomfortable with the idea of a female doctor (20 percent) or a female lawyer (34 percent).[46] Respondents to a 1960 poll overwhelmingly (70 percent) agreed that married women should *not* be given equal opportunity with men for jobs.[47] And none of these polls framed the issue as a human right. The first polling on same-sex couples did not ask about rights but instead asked about whether homosexual behaviour (conducted in private) should be criminalized: 41 percent answered yes in 1968, and 42 percent said no.[48] Abortion, as well, was not framed in terms of women's rights. Instead, pollsters asked whether abortion should be permitted if the child was deformed (46 percent answered yes in 1962), or if the mother's mental or physical health was in danger (72 percent answered yes in 1965, and 88 percent answered yes in 1972); or whether a woman and her doctor alone should decide (66 percent answered yes in 1972).[49]

The rights revolution was, at best, in its infancy. Of Toronto's more than 1,100 firefighters, only two were visible minorities. The forced relocation of African Canadian residents from the Halifax suburb of Africville between 1964 and 1967 was, according to some people, an opportunity to improve the residents' poor living conditions. Others saw the relocation as the destruction of a community. In either case, the relocation demonstrated that African Canadians had little influence even in their own community. Foreign policy continued to prioritize state sovereignty to the detriment of human rights. Landmark human rights statutes contained many flaws. Several jurisdictions, including Quebec and the federal government, had not yet even introduced human rights legislation. The federal *Bill of Rights* was a lame duck. In 1969, in the midst of a surge of protests, Montreal City Council passed Bylaw 3926, which allowed the Executive Council to take special measures if there were "reasonable grounds to believe that the holding of assemblies, parades or gatherings will cause tumult, endanger safety, peace or public order."[50] The Executive Council immediately introduced an ordinance banning the "holding of any assembly, parade or gathering on the public domain of the City of Montreal for a time period of thirty days."[51] Montreal had, in effect, banned freedom of assembly for a month. And it would do so again in 1971. Nonetheless, the seeds of change were evident. The inexorable evolution of human rights would soon lead to a moment in history that revolutionized Canada's rights culture.

CHAPTER 4

The Rights Revolution

IT SEEMS TRITE TO FOCUS on any one group in society when discussing Canada's rights revolution. Still, to understand the context and implications of this revolution, it is worth beginning with how it impacted women, especially in the workplace. Consider, for instance, Doris Anderson, who was hardly typical of most Canadian women in the 1970s. As editor of *Chatelaine* from 1957 to 1977, she was instrumental in turning it into the most successful magazine in the country. Yet throughout her career she faced many of the same obstacles and frustrations most women encountered in the male-dominated workplace. As an associate editor in the mid-1950s, she had to endure weekly lunch meetings with her male editor: "He insisted I match him drink for drink, although he must have weighed a good hundred pounds more than I. In those days I could hold my own—as most women in my business had to learn to do. After lunches with Clare, though, I always took a trip to the washroom, put my finger down my throat, and threw up; otherwise I would never have been able to go back to the office and function with any degree of efficacy."[1] Although she led the most successful magazine in the Maclean-Hunter corporation, she was never promoted above editor of *Chatelaine*, earned 20 percent less than other editors in the company, and was almost fired when she became pregnant. Sexual harassment was rampant to the point of being commonplace: "Some men simply assumed sexual harassment was a perk

of being boss ... Every single woman I knew had been proposi-
tioned at some time, mostly by married men."[2]

Sexual harassment would eventually be prohibited under
human rights law in Canada, but at the time, it was a non-
issue. The term "sexual harassment" was not even used until a
speak-out rally in Ithaca, New York, where a group of women
were protesting intimidation at work. The first Canadian study
of it was not published until 1979.[3] One woman, testifying before
the British Columbia Human Rights Commission, recounted
her most vivid experience with sexual harassment, which took
place in 1978:

> I was working as a cashier for one of the large chain drug
> stores. The boss was continually propositioning women. There
> was a narrow pathway between where the cash register was and
> a wall. One time I was walking through the pathway and he
> was coming through the other way. He continued and instead
> of allowing me time to back up he pressed me against the wall
> and as he went by he grabbed my behind. I told him to take
> his "paws" off me. He looked rather stunned and walked away.
> Later the assistant supervisor came over and told me I was
> fired.[4]

Another woman, also testifying before the commission, had suffered a similar experience in 1980:

> My experience occurred during the first few months of employ-
> ment. It happened in a locked supply office. The man was very
> strong, picked me up and took me into a little room (with
> me protesting). I didn't think he would actually do anything,
> I thought he was just fooling around. He held my arms and
> proceeded to feel my body. After I finally convinced him to put
> me down (in tears), he informed me that before he got trans-
> ferred he would make love to me whether I wanted to or not.[5]

Sexual harassment perfectly captures how ideas about rights
change over time. One activist in the 1970s described sexual
harassment as "so common that it was rarely even talked about."
It often appeared in the form of pin-ups or graffiti if not outright

groping and propositions from male workers.[6] Julie Webb, for
example, faced sexual harassment on a daily basis at her job at
Cypress Pizza in Vancouver. Her boss, Rajinder Singh Roopra,
touched her hair repeatedly; put his arm around her and held her
against her will; made suggestive sexual remarks; leered, ogled,
and made suggestive gestures; asked her several times for dinner
dates and to visit a motel to watch pornographic videos; and
continually inquired about her sex life.[7]

For a long time—most of the 1970s and 1980s—the largest
number of human rights complaints involved sex discrimination.
Discrimination for many women began early in life. At school
they could see that their male teachers received better pay and salaries and that female teachers were forced to quit when they got
married or had children. Sex discrimination continued at university, where women faced exclusion and segregation in classes.
Shelly Rabinovitch recalled one experience in 1973 when she was
a senior at university:

> Dr. Stuckey held a fourth-year seminar—that I was given per-
> mission to attend—analyzing the ways in which women were
> portrayed in erotica and pornography. Despite York's repu-
> tation as a liberal university, we were not allowed to hold the
> seminar on university property. So about a half dozen women
> would bus to Dr. Stuckey's home where we would drink tea,
> eat cookies, and discuss hard-core depictions of women from
> North America and Europe.[8]

In 1920 there were 3,716 female university graduates in Canada
compared to 19,580 men; in 1960, the ratio was 26,629 to 80,582;
by 1975 there were still only 140,268 female and 190,696 male
university graduates.[9]

Transitioning from school to work in 1980 was, as Shari
Graydon remembered, equally perilous:

> A year after I joined an international public relations firm at
> an entry-level position with a salary to match, I experienced a
> little sisterhood from one of the secretaries. She informed me
> that the agency's newest hire—a man who couldn't write a press

release to save his life—was being paid $8,000 a year more than
me. She also confided that he'd cleverly found an opportunity
to reveal to her that he didn't wear any underwear.[10]

The percentage of women in the total Canadian workforce
climbed from 20 percent in 1941 to 34.3 percent in 1971.[11]
Employment discrimination was rampant. Women were denied
jobs as taxi drivers because it was too dangerous or as bus drivers
because the seats were too large; prevented from joining police
or fire departments by minimum height and weight requirements; and banned from work deemed suitable only for men,
including construction, mining, surveying, and a host of others.
One rather creative school board in St. John's, Newfoundland,
justified paying female janitors less than men because the former were assigned smaller brooms. The idea that unequal treatment for women was common sense rather than discrimination
was so ingrained that one Ontario High Court judge rejected a
policewoman's request for equal pay in 1968 on the following
basis: "She is not being discriminated against by the fact that
she received a different wage, different from male constables, for
the fact of difference is in accord with every rule of economics,
civilization, family life and common sense."[12] In 1974, women
constituted barely 20 percent of enrolments in law schools and
less than 5 percent of practising lawyers and were virtually absent
among the judiciary.[13] Between 1919 and 1972, women never
held more than 5 percent of the seats in the federal House of
Commons; between 1968 and 1972, Grace Macinnis was the only
woman in Parliament.[14] By 1974, women working full-time jobs
earned less than 66 percent of a male wage; women with a university degree earned an annual average salary of $21,000 compared
to $30,000 for their male counterparts.[15] At a time when one
Canadian in five was poor, 42.5 percent of single women and 74.4
percent of women over sixty-five earned less than $1,500 a year.
One-third of single mothers were impoverished.[16]

The rights revolution affected all Canadians. At the same
time, it is easy to appreciate how women and other marginalized

people might have especially benefited from fluctuating notions
of rights. Not only had antidiscrimination law initially failed to
acknowledge sex discrimination, but most activists (including
many feminists) did not even campaign for banning sex discrimination until the 1960s. British Columbia became, in 1969, the
first province to ban discrimination on the basis of sex.

The passage into law of British Columbia's 1974 *Human Rights
Code* was yet another critical moment in Canadian human rights
history. It was perhaps the most progressive human rights law in
the world. It contained all the strengths of the Ontario model,
including a viable enforcement mechanism, but it also incorporated a "reasonable cause" section.[17] Whereas other human rights
statutes in Canada were limited to specific grounds, such as race
or religion, the reasonable cause provision banned *all* forms of
discrimination unless the accused could demonstrate reasonable
cause.[18] But legal reform was only one example of how human
rights was changing Canadian society. A generation after the federal government almost rejected the UDHR, it embraced human
rights as a legitimate component of foreign policy. Meanwhile,
a vigorous social movement sector had emerged whose various
advocates in large part framed their grievances in the language of
human rights. And after several failed attempts, the constitution
was patriated with an entrenched bill of rights.

Social movements embodied the rights revolution. An astound-
ing number of social movements had emerged by the 1970s. An
energized student movement contributed to the creation of a
New Left; the number of women's groups in British Columbia
alone increased from two in 1969 to over two hundred within a
decade; the first gay rights organizations were formed in Vancouver and Toronto, and a national association was established
in 1975; and the founding of Greenpeace marked the birth of
the modern environmental movement. There were at least four
national Aboriginal associations and thirty-three provincial

organizations.[19] African Canadian social movement organizations (SMOs) spread across the country, while advocates for children's rights, prisoners' rights, animal rights, peace, poverty, and official languages organized in unprecedented numbers. The federal Secretary of State alone was providing funding to more than 3,500 SMOs by the early 1980s.[20] All of these movements employed the language of rights. Vancouver Status of Women, for example, campaigned for a Ministry of Women's Rights and framed freedom from sexual harassment as a human right. Even Canada's churches were deeply implicated in the rights revolution. Several Christian churches, most notably the United Church of Canada, replaced missionary work with humanitarian and rights-based activism overseas.[21]

Notable in Canada's social movement landscape was the emergence of civil liberties *and* human rights organizations, with at least one in each province. This development was all the more surprising given that there was no strong tradition of such advocacy. It was not simply a rhetorical distinction; in fact, it symbolized some of the changes within Canada's rights culture. Civil liberties groups fought to remove unfair restrictions on, for instance, single women who lost their welfare support if there was evidence they were living with a man. But their advocacy ended at ensuring equal treatment for welfare recipients. In contrast, human rights groups argued that individuals had a right to economic security and could not exercise their political and civil rights without proper resources. Human rights advocacy went beyond equal treatment to framing poverty as a rights violation. The differences mattered. Human rights organizations clashed with civil liberties groups on a host of issues, from pornography to sexual assault laws. Whereas human rights groups sought to ban pornography or hate speech, civil liberties groups saw any restrictions as a violation of free speech. Similarly, human rights organizations wanted to ban any evidence in sexual assault trials of a victim's sexual history, whereas civil liberties groups resisted such policies as a violation of due process.[22]

Montreal's Ligue des droits de l'homme exemplifies this distinction as well as how the rights revolution would influence social movements. This group began as a civil liberties association (its original English name was the Quebec Civil Liberties Union), but in 1974 it explicitly rejected its civil libertarian roots and embraced a human rights platform. Its new mandate was to adapt to the changes occurring in Quebec society and consider the unique problems facing the poor, women, the elderly, youth, and minorities. With this new mandate, economic and social rights were given the same priority (if not greater) as civil and political rights. The Ligue believed that equality would be achieved not by focusing on individual rights but by improving the social conditions in which those rights were exercised.[23] This reflected broader developments within Canada's social movement landscape.

Social movements led by women, gays and lesbians, Aboriginal peoples, churches, and a host of others embraced human rights as a vision for social change.[24] At the most basic level, the language of rights united all of these movements around the principle that non-discrimination was a fundamental human right. Although they often sought to strengthen and enforce human rights laws, this was not their only strategy for advancing new rights claims. In many provinces, social movements played a leading role in human rights education. British Columbia's Human Rights Commission, for instance, depended heavily on SMOs throughout the 1970s and early 1980s. The commission provided grants to organizations to host conferences, conduct research on issues such as mandatory retirement, or produce educational materials. By the early 1980s, these organizations were essentially carrying out the commission's statutory mandate for education. Emerging rights claims, involving issues ranging from sexual harassment to non-discrimination for people with disabilities, were integral to these educational efforts long before they were recognized in law.[25] Moreover, the women's rights movement, if defined as any organized non-governmental activities promoting women's equality, was extraordinarily diverse. The movement encompassed women's centres, transition homes, rape crisis centres, music festivals, self-defence classes, publishing houses, newspapers, books, advocacy groups, rallies, films, book cooperatives, professional associations, and much more.

This is not to say that all activists embraced human rights. A collective of women's liberationists from across Canada, for example, published an anthology in 1972 explicitly rejecting rights discourse as a vision for social change: "The philosophy of the women's rights groups is that civil liberty and equality can be achieved *within* the present system, while the underlying belief of women's liberation is that oppression can be overcome only through a radical and fundamental change in the structure of our society."[26] Queer activists were similarly divided between liberationists and rights activists. Many of the former largely eschewed rights activism in favour of a more radical agenda.[27] The National Indian Brotherhood adopted the Assembly of Indian Chiefs of Alberta's "Red Paper" in 1970, which famously rejected the federal government's human rights approach to Aboriginal peoples. Women Against Pornography, a grassroots organization founded in Victoria in 1982 dedicated to eliminating pornography, is another example. The organization's opposition to censorship was "not for civil libertarian (male) reasons, but because we believe state censorship is never in women's best interests, but rather will be used by the ruling elite to further oppress minorities."[28] Any support they expressed for human rights was only meant to demonstrate the futility of framing grievances as rights.[29] These and similar social movement organizations preferred grassroots activism for social change: establishing information services and drop-in centres; distributing leaflets to consumers in downtown stores that discriminated against female workers; supporting strikes or boycotts; picketing pornography stores; hosting consciousness-raising groups; engaging in civil disobedience; harassing rapists with poster campaigns; and organizing rallies, walkathons, marches, and protests as well as Take Back the Night vigils.

The rights revolution was not restricted to Canada. Human rights, as many historians have argued, "played virtually no role as a protest language in the decades after the Second World War."[30] Not until the 1970s did human rights become an integral component of international politics. Amnesty International symbolized this new era. Membership in AI expanded dramatically, from 20,000 in 1969 to 570,000 in 1983. Also, the organization shed its earlier focus on prisoners of conscience to become a truly human rights association addressing a range of violations.[31]

Among the most visible human rights campaigns were those in Eastern Europe and South America.[32] One of AI's first and most successful campaigns was against Augusto Pinochet's brutal dictatorship in Chile (1973–89). After overthrowing Salvador Allende, the military junta imposed a state of terror that included eliminating political opponents, engaging in torture and indiscriminate killings, banning political parties and trade unions, and censoring the media.[33] Chile, much like Argentina, adopted a practice of "disappearances": the intelligence services would kidnap people, deny that they were incarcerated, and dispose of the victim's bodies (sometimes by throwing them out of planes into the ocean) to conceal the evidence. One of the more gruesome practices of the Argentinian regime involved imprisoning pregnant women until they gave birth; then, after killing the mother and disposing of her body, the state would give the baby to a couple seeking adoption. The prison guards were, in essence, feeding a pregnant woman to keep her alive until they could harvest her offspring. Although AI and its network of transnational human rights organizations failed to undermine the regime in Chile, it did much to foster international condemnation of it. Later, in the 1980s, AI would play a critical role in undermining Argentina's junta.

There had been international human rights movements before this—most notably, the antislavery and suffragette movements. But the 1970s saw the birth of a truly transnational human rights movement. By gathering information and leveraging countries against one another, newly emerging transnational networks brought pressure to bear against apartheid in South Africa, disappearances in Chile and Argentina, Indonesia's oppression of the East Timorese, and the suppression of political dissent in the Soviet Union and the Philippines.[34] By drawing attention to horrific narratives of torture, killings, and imprisonments, AI and various transnational advocacy networks inaugurated a new era of global human rights politics.

It was also during this period that the modern international human rights regime was born. Many of today's "core" human rights treaties came into force during this period: the *International Convention on the Elimination of All Forms of Racism* (1969); the *International Covenant on Civil and Political Rights* (1976); the *International Covenant on Social, Economic and Cultural Rights* (1976); the *Convention on the Elimination of All Forms of Discrimination Against Women* (1981); and the *Convention Against Torture and Other Cruel, Inhuman or Degrading Treatment or Punishment* (1987). Ratification of these treaties had increased exponentially by the 1980s. In 1948, most states had questioned the legitimacy of the UDHR; by the 1980s, it had become almost compulsory for any liberal state to ratify a human rights treaty.

It was almost inevitable, given such developments, that Canadian foreign policy would begin to incorporate human rights. In 1975, the federal government established a Federal/Provincial/Territorial Continuing Committee of Officials on Human Rights to consult over international treaties.[35] After securing provincial consent, Canada in 1976 acceded to the *International Covenant on Civil and Political Rights*, as well as the *International Covenant on Social, Economic and Cultural Rights*.[36] Canada later supported declarations or conventions relating to racism, children, and women's rights. This meant that officials had to prepare speeches for ministers commemorating anniversaries or special human rights initiatives, and officials from the Department of

External Affairs had to meet with human rights SMOs regularly to prepare for UN Commission on Human Rights meetings. Canada demonstrated its commitment to promoting human rights abroad through interventions in sessions of the Commission on Human Rights and similar international forums.[37] Canadians also played a key role in drafting the *Declaration on the Elimination of All Forms of Intolerance and Discrimination Based on Religious Belief* (1981).[38] These initiatives indicated a profound shift in foreign policy, which in the past had rejected human rights as a legitimate component of international politics.[39]

Canada participated in the negotiations that led to the Helsinki Accords in 1975 with the Soviet Union. Among other things, those accords committed each country to a set of human rights principles.[40] These international commitments provided a unique opportunity for parliamentarians to involve themselves in foreign affairs. Before this, MPs had responded to human rights violations in Eastern Europe with vague calls for self-determination or minority rights. Now, MPs were able to draw on the language contained in the Helsinki Accords to introduce resolutions in Parliament dealing with family reunification, free movement of people, religious freedom, and other equally precise reforms that demonstrated an evolving understanding of the issues.[41] MPs also participated in increasing numbers in international human rights conferences as part of Canadian delegations to the UN and as members of various monitoring groups abroad.[42] Over time, many MPs gained valuable experience and expertise on human rights issues, and they brought this knowledge to Parliament, where they continued to pressure the federal government to integrate human rights into foreign policy.[43] A private member's bill was introduced in 1978 to prohibit foreign aid to countries with poor human rights records. Although the federal government immediately rejected the idea, the bill remained on Parliament's agenda, where it drew attention to the human rights component of Canadian foreign policy. As a result, the government was forced to defend and elaborate its aid policies in public.

There were also many instances when international developments had an impact on domestic policy. Among other things, policy-makers could appeal to international human rights law when implementing controversial domestic legislation. The International Year for Human Rights, besides facilitating the emergence of numerous human rights organizations, was the impetus for human rights legislation in British Columbia, Alberta, New Brunswick, and Newfoundland. Political leaders often cited international human rights treaties when justifying the introduction of human rights laws, including the federal *Bill of Rights* (1960), the *Ontario Human Rights Code* (1962), the *Quebec Charter of Human Rights and Freedoms* (1975), and the *Yukon Human Rights Act* (1987).[44] British Columbia would use the International Year of the Disabled as an incentive to ban discrimination on the basis of physical and mental disability.[45] And most of the provinces introduced legislative reforms in response to Canada's acceding to the *Convention on the Elimination of All Forms of Discrimination Against Women.*

The rights revolution in foreign policy was abetted by the actions of SMOs headquartered in Canada and operating abroad. MATCH International was established following the 1975 United Nations for Women conference in Mexico City.[46] This was the first ever conference of its kind: run for women and by women in partnership with women in poor countries. The federal government provided funding for SMOs such as MATCH International to promote human rights and humanitarian work abroad. Churches also became integral to Canada's new focus on human rights and humanitarianism around the world. In 1968 the federal government embarked on a strategy to use churches as conduits for humanitarian aid, beginning with a $100,000 grant to the United Church to manufacture water-drilling rigs in India. Within a few years the Canadian International Development Agency was operating a permanent SMO division.[47] These developments were part of a shift among Canadian churches away from missionary work in favour of humanitarian efforts.

And the churches, in turn, sought to influence policy and generate public support for human rights–based foreign policy.[48] Christian churches in Canada formed a multitude of SMOs to promote human rights abroad: the Inter-Church Committee for Human Rights in Latin America, the Canada–Asia Working Group, the Inter-Church Coalition for Africa, the Inter-Church Committee on Refugees, the Consultative Committee on Human Rights, and the Task Force on Corporate Responsibility. One project, Ten Days for World Development, launched in 1978, was especially successful in generating support for foreign policy based on human rights and humanitarianism.[49] As a result of these developments, Canada became one of a small group of "like-minded countries" (including Norway and the Netherlands) that linked development aid to human rights.[50]

There were subtle but nonetheless notable examples of how human rights were beginning to inform foreign policy. In 1976, the Canadian government inserted a section on refugees into its immigration law; in 1978, it took unilateral action to restrict Canadian companies from operating in South Africa and withdrew aid from the Amin regime in Uganda; in 1977, it imposed economic restrictions (including bans on food exports and a curtailing of credits) on Poland and the Soviet Union; in 1981, it suspended aid to Guatemala, El Salvador, and Sri Lanka.[51] In the midst of these debates, the Progressive Conservative Party, then in opposition, committed itself to a more rights-based foreign policy. When that party came to power in 1979, it honoured this commitment by, among other things, withholding aid from Vietnam for gross human rights violations.[52] In the course of the 1980s, Canada would impose sanctions on twenty-two countries.[53]

To be sure, human rights concerns never trumped economic and geopolitical interests. Major policy speeches on human rights in foreign policy were notably lacking in substance and often reflected a reluctance to interfere in the internal affairs of other nations, no matter how repressive.[54] The federal government vigorously resisted domestic pressure to intervene in the internal affairs of even the most repressive regimes, including when it came to human rights in Latin America.[55] It quickly reintroduced foreign aid for both Guatemala and El Salvador.[56] In addition to widespread human rights abuses in the Soviet Union, atrocities were committed under Idi Amin in Uganda (1971-79), Macias Nguema in Equatorial Guinea (1969-79), and the socialists in Ethiopia after 1974. There was also the Cambodian genocide (1975-79), the Hutu massacres in Burundi (1972), the Indonesian army's mass killings in East Timor (1975), and famine in China under Mao (1949-76). Canada also failed to impose sanctions against Chile. Even so, Canada's initial attempts to link human rights to foreign aid constituted an astonishing change for a country that, not so long ago, had no human rights movement, no human rights law, no concern for human rights abuses abroad, and had opposed the UDHR. In a complete reversal of its policy of the 1950s, Canada chaired a committee of the Commonwealth in 1984 to impose further sanctions on South Africa.[57]

The 1970s saw the beginning of a period of unprecedented legal reform. At no other time in Canadian history had policy-makers committed themselves so thoroughly to codifying rights in statute. This was a genuine rights revolution in law. British Columbia's *Human Rights Code* was a product of a new stage in Canada's rights culture. Women were able to use the reasonable cause section to set precedents in areas such as pregnancy and sexual harassment.[58] That people now spoke of sexual harassment as a human rights violation—and that it was recognized in human rights law—was remarkable. The reasonable cause provision was also used to ban discrimination on the basis of physical appearance, disability, age, language fluency, sexual orientation, and immigrant status.[59] This was a far cry from earlier legislation that recognized only race, religion, and ethnicity.

Saskatchewan had already passed a *Bill of Rights* in 1948, as had the federal government in 1960. In 1971, the first bill introduced in Alberta after Peter Lougheed's Progressive Conservative Party defeated the Social Credit Party, which had been in power for thirty-six years, was a *Bill of Rights*.[60] Four years later, the Quebec government passed its own human rights law: the *Charter of Human Rights and Fundamental Freedoms*. Each of these bills went beyond prohibiting discrimination and recognized civil liberties such as speech, association, assembly, religion, due process, and the right to vote. True, these bills were statutory rather than constitutional law, and it was questionable whether the provinces had the jurisdiction to legislate on civil liberties. Still, they were powerful symbols. Quebec's human rights legislation, in particular, set a new standard. The statute prohibited discrimination on the basis of social condition, language, and political opinion; affirmed employment equity and equal pay for work of equal value; recognized a wide range of civil and political rights (e.g., life, security, religion, expression, association) as well as economic and social rights (e.g., education, culture, social assistance, reasonable conditions of employment); and provided special protection for children, the mentally infirm, and the elderly.[61] Quebec was also the first province to make its legislation paramount above all other laws and to have the commission report directly to the legislature (for greater independence).

Trudy Ann Holloway's case was typical of the new human rights legal regime in Canada.[62] She began working full-time at the Shop Easy grocery store in 1975 as a cashier. When Clarico Foods Ltd. purchased the store in June 1980, Clair McDonald became the new owner and Rob Johnson was hired as the store manager. Holloway was pregnant at the time, but she suffered a miscarriage within a few weeks. In August 1980, Holloway became pregnant again. Fearing another miscarriage, Holloway's doctor recommended that she take five weeks off work, and in mid-November she returned to the store in good health. On 2 January 1981 she asked for the same raise as the two junior cashiers but was rebuffed because, according to McDonald, she would be leaving soon and could not keep up with the work. A week later, Holloway was called to McDonald's office and fired.

Holloway visited the Vancouver offices of the Human Rights Branch and filed a complaint under the *Human Rights Code*. She alleged that McDonald had fired her for being pregnant. At the time, pregnancy was not an enumerated ground under the law. Alan Andison, a human rights investigator, was assigned the case. Over the next three months, Andison met several times and exchanged letters and telephone calls with McDonald, Johnson, the other cashiers, and Holloway. McDonald told Andison that he fired Holloway because "she was leaving anyway" and "she didn't look good being pregnant." Johnson, the store manager, explained that they would have fired one of the junior cashiers if Holloway had not been pregnant (during his investigation, Andison discovered that one of the other cashiers was pregnant but had not told the owner out of fear of losing her job). If Andison had doubts about Holloway's case, they were quickly put to rest. Johnson told Andison that "I wouldn't let my own wife work while pregnant" and that Holloway "couldn't wear her uniform and wore an over-sized shirt. She was getting large and had a hard time bending. It was best to lay her off and let her collect [unemployment insurance]." McDonald did not hesitate to tell Andison that "Trudy was the logical one to go because she was pregnant" and that "she could not wear her uniform. She wore unsightly pants [elasticized pants]." Yet McDonald's position was that, because of the city's new ban on Sunday shopping, he had to let go some staff to save money (although he had hired a new cashier two days after the bylaw came into effect and nine days before firing Holloway). There had been no complaints about her work performance.

Andison concluded that Holloway had been fired because she was pregnant, and attempted to conciliate an informal settlement that included lost wages, an apology, a change in store policy, and a letter of recommendation.[63] McDonald refused. Hanne

Jensen, the director of the Human Rights Branch, in her letter
to the Minister of Labour recommending a board of inquiry,
wanted to use the case to send a signal to others: "The unwillingness of the respondent to deal with settlement of this complaint demonstrates the need for a strong statement of intent
to protect pregnant women in the work force from termination
for discriminatory reasons."[64] On 8 December 1982, a board of
inquiry appointed by the Minister of Labour and chaired by law
professor William Black was held at the University of British
Columbia Faculty of Law's moot court room. Holloway, Andison, McDonald, Johnson, and Hanne Jensen were present. The
branch provided Holloway with a lawyer, and McDonald brought
his own legal counsel. After two days of argument, Black declared
that Holloway had been fired because she was pregnant. That, he
continued, had been a violation of the Code's reasonable cause
section and could also be considered sex discrimination. Black's
decision was one of the first rulings in Canadian history to recognize pregnancy as sex discrimination.

Human rights law was evolving beyond formal equality
towards substantive equality. Other boards of inquiry recognized that systemic discrimination could also take the form of
patterns of behaviour or institutional practices that exacerbated
the disadvantages of marginalized communities. Lack of intent
and honest belief were rejected as legitimate defences. Seemingly
neutral practices, such as arbitrary height and weight requirements, were defined as discriminatory. Affirmative action programs, sanctioned by human rights commissions, were created
to address the legacy of generations of discriminatory treatment.

The federal *Human Rights Act* (1977) completed a nation-
wide effort to entrench human rights in law.[65] In less than a
generation, Canadians had established the most sophisticated
human rights legal regime in the world. There was surprising
uniformity across the country: federal and provincial legislation
was, with a few notable exceptions, based on the original Ontario
model. Human rights laws prohibited discrimination in services,

employment, accommodation, advertising, and signs. They also incorporated existing antidiscrimination laws into a single statute. Specially trained human rights officers were hired to investigate complaints. They were told to make every possible effort to conciliate complaints informally; if conciliation failed, the government could appoint a formal inquiry (and the commission would represent the complainant before the inquiry). Offenders might pay a fine, offer an apology, reinstate an employee, or agree to a negotiated settlement. Inquiries were not courts. The entire process was designed to be efficient and accessible and to absorb the cost of resolving complaints. Commissions were given the resources to pursue vigorous human rights education programs. This was the basic model for human rights law across Canada. The federal legislation also reflected the increasing diversity of human rights in Canada: the statute incorporated enumerated grounds such as sex (including sexual harassment and pregnancy), ethnic origin, age, marital status, physical disability, pardoned conviction, and a mandate for equal pay for work of equal value. In this way, the federal statute was the product of decades of human rights legal reform at the provincial level.[66]

The Canadian human rights system was among the most comprehensive in the world. Equality commissions in Britain, Australia, and the United States had far more restrictive mandates and less effective enforcement mechanisms. For instance, had Holloway lived in the United States, she would likely have had to hire her own lawyer and seek restitution in court, which was far more intimidating, expensive, and time-consuming than a board of inquiry. Moreover, unlike people who chaired boards of inquiry, many judges had no expertise in discrimination cases.[67] The 1970s was also marked by a proliferation of domestic human rights laws around the world, especially among Eastern European and Third World countries. Thomas Pegram, a political scientist who specializes in international law, describes this diffusion of human rights law as a "contagion effect": a process arising from a "complex domestic, regional, and international interaction of

actors, arenas, and modalities of diffusion" that resulted in a
"wave phenomenon of varying intensity across regions," beginning in Europe and North America.[68] Few other countries in the
world, however, incorporated all of the strengths of the Canadian system: professional human rights investigators; public
education; research for legal reform; representing complainants
before inquiries; jurisdiction over the public and private sector;
a focus on conciliation over litigation; independence from the
government; and an adjudication process as an alternative to the
courts.[69] This was a far cry from the lack of any effective statutory or constitutional recognition of human rights in Canada
in the 1940s.

This is not to say that innovations in human rights policy
went uncontested.[70] The federal *Human Rights Act*, for example,
was in many ways more progressive than its provincial counter-
parts: it was one of the first such acts in Canada to recognize discrimination on the basis of a pardoned criminal conviction, and
of physical disability. It was also the first to include equal pay for
work of equal value. And the statute created an independent commission that did not report to a cabinet minister. Ironically, the
justice minister insisted before Parliament that the government's
objective was to avoid any innovations: "A prime objective has
been to allow the Commission to establish itself without being
initially overburdened ... It would not be desirable to impose initially upon the Commission the responsibility of dealing with
too many concepts in the human rights area for which there
are no guiding precedents."[71] Many Parliamentarians, though,
insisted that the government had not gone far enough. All six
organizations that made representations to the committee, as
well as critics within Parliament, chastised the government for
not including sexual orientation or political affiliation; for not
applying the legislation to the *Indian Act* to end discrimination
against women; and for failing to ban mandatory retirement.[72]
That most of the critics shared the same concerns suggests that
a consensus was emerging around these new rights claims.

What is especially noteworthy about these debates is that no one objected to the *Human Rights Act* in principle. Thirty years earlier, opponents of antidiscrimination law had insisted that discrimination was non-existent, or that it was impossible to legislate morality, or that it was an unjust interference by the state.[73] Support for human rights legislation constituted a genuine shift in Canada's rights culture.

A similar consensus surrounded the *Charter of Rights and Freedoms.* By the 1980s, hardly anyone challenged the legitimacy of a bill of rights on the basis of Parliamentary supremacy.[74] The evolution of Canada's rights culture is especially striking when we consider how Parliamentary hearings in 1980 and 1981 differed from the hearings in the 1940s and 1950s on a bill of rights.

The federal government called a Special Joint Committee (of the House of Commons and the Senate) on the Constitution to consult Canadians regarding the proposed Charter. It was supposed to last a few weeks. In the end, it took almost a year to finish: hundreds of people submitted letters or came to Ottawa to present briefs. Whereas six social movement organizations had made presentations to Parliament on the *Human Rights Act* in 1977, ninety organizations came to Ottawa in 1980. In total, 323 organizations and 639 individuals made submissions. At no other time in Canadian history had the state engaged in such an widespread consultation with Canadians about human rights.

In the 1940s, discrimination on the basis of race and religion dominated public debates surrounding a bill of rights. Social movement organizations pointed to instances where Blacks, Japanese, Jews, and other minorities had been denied services or employment. Organizations such as the National Black Coalition were still part of the conversation in 1980, and insisted during the hearings surrounding the Charter that affirmative action was necessary to "redress historical disadvantages."[75] However, in 1980, far more ethnic organizations were engaged in these debates. The Baltic Federation of Canada, Canadian Polish Congress, and Canadian Slovak League, for example, challenged the idea of "founding races."[76] Language rights, they insisted, had to include people whose mother tongue was neither English nor French.[77] One of their primary contributions to the dialogue was to frame the retention of culture and identity as a human right.

Debates surrounding religion and a bill of rights in the 1940s had focused primarily around eliminating the overt repression of religious minorities. By 1980 the discussion had expanded to include the right to maintain separate state-funded schools, hospitals, and child care institutions.[78] Key players in the 1940s had included organized labour and business. Again, by 1980, the debate had shifted. The British Columbia Federation of Labour suggested that the Charter should recognize all forms of workplace discrimination, including disability and political belief.[79] Meanwhile, organizations representing business raised a host of new issues in terms of human rights: free markets and trade; the mobility of persons to pursue a livelihood; the mobility of capital and professional accreditation; property; and the free circulation of goods and services.[80]

When representatives from the country's leading women's rights organization, the National Action Committee on the Status of Women, sat down before the committee to present their brief, Senator Harry Hayes (the co-chairman) could not resist saying "Well, it is all fine and good for you girls to be here, but who is looking after the kids?"[81] But Hayes was a relic of an older generation, and women's organizations used the hearings to forward a more robust definition of human rights. The Canadian Committee for Learning Opportunities for Women framed economic independence, meaningful work, and equal participation in public life as human rights.[82] Other organizations sought recognition of a human right to learning and training; the right to an annual income; the right to parental leave; and the right to free and quality child/day care (especially for single mothers).[83] Children were also represented by organizations such as a the Canadian Council on Children and Youth and the Canadian Council for Exceptional Children, which defined child care and education for children with disabilities as human rights.[84] Whether or not abortion was a human right was an especially divisive issue throughout the hearings. It pitted women's rights organizations, including the Canadian Abortion Rights Action League, against pro-life associations and the Canadian Conference of Catholic Bishops.

Sexual minorities and people with disabilities had been absent during the hearings in the 1940s, but they were prominent in the Charter debates. The Canadian Council on Social Development wanted to prohibit discrimination against "handicapping conditions," socio-economic status, marital status, sexual orientation, and political belief. It also favoured a human right to employment, protection against unemployment, healthy working conditions, an adequate standard of living, health care, education, social insurance, and privacy.[85] The United Church petitioned for the rights of refugees, immigrants, and inmates as well as for minimum standards for housing, nutrition, and income.[86] The National Anti-Poverty Organization lobbied for socio-economic and labour rights, including the right to rest and leisure, paid holidays, and mobility rights for welfare recipients.[87] For gay and lesbian organizations, the hearings provided the first major national forum to advance new rights claims since they had begun to organize in large numbers in the 1970s. The Canadian Association of Lesbians and Gay Men sought the same basic right against discrimination that had already been accorded to women and people with disabilities as well as to visible, ethnic, and religious minorities.[88] Meanwhile, the Canadian Council of the Blind and the Canadian National Institute for the Blind highlighted discrimination against people with visual impairments in employment. Both groups also drew attention to a host of other practices: blind people were banned from sitting on juries, confronted with harsh immigration policies, and denied the minimum wage. They also noted the prohibitions on marriage for the people with mental disabilities.[89] Other organizations pointed out that people with auditory impairments were routinely denied goods and services as well as access to facilities, accommodations, and employment.[90]

The Special Joint Committee on the Constitution was another critical moment in Canada's human rights history. The hearings highlighted a host of new rights claims; they also demonstrated how Canadians were building on earlier claims. After their success in the 1970s in banning direct forms of sex discrimination, especially in the workplace, women now put forward rights claims on a number of other issues, from abortion to day care. Of course, women had been mobilizing around these issues for generations. But it was indicative of the impact of the rights revolution that they were now framing their demands in the language of human rights.

But it was Aboriginal peoples who provided the most impactful moments during the hearings. Aboriginal peoples' organizations had never before engaged with human rights policy in a meaningful way. True, they had participated in public discussions surrounding the federal *Human Rights Act*, but only to oppose any provisions that might apply to the *Indian Act*. Most Aboriginal peoples' organizations insisted on completing negotiations over outstanding claims before addressing human rights legislation. Complaints to human rights commissions involving Aboriginal peoples had always been few in number: a survey of complaint files in British Columbia, Alberta, Ontario, New Brunswick, and Newfoundland reveals that by 1982, human rights commissions had rarely investigated complaints involving Aboriginal peoples.[91] One of the most widespread consultations on human rights law in the 1970s, the Ontario Human Rights Commission review titled "Life Together," received few briefs or letters from Aboriginal organizations.[92] Aboriginal peoples' refusal to engage with human rights policy may also have been due to the lack of any cultural tradition of rights.[93] To be sure, Aboriginal peoples had legitimate reasons to be skeptical of the benefits of framing their issues using rights language following the debacle over the 1969 White Paper. And for obvious reasons, most Aboriginals mistrusted government agencies.[94]

Nonetheless, several Aboriginal peoples' organizations participated in the hearings. The Association of Métis and Non-Status Indians of Saskatchewan drew attention to the deplorable living conditions on reserves and demanded recognition of Aboriginal peoples' right to control natural resources, economic development, and education.[95] The National Indian Brotherhood framed their exclusion from political life as a form of collective discrimination, while insisting on hunting rights and a repeal of the ban against ceremonies.[96] Human rights, they insisted, had to include self-determination and a positive recognition of treaties.[97]

The organizations that made presentations to the committee ultimately had a considerable impact on the Charter. Aboriginal peoples' organizations secured a section on Aboriginal rights, while women's groups led an impressive campaign to save the equality section. French- and English-language rights associations provided important rhetorical support for entrenching minority-language rights in the constitution. Civil liberties groups, lawyers' associations, and human rights commissions had a direct impact on the wording of several sections. One of the first concerted campaigns by people with disabilities resulted in an explicit reference to their equality rights, while ethnic minorities' efforts resulted in a section on multiculturalism.[98] Public discourse surrounding human rights in the 1950s had been dominated by references to civil liberties (speech, association, assembly, press, religion, due process, and voting) and to racial, religious, or ethnic discrimination; the Charter debates revealed how Canada's rights culture had evolved and how social movements were continuing to push at the boundaries.[99]

Canada became the first country to recognize multiculturalism in its constitution and one of the few in the world with a bill of rights incorporating education, language, Aboriginal peoples, and equality between men and women. There was emerging in Canada a consensus around many new rights claims. In a poll conducted in 1982, 69 percent of respondents agreed that discrimination against racial minorities should be prohibited;

89 percent thought that the Charter should protect against discrimination against those aged sixty-five or older; and 77 percent agreed that the constitution should ban sex discrimination.[100] In contrast, support for language rights (61 percent), religion in schools (58 percent), and especially sexual orientation (32 percent) was more contested.[101] Opinion polls did not even bother to ask Canadians about entrenching economic and social rights. Only a few SMOs and parliamentarians suggested that the *Charter of Rights and Freedoms* should include economic and social rights. The Canadian Bar Association reflected the country's continued ambivalence to these rights claims: "Thus most economic rights, such as the right to a basic standard of living or the right to work, can best be protected by positive state action by legislatures ... [A] Bill of Rights should be carefully drafted so as to minimize the possibilities of judicial interference in economic and social welfare policy."[102] But even this deficit in Canada's rights culture did not go uncontested. Quebec had already set a new standard when it incorporated economic and social rights in its human rights legislation in 1975.

It is difficult to overstate the impact of the rights revolution on Canadian law between 1974 and 1984. After decades of moratoriums on the death penalty, Parliament abolished capital punishment in 1976. Children were recognized as having their own rights as well. Quebec's *Youth Protection Act* of 1977, for instance, guaranteed youths the right to be consulted about switching foster care parents and to consult a lawyer before judicial proceedings, while the *Ontario Child Welfare Act* of 1978 protected the privacy of adopted children.[103] People with mental disabilities became rights-bearing citizens; in some jurisdictions, they were included in minimum wage laws, and greater restrictions were placed on forcible confinement. In Quebec in 1979, prisoners were granted the vote for the first time. The federal government introduced freedom of information legislation in 1982; soon after, all of the provinces followed suit.[104] Every jurisdiction also established an ombudsman's office.

These developments occurred in the context of an international rights revolution. Social movements proliferated around the world in the 1970s, and many of them explicitly framed their grievances in the language of rights. Other, more established organizations such as religious groups and trade unions established programs and committees with a mandate to pursue human rights. "Human rights," explains historian Jan Eckel, "increasingly served as a unifying term, under which civil organizations subsumed their activities."[105] Amnesty International was especially effective at turning domestic state crimes into international causes that generated widespread public debate. It often did so by framing the issue at hand around an individual's life story. "Never before had a single organization possessed such detailed knowledge about such a vast number of victims of state repression as Amnesty did in the 1970s and 1980s."[106] As was the case in Canada, these were often the same grievances that, for instance, women's organizations had been advocating for generations. But as Eckel notes, "they had just never before called them 'human rights.'"[107]

Human rights had, by this time, largely trumped civil liberties in the public discourse on rights. But the rights revolution was no panacea. Narcotics legislation granted police enormous latitude for search and seizure; tenants had few statutory protections against their landlords; insurance policies discriminated on the basis of gender; and mandatory retirement policies denied some people much-needed income in their old age.[108] The lessons of the October Crisis did not prevent the city of Montreal from restricting freedom of assembly when, in 1971, it again resorted to Bylaw 3926. The RCMP was found to be complicit in a host of illegal activities designed to undermine perceived subversives, going so far as to illegally open mail and secretly raid the offices of newspapers and the Parti Québécois (to copy subscriber and membership lists). The high point of absurdity was when the

RCMP burned down a barn in rural Quebec to prevent a gathering of radical activists. The federal government established a Royal Commission in 1977 to investigate the RCMP; it eventually confirmed that the RCMP had acted illegally. Not a single officer was prosecuted, however.[109]

The state's tendency to disregard human rights during times of perceived danger had not changed much since the nineteenth century. In 1976, Montreal hosted the Summer Olympics. This was, by far, the largest international event ever hosted on Canadian soil. It was also the largest security operation in Canadian history. In the aftermath of the October Crisis, the state's security apparatus was determined to use extraordinary measures to police the games. A security force of 17,224 was assigned to protect 6,000 athletes. The operation included the army, five separate police forces, and at least a half-dozen federal agencies, from harbour patrol to immigration.[110] The federal government passed special legislation allowing the immigration minister to deport anyone who might engage in violence during the Olympics. It was an unusual statute: the entire law was a single sentence that gave the minister the unfettered authority to deport non-citizens with no right to appeal.[111] Even by global standards, the security apparatus for the Montreal Olympics was impressive. It was also vastly disproportionate to the threat: not only was there no incident of note, but the crime rate in Montreal dropped by more than 20 percent during the games.[112]

Nevertheless, the rights revolution was transforming Canadian social movements, political culture, and law. Opinion polls suggest that, beginning in the 1970s, Canadians increasingly embraced the principles embodied in human rights policy. In a poll taken thirty years after Ontario's groundbreaking *Racial Discrimination Act*, 41 percent of respondents agreed (35 percent disagreed) with the statement that immigrants were often discriminated against because "police and courts are not prepared to take a strong stand against discrimination."[113] In 1981, 82 percent of respondents supported affirmative action legislation to prevent discrimination based on race, colour, and ethnicity.[114] Ten years later, in 1991, 20 percent of Canadians reported that racism was one of the worst social problems in Canada; 47 percent indicated that it was a fairly serious problem; and 50 percent believed that racism had increased in Canada over the past five years.[115]

Human rights were also proving to be a useful approach to framing grievances against the state for intruding on people's private lives. Abortion had been technically legal since 1969, although women had to secure the permission of a hospital-based Therapeutic Abortion Committee. A federal inquiry in 1977 uncovered serious problems with the law. Abortion services, it turned out, were not equally available to all women: "There was considerable confusion, unclear standards or social inequity involved with this procedure ... These factors have led to: sharp disparities in the distribution and the accessibility of therapeutic abortion services; a continuous exodus of Canadian women to the United States to obtain this operation; and delays in women obtaining induced abortions in Canada."[116] Despite the law, Dr. Henry Morgentaler established abortion clinics in Ontario, Manitoba, and Quebec. He was soon prosecuted for performing abortions outside a hospital. Morgentaler faced three indictments in Quebec alone. Juries, however, acquitted him every time. Then in 1974, the Quebec Court of Appeal surprised everyone when it exploited a rarely used provision of the Criminal Code to substitute the jury's not-guilty verdict with a verdict of guilty (the Supreme Court affirmed this decision in 1975). The federal government, although unwilling to amend its abortion law, was sufficiently shocked by the court's audacity that it removed the provisions that permitted a court to substitute a jury verdict. After it was elected in 1976, the Parti Québécois announced that it would halt all proceedings against the by now famous abortion doctor.

Quebec also led the country in another critical human rights legal reform: the province banned discrimination on the basis of sexual orientation in 1977. The amendment was in response to an especially brutal police raid on a gay bathhouse called Truxx. The raid was widely publicized and threatened the newly elected Parti Québécois's image as a progressive party.[117] At the time, no other province considered sexual orientation as a human right. Neither the federal *Human Rights Act* nor the *Charter of Rights and Freedoms* recognized sexual orientation. When the Saskatchewan Federation of Labour adopted a non-discrimination policy on the basis of sexual orientation in 1976, for instance, it was the only labour federation in the country to acknowledge this form of discrimination for many years to come.[118] Yet discrimination against gays and lesbians was not uncommon in Canada. In February 1981, in what was later characterized as the largest police action since the October Crisis, 150 Toronto police officers raided four bathhouses and arrested hundreds of gay men. *The Globe and Mail* characterized the raids as an "ugly action" and a clear case of discrimination against homosexuals: "This flinging of an army against the homosexuals is more like the bully-boy tactics of a Latin American republic attacking church and lay reformers than of anything that has a place in Canada."[119] But unlike its neighbour, the Ontario government refused to include sexual orientation in the *Human Rights Code*, despite a recommendation from its own Human Rights Commission.[120]

The Parti Québécois's rise to power symbolized yet another profound challenge to Canada's rights culture. French Canadians' demand for recognition of their collective rights defied English Canadians' fundamental notions about rights. The PQ's 1979 proposal for sovereignty-association argued that English Canadians placed "the accent on individual rights and preferred to ignore any reference to collective rights."[121] The first legislation passed by the PQ placed widespread restrictions on the use of English in the province, most notably in education. Similarly, throughout the 1980s, the Ligue des droits de la personne not only endorsed the right to self-determination but also campaigned for unilingual French education in Quebec as a fundamental human right.[122] Lucie Lemonde, president of the league in the 1990s, became increasingly frustrated by her inter-actions with human rights organizations outside Quebec and their willingness to allow individual rights to trump collective rights: "c'était la conception anglaise des droits civils (civil liberties) qui prévalait."[123] The debate surrounding French Canadians' collective rights would haunt the nation for a generation, from the referendums to the constitutional negotiations to court challenges on language rights. As we will see, this debate would have a profound impact on those rights recognized in the new constitution and come to represent a defining feature of Canada's rights culture.

Of greater concern by the late 1970s, though, was the stirrings of a backlash against the rights revolution. In Vancouver, a columnist for the *Vancouver Sun* named Doug Collins unleashed a stream of vitriolic attacks on the provincial Human Rights Branch between 1977 and 1983. Referring to that branch as a "noble band of manipulators," he attacked the principle that governments could regulate employers' hiring practices, at one point insisting that "these idiocies are quite in line with [the Director's] ridiculous whine that Super-Value's newspaper advertising shows only white women and no men."[124] Collins, who opposed a human rights tribunal decision that found a couple in Lillooet guilty of discrimination for refusing to rent space in a trailer park to two Aboriginals, wrote that the "human rights process, as now set up in BC, stinks and provides opportunity for intimidation and persecution of honest and straightforward people."[125] Six years later, Collins was still launching invectives against the branch (which he described as an "evil industry") for "thrusting stuff down our throats that we gagged on ... You could fill a telephone book with the excesses and stupidities of the human righters."[126] Collins was not alone, though he was certainly one of the most rancorous critics. By the 1980s, there were many voices in the media critical of human rights law. Ian Hunter, a professor of law at Western University, had written several articles on human rights in the 1970s and consulted for the Ontario Human Rights Commission. But he broke with the commission after 1983 when it began to address systemic discrimination and affirmative action programs, which he believed imposed excessive regulation on employers.[127]

The backlash took many forms. The Saskatchewan Court of Queen's Bench in 1976 and a Manitoba Board of Adjudication in 1983 ruled that sex discrimination did not include sexual orientation.[128] Employers fought human rights law in the courts using defences such as vicarious liability and honest belief. In the case of the former, they argued that employers should not be held responsible for the actions of their employees. In the case of the latter, the defendants acknowledged that their actions were discriminatory but claimed that they had been founded on an honest belief and were therefore reasonable and not violations of the law.[129] Although neither defence gained much traction, the latter received a sympathetic ear among some judges. In at least one case in 1977, the judge employed a twisted logic based on the honest belief defence to justify discrimination: "Many people in our society may well entertain a bias or some predisposition against homosexuals or homosexuality on moral and/or religious grounds. It cannot therefore be justly said that a bias so held has no reasonable foundation."[130]

A far more serious challenge was a Fraser Institute publication in 1982 that provided a carefully crafted critique that, while profoundly misleading, nonetheless offered a philosophical challenge to human rights. A senior economist for the institute, in a co-authored book titled *Discrimination, Affirmative Action, and Equal Opportunity*, argued that equal pay laws "banish the ability of a group, in this case females, to counteract the economic discrimination they may suffer." In other words, the law denied women the opportunity to work for a lower wage and thus exploit their advantage as cheap labour.[131] He was especially critical of affirmative action, which the book described as reverse discrimination (both authors were men). The authors, who insisted that discrimination was not as pervasive as was commonly believed, argued that human rights legislation would "harm the very minority groups they were designed to help."[132] These and other critiques of human rights legislation provided the language for a more sustained attack on human rights. Ironically, similar arguments had been used in 1944 to oppose Ontario's *Racial Discrimination Act*.

The epicentre of the backlash was in the province with the country's most progressive human rights law. British Columbia's Social Credit government earned the dubious distinction of becoming the first jurisdiction to eliminate its human rights commission. The *Human Rights Code*, with its famous reasonable cause section, was repealed and replaced in 1984 with legislation designed to punish individuals rather than conciliate or address systemic discrimination. The move was bitterly contested within the province and was denounced across Canada and abroad. Almost no one supported the legislation; in the provincial legislature, not even the government's own members spoke in support of it. Gordon Fairweather, the Chief Commissioner of the Canadian Human Rights Commission, criticized the changes, which he characterized as "emblematic of a police state."[133] Ken Norman, Chief Commissioner of the Saskatchewan Human Rights Commission, maintained that "tearing apart the institutional fabric of the human rights commission and human rights branch is a very regressive step."[134] The International Association of Human Rights Agencies passed a resolution condemning the amendments.[135] Doug Collins, on the other hand, applauded the government's actions.[136]

The controversy in British Columbia in 1984 exemplified the contested nature of human rights in Canada. Over the next decade there would be increasing pressure to expand the scope of human rights law as Canadians appropriated rights discourse to advance new claims. But there was a powerful countermovement determined to resist such claims.

CHAPTER 5

Contesting Human Rights

GILLES FONTAINE HAD HUMAN IMMUNODEFICIENCY VIRUS (HIV). At first he experienced bed sweats and frequent diarrhea, but otherwise he had no symptoms. He was eventually diagnosed in 1985 when the AIDS epidemic was making international headlines. At the time, most people knew almost nothing about the disease. Individuals with HIV were vilified, while unfounded fears spread throughout the population regarding how the disease could be contracted. Fontaine, who was a professional cook, asked his doctor if there was a risk he might infect other people. His doctor assured him that he would not infect anyone in this way. He also advised Fontaine that he was under no obligation to inform employers of his condition. At no time did his condition affect his ability to work.

Two years later, Fontaine responded to a newspaper advertisement for cooks to work on railway crews for Canadian Pacific. He was hired soon after and was sent to Broadview, Saskatchewan, to join a railway crew. Their job was to travel to Moose Jaw and maintain the rail line. Fontaine was responsible for providing three meals a day to a crew of sixteen men, maintaining the kitchen and ordering supplies. When Fontaine arrived in Broadview he met the roadmaster, Jeff Fowlie, who assigned him sleeping quarters in a railcar with the other members of the road crew. By all reports Fontaine was a diligent and hard worker in his first month of employment. During a casual conversation with another member of the road crew, however, he mentioned that he had HIV. The news quickly spread among the crew. The next day the entire crew refused to eat the food he had prepared. Fowlie, who also refused to eat breakfast the next day, told Fontaine there were concerns he would infect the men. Fowlie drove to town to phone Rita Berthelette at the catering company and warned her that he would be unable to control the men if they decided to attack Fontaine. When he returned to the camp, Fowlie parked his truck to block any of the men from taking their car to town and advised Fontaine to leave the campsite. Fontaine fled to the nearest town and hid in a hotel's laundry room until the bus arrived to take him to Winnipeg. When he met Berthelette the next day in her office, she suggested that he stop working as a cook because of his illness. According to later reports, it was unclear whether Fontaine was fired or resigned. But when he returned to the office to collect a Record of Employment (for Unemployment Insurance), Berthelette wrote on the form that Fontaine was "dismissed by Roadmaster for having AIDS."[1]

Fontaine submitted a complaint to the Canadian Human Rights Commission. A tribunal concluded in 1989 that HIV was a disability as defined under the legislation. The tribunal awarded Fontaine $23,160 in compensation and $2,000 for pain and humiliation. They also directed Canadian Pacific to apologize. The decision set a critical precedent in expanding the definition of disability as a human rights violation.[2] However, attempts to assert new rights are often contested. Conflicts over the boundaries of Canada's rights culture because especially salient in the 1990s, particularly over the issue of sexual orientation. Moreover, as we will see, the contested nature of human rights means that attacks on existing rights are as common as new rights claims. Human rights history is not a linear narrative: it is as much about defending past claims as it is about asserting new ones.

Human rights are, as we have seen, a particular type of social practice. Those moments in Canada's human rights history that have transformed our rights culture can often be attributed to wider changes in society. For instance, by the 1970s, most complaints filed under antidiscrimination laws dealt with race. In this way, the law reflected public discourse surrounding rights at the time. Sex discrimination, although common, was never included in the law; it was not even part of most campaigns for antidiscrimination legislation. Sex discrimination was only added to human rights law following the influx of women into post-secondary education and the workforce and the rise of second wave feminism. The results were dramatic. As soon as sex discrimination was included in human rights law, more than 50 percent of complaints in any given year dealt with discrimination against women (even though most jurisdictions recognized a dozen or more grounds).[3] Similarly, the federal government's 1977 *Human Rights Act* set an important precedent: the statute included physical and mental disability as prohibited grounds of discrimination.[4] Ontario (1981) and British Columbia (1984) soon followed Ottawa's lead, and it was not long before every other jurisdiction incorporated disability into human rights legislation.[5] These developments coincided with the International Year for Disabled Persons (1981), widespread programs in public schools for students with disabilities, campaigns for better public services, and the emergence of the disability rights movement.[6] Disability was one among several new issues that entered Canadians' human rights lexicon in the 1980s. It would later supplant race and sex as generating the largest number of human rights complaints in the country.[7]

Another seminal event, in 1984, was Justice Rosalie Abella's Royal Commission report on employment equity.[8] It affirmed growing support for the principle of substantive equality. Abella was critical of the human rights legislative model as it existed:

> This approach to the enforcement of human rights, based as
> it is on individual rather than group remedies, and perhaps

confined to allegations of intentional discrimination, cannot deal with the pervasiveness and subtlety of discrimination ... Neither, by itself, can education. Education has been the classic crutch upon which we lean in the hopes of coaxing change in prejudicial attitudes. But education is an unreliable agent, glacially slow in movement and impact, and often completely ineffective in the face of intractable views. It promises no immediate relief despite the immediacy of the injustice.[9]

Abella's report began with a plea for a broader approach to rights adjudication, one that would address systemic discrimination:

The systemic approach acknowledges that by and large the systems and practices we customarily and often unwittingly adopt may have an unjustifiably negative effect on certain groups in society. The effect of the system on the individual or group, rather than its attitudinal sources, governs whether or not a remedy is justified.[10]

She did not recommend quotas. Rather, she called for widespread reform to public and private employment practices to eliminate systemic barriers to marginalized groups.[11] A year later, the Supreme Court of Canada upheld the concept of systemic discrimination and several provinces incorporated a mandate to address it in their human rights legislation.[12] Meanwhile, British Columbia, Saskatchewan, and New Brunswick had begun promoting equal opportunity programs. By 1986 the federal government had fulfilled Abella's primary recommendation and passed the *Employment Equity Act* to enhance women's and minorities' representation in federally regulated industries with more than one hundred employees.[13]

Meanwhile, feminists were at the forefront of advancing a more nuanced understanding of discrimination: intersectionality. Human rights legislation, as we have seen, evolved largely in reaction to particular circumstances. Except for British Columbia's reasonable cause provisions, these laws were designed to respond to specific types of discrimination.[14] An intersectional analysis recognized that reducing discrimination to one factor, such as sex, failed to account for how some individuals experienced discrimination.[15] Someone might be discriminated against not because she was a woman or a person with a disability but because she was a woman with a disability.[16] Discrimination might also arise as a result of stereotypes associated with the intersection of race and gender. Human rights law, however, defined discrimination through a list of independently enumerated grounds that had been incorporated ad hoc over many years.[17] Adjudicators were encouraged to examine a case through a single ground at a time, and complainants had to define themselves in narrow terms.[18] The problem was not merely academic: it had profound real-life consequences. Nitya Duclos surveyed federal human rights cases from 1994 to 2004 and found a shocking underrepresentation of racial minority women.[19] Moreover, human rights law was not criminal law, and its primary purpose was not to punish. Instead, the hope was that victims would benefit from having their grievances acknowledged and that the perpetrators would accept that their behaviour had been discriminatory and change their practices. Sexual harassment cases, for example, involved determining not only what happened and where, but also *why* it happened, the motivation, and the nature of the harassment. Duclos cites a case involving a teenage East Asian woman who complained about sexual harassment while working at a grocery store. It was probable that the harassment derived partly from the stereotype that Asian woman are passive. However, an investigator who did not consider the intersectionality of race and gender might determine that there was no sexual harassment if no evidence was found that the accused harassed the other (white) women in the store. In such situations, it is essential to consider racial and sex discrimination as interrelated.[20]

In *Alexander v British Columbia*, an Aboriginal woman was refused service at a liquor store because the owner thought she was drunk when, in fact, she was partly blind and had a mobility impairment that gave the impression of intoxication.[21] A human rights tribunal ruled that she had been discriminated against on the basis of disability; it rejected the allegation that the discrimination was due to her race. If Alexander had claimed only racial discrimination, would her case have failed? Similar inquiries might misunderstand the causes of discriminatory acts or the nature of the harm, remedies might be affected, victims might be forced to frame their complaints in ways that did not reflect their actual experiences, and the case might be dismissed because adjudicators had failed to account for the underlying cause.[22] A landlord, for instance, might rent apartments to black people and white people but refuse to rent a unit to an interracial couple. It would be easy to dismiss the case unless the adjudicator considered the intersection of sex and race as the underlying cause of discrimination.[23] In effect, traditional approaches to human rights adjudication sometimes misunderstood the nature of the violation and reinforced dominant norms.[24] Human rights law needed to define discrimination as a *set* of relationships instead of viewing it in terms of a single immutable characteristic. For this reason, in 1998, the *Canadian Human Rights* Act was amended to expand the definition of discrimination to include an intersectional analysis.[25]

The *Charter of Rights and Freedoms* had a profound impact on Canadian law.[26] Even its very existence was noteworthy. As we saw in Chapter 1, Canada's rights culture had once been premised on the principle of Parliamentary supremacy. It was a foundational principle of the Canadian state that rights were best protected through Parliament rather than the courts. Attempts in the nineteenth century to, among other things, have rights codified in a written constitution were violently resisted. Yet almost 150 years later, Canadians embraced the notion of using the courts to enforce a written bill of rights, even if this meant frustrating the will of Parliament.[27]

It was a testament to the implications of the new constitution that governments needed several years to change their laws to ensure conformity with the equality section. The implementation of Section 15 was delayed for three years. British Columbia, for instance, had to amend forty-nine statutes. Two of its long-standing laws—the *Barber's Act* and *Hairdresser's Act*—had banned women from cutting the hair of a girl or boy under seven years old.[28] Over the next few years, the equality section would redefine family law, criminal law, employment law, and a host of other legal regimes on a range of issues from sexual orientation to poverty and disability. It would also produce some of the most controversial Charter jurisprudence: same-sex marriage; sexual orientation as a prohibited ground of discrimination; spousal benefits for common law and same-sex couples (one case, *M v H*, led to the amendment of fifty-eight federal and hundreds of provincial statutes); prisoners' voting rights; girls' right to play in boys sports leagues; sign language in hospitals; and pay equity for women. These cases exemplified how grievances that might have been framed as moral issues in the past had, over time, come to be framed in terms of human rights.[29] The courts have also become a site of contestation regarding the human rights of Aboriginal peoples. In one of its most important decisions, the Supreme Court of Canada affirmed Aboriginal people's land rights unless an argument could be made that the government had extinguished the right in the past.[30]

The Charter's influence on Canadians' values over the years has undoubtedly been significant, but it is also impossible to fully measure. Its legal implications are far easier to identify, and these alone are impressive.[31] One of the first battlegrounds was language rights. The Supreme Court of Canada struck down key elements of the Parti Québécois's signature legislation, Bill 101, which among other things would have forced children to be educated in French.[32] The Charter also created new rights for minorities outside Quebec. The Court determined that French-language minorities have a right to education (where numbers warrant), as well as a degree of control over that education because such "management and control is vital to ensure that their language and culture flourish ... [M]inority language groups cannot always rely upon the majority to take account of all of their linguistic and cultural concerns."[33] A year later, the Court held that all of Manitoba's laws were invalid because they were not published in English and French. To avoid the inevitable legal chaos, the judgment was delayed until the province could translate its statutes.[34]

The Supreme Court of Canada was especially assertive in expanding the scope of due process. For instance, although the right to silence during police investigations had been purposefully excluded from the Charter, the Court interpreted the Charter as guaranteeing that right as part of the right to counsel. More than half of its Charter decisions between 1983 and 2003 involved the conduct of police officers.[35] The Court mainly addressed the right to counsel, burden of proof, trial within a reasonable time, the right to a hearing, and the admissibility of evidence. These judgments have led to a host of new due process rights: police are required to inform detainees of their right to a lawyer, their right to contact a lawyer of their choosing, and the availability of legal aid. Also, defendants have the right to a speedy trial (which has led to the dismissal of tens of thousands of criminal charges due to delays); a right to silence during pretrial investigations; and a right against self-incrimination, including as this relates to blood samples, DNA, and interrogations when intoxicated (in one case, the Court dismissed the evidence given by an undercover officer who had been placed in a prison cell to solicit a confession).[36] Prisoners have a right to a lawyer during disciplinary hearings, and refugee claimants have the right to an oral hearing. The Court struck down the reverse-onus-of-proof provisions in the *Narcotics Control Act* (which required people caught with drugs to prove they were not traffickers) and nullified minimum jail sentences for importing narcotics on the grounds that the practice was cruel and unusual. The Court also frustrated Parliament's initial attempt to ban a woman's sexual history (and medical records) in sexual assault cases because it violated the accused's right to a fair trial. It then forced Parliament to revise the legislation that prohibited sex with minors under the age of fourteen years, but affirmed the right against publicizing the names of rape victims.[37] Over the years, the court has not hesitated to dismiss confessions and overturn convictions if there was evidence of coercion or police misconduct. At the same time, there has been a noticeable decline in the number of laws nullified under the Charter since 1990. The Court has sought to balance public policy and rights under the Charter. [38] Judges, for instance, can admit evidence if errors were made in good faith or if excluding evidence might bring the administration of justice into disrepute.[39]

The Charter has also transformed the right to privacy. The law criminalizing abortion had survived multiple challenges in the 1970s; but in 1988, the Supreme Court of Canada declared the law inoperative on the basis that it violated the right to privacy and that the procedural delays violated the right to security of the person (the Court also rejected subsequent attempts to restrict women's access to an abortion).[40] The Court had ruled four years earlier that the right to privacy required that searches or eavesdropping be authorized under statute or common law. In one case, a police officer entered a man's trailer while he was asleep on the couch and found a bloody shirt, shoes, a cigarette package, and money linking him to a murder. The Court ordered a retrial and excluded some of the evidence. The Court has further restricted the search powers of regulatory bodies and excluded DNA or blood samples that were obtained under coercion (or, in a few cases, while the accused was unconscious) because individuals have a high expectation of privacy.[41] In one case, the police used a traffic violation to affect a body-cavity search on a suspected heroine dealer. The court ordered a new trial and excluded the evidence.[42]

These rights—equality and language rights, and the right to both privacy and due process—are a product of the rights revolution.[43] With the obvious exception of basic due process (such as habeas corpus), they were not historically part of Canada's rights culture. Under the Charter, the Supreme Court of Canada has dramatically expanded the scope of free speech in the context of secondary picketing; advertising to children under thirteen years old; the publishing of polling data within three days before an election; advertising by dentists; spending during a referendum; importing literature deemed obscene; English-language signs in Quebec; and the promotion of hate speech.[44] To protect freedom of religion, the court ruled that federal Sunday closing laws were invalid and struck down the requirement that home schooling instructors have a certificate issued from a school board. It has also redefined the duty to accommodate, for example, by creating a teenager's right to wear a kirpan (ceremonial dagger) to school, and by requiring employers to accommodate people with disabilities (the standard being whether or not accommodation causes undue hardship).[45] The right to a free press has led to the nullification of laws restricting media coverage of matrimonial disputes and pretrial civil hearings. The Court has also determined that there is a right to have sign-language interpreters in hospitals.[46] Non-citizens also have rights. Through a creative interpretation of the equality section, and by applying the doctrine of analogous grounds, the Court has extended equality rights to new groups of people, including gays and lesbians, non-citizens, and unmarried couples.[47]

Curiously, the Supreme Court of Canada was initially hostile to any suggestion that the Charter's guarantee of freedom of association included the right to strike or to collective bargaining. The Court ruled against organized labour in a series of challenges to wage controls, prohibitions on strikes, union recognition, decertification, and back-to-work legislation. Although Chief Justice Brian Dickson acknowledged that the "role of association has always been vital as a means of protecting the essential needs and interests of working people," the Court did not accept that freedom of association included the right to strike.[48] This did not prevent the Court from extending freedom of association to advertising or to the right of two companies to merge. In fact, only a year earlier, an Ontario judge had ruled that a union could not use its members' dues to support a political party even though such a restriction would not apply to a professional organization or a corporation (the Supreme Court of Canada overruled the decision in 1991).[49] However, in 2007, the Court ruled that freedom of association included a procedural right to collective bargaining.[50] Then, in 2015, the court completely refuted its earlier position and declared that the right to freedom of association did in fact include the right to strike.[51]

Clearly, the Charter has become a vehicle for advancing new rights claims. According to a group of legal scholars who conducted a quantitative study of the Supreme Court of Canada's jurisprudence, the number of rights-related cases increased from 20 percent of the court's docket before 1975 to more than 60 percent after 1982.[52] During the peak of the Court's rights litigation, between 1982 and 2003, the Court invalidated sixty-four statutes, of which 44 percent dealt with due process and 27 percent dealt with civil liberties.[53] In most years before 1982, the Court often did not find a single statute invalid; since 1982, the Court has invalidated at least one statute every year.[54] The rate of judicial review has expanded dramatically under the Charter. So the Court's impact has been profound. Alongside its landmark right-to-strike decision, it has struck down Criminal Code prohibitions against solicitation (prostitution) and assisted suicide.[55] In all three cases, the court has created a human right after having declared years earlier that no such human right existed.

At the same time, we need to recognize that this was a social process. Social movement organizations initiated a great deal of this litigation. They influenced the Court's decisions through a combination of research and briefs to the Court. Among the leading interveners in Charter cases before the Supreme Court of Canada since 1982 have been the Women's Legal Education and Action Fund and the Canadian Civil Liberties Association. Many of these organizations have received generous funding from the federal Secretary of State or Canadian Heritage since the 1970s. The federal government also created a Court Challenges Program that, for decades, provided funding to social movement organizations to pursue litigation for language and equality rights. Between 1985 and 2006, the program funded 586 equality cases alone, including several dozen that would reach the Supreme Court of Canada.[56] The history of the *Charter of Rights and Freedoms* exemplifies how a rights culture is a social process and how change is often initiated by those who are the victims of rights abuses.

The Charter was not the only source of human rights law in Canada.[57] Provincial and federal human rights legislation also reflected popular discourse surrounding human rights. Sexual harassment, disability, social condition, addiction, source of income, and family status were added to human rights statutes during this period (albeit this varied by jurisdiction).[58] British Columbia's decision to include people with disabilities in its *Human Rights Act* was unopposed among legislators, and similar amendments in other jurisdictions received virtually unanimous support. In contrast, grassroots movements to have sexual orientation recognized as a human right faced bitter opposition. Like religion in the nineteenth century, sexual orientation symbolized the contested nature of human rights in Canada.

Politicians in Canada had, for many years, rejected sexual orientation as a human right. In 1974, British Columbia had produced one of the most innovative human rights laws in the world, yet the government refused to include sexual orientation.[59] Members of Parliament and SMOs lobbied to have sexual orientation included in the federal *Human Rights Act* and the *Charter of Rights and Freedoms*, only to be rebuffed. When the Ontario Human Rights Commission initiated provincewide public consultations in the mid-1970s on possible reforms to the Code, the most contentious issue by far was sexual orientation.[60] In its 1977 report, *Life Together*, the Ontario Human Rights Commission recommended that the government include sexual orientation in the Code. The response was swift and highly critical. This one issue received disproportionate attention in the media, and so critical was the public response that the Ontario government rejected this recommendation from its own commission.[61] Instead, it was Quebec that became the first jurisdiction to ban discrimination on the basis of sexual orientation. It would be almost another decade before Ontario did the same. Even then, it was only the beginning. In 1993 a judge in Ontario applied a twisted logic to reject the contention that a prohibition on same-sex marriage was discrimination on the basis of sexual orientation: "The law does not prohibit marriage by homosexuals, provided it takes place between persons of the opposite sex."[62] Still, banning discrimination on the basis of sexual orientation was an important symbolic first step.

In the 1990s many provinces continued to refuse to recognize sexual orientation as a human right. A major overhaul of Newfoundland's *Human Rights Act* in 1988 was almost jettisoned entirely when the Cabinet became embroiled in the debate over sexual orientation.[63] The province's justice minister in 1990 feared that the amendment would protect pedophiles, while also insisting that such discrimination did not exist in Newfoundland. The Newfoundland Human Rights Commission's files indicate that it never investigated a single case of discrimination against gays and lesbians before 1993, even though the Newfoundland Human Rights Association had documented several incidents.[64] When the government relented and amended the law in 1997, only Prince Edward Island and Alberta remained. The government of Alberta was especially vocal in its refusal to amend its human rights legislation.[65]

Alberta was already a key battleground in the fight for the rights of sexual minorities. When the first gay rights groups appeared in Canada's largest cities in the early 1970s, they included the Gay Alliance Towards Equality (GATE) in Edmonton, founded in 1971. GATE organized the first campaigns to have sexual orientation included as a prohibited ground for discrimination.[66] Both GATE and Calgary's People's Liberation (founded in 1973) operated phone lines and offered peer counselling, and in some cases held social events and hosted drop-ins.[67] The Womyn's Collective, founded in Calgary in 1977, held its first all-women dance that year and hosted meetings, social events, and consciousness-raising groups, in addition to operating a drop-in centre and the Lesbian Information Line.[68] A Lesbian Mothers' Defence Fund was launched in Calgary in the 1980s, and in 1983, Calgary hosted the province's first conference on lesbian rights. Meanwhile, the first lesbian organization in Edmonton, Womonspace, was established in 1982. Similar organizations emerged in Red Deer, Grande Prairie, Medicine Hat, and Lethbridge in the 1990s.[69] The proliferation of gay and lesbian rights organizations illustrates how minorities appropriated rights discourse to advance their claims. By the 1990s there was a flourishing gay rights movement in Alberta.

Virtually every success in the fight for equal rights for sexual minorities in Alberta can be attributed to the efforts of activists. Certainly the province's political leaders were unwilling to follow other provinces in legislating equal rights for gays and lesbians. The Progressive Conservative government had refused to address sexual orientation despite a 1976 recommendation from the Alberta Human Rights Commission that the law be amended. The party refused to budge on the issue. Activists wrote briefs, mounted letter-writing campaigns, held meetings with members of the legislature, and formed a provincial organization in 1979 called the Alberta Lesbian and Gay Rights Association. Undeterred, the government appointed a chairman to the Human Rights Commission who was openly hostile to gays and lesbians. The commissioner insisted that sexual orientation was a choice and that people who flaunted their sexual orientation should expect discrimination.[70] One cabinet minister declared in 1989 that the province would never ban discrimination if it meant allowing homosexuals to teach in schools. Another cabinet minister insisted that "two homosexuals do not constitute a family."[71] Ten years later the government went so far as to introduce legislation restricting common law marriages to heterosexual couples.[72]

Politics aside, the social context in Alberta was another obstacle for the gay and lesbian rights movement. On national television, religious groups attacked Calgary's 1995 lesbian and gay film festival (which had received a $4,000 federal grant) for being a "pornographic film orgy." One minister insisted that "I'm not after the homos or the bi's, I'm after the fact they're showing porno movies in a tax-funded situation."[73] Two years later, a group of evangelical Christians convinced the chief superintendent of the Calgary Public School Board to ban two books from school libraries that dealt with homosexuality because they were "pro-gay."[74] Public opinion was also divided. A 1999 opinion poll found that a vast majority of people in Quebec and Atlantic Canada (over 87 percent) supported the inclusion of sexual orientation in human rights legislation, and 75 percent in Ontario. The weakest support, 65 percent, was on the prairies.[75]

Given such a hostile climate, it was almost inevitable that the courts would have to intervene. By 1998, Alberta was the only jurisdiction (except for the Northwest Territories) where discrimination against gays and lesbians was legal. Delwin Vriend, a professor, was fired from King's College in Edmonton for being gay. According to the college, "homosexual practice goes against the Bible, and the college's statement of faith."[76] The Human Rights Commission initially refused to hear his case, but a new commissioner and a vigorous campaign on behalf of activists led the commission to change its position on investigating sexual orientation cases. Meanwhile, Vriend convinced the Alberta Supreme Court that the commission's initial refusal to consider his case violated his rights under the *Charter of Rights and Freedoms*. Although the Alberta Appellate Court overturned the ruling, the

Supreme Court of Canada ruled in 1998 that Alberta's human rights law's omission of sexual orientation violated Section 5 of the Charter. That Court ordered the government of Alberta to interpret its human rights legislation as if it included sexual orientation. As of 1998, for the first time in Alberta's history, it was illegal to discriminate on the basis of sexual orientation. Prince Edward Island formally amended its statute two months later; meanwhile, Alberta, while it enforced the law as the Court required, stubbornly refused to formally amend the legislation.

Human rights, which had not been a serious consideration in foreign policy until the 1970s, gained much greater prominence in Canada's external relations. International human rights politics led many states during this period to engage in diplomatic pressure, sanctions, and military action (humanitarian intervention as well as peacekeeping) against states responsible for widespread human rights violations. However, as in all aspects of the rights revolution, this was a contentious process. Policy-makers struggled with how to promote human rights abroad while, at the same time, respecting the principles of state sovereignty and non-interference.

Jimmy Carter, as President of the United States from 1976 to 1980, had made human rights a central tenet of American foreign policy. Although it is difficult to identify any lasting legacy, there is no question that he played an important role in raising the profile of human rights in international politics. Norway, the Netherlands, Sweden, and Switzerland were among the first countries to link human rights to humanitarian aid. Each of these countries declared human rights to be an integral component of its foreign policy and supported human rights campaigns abroad.[77] The collapse of the Soviet Union and the emergence of democratic movements in Asia, Latin America, and Africa created additional opportunities to incorporate human rights into foreign policy.[78] There was less pressure on Western states to support brutal dictatorships like Argentina out of fear that they would fall under the influence of the Soviet Union. The United States, Britain, France, and Germany increased their aid and rhetorical support to states committed to promoting democracy and human rights. The World Bank and the Organization for Economic Co-operation and Development integrated good governance into their criteria for providing loans to poor nations. Some nations, however, resisted. Many African and Asian countries at first appealed to human rights to denounce colonialism and then asserted a right to development when Western nations criticized their domestic policies. Some countries insisted that it was necessary to limit certain freedoms to ensure economic development; others simply rejected human rights as a Western invention designed to cloak continued Western hegemony.

In a report on human rights and foreign policy written in 1984, Hugh Keenleyside and Patricia Taylor lambasted the Trudeau government for its hypocritical and inconsistent approach to human rights. In particular, they noted the government's unwillingness to take action against countries for human rights abuses where Canada had strong commercial interests.[79] Three years later, both the Standing Committee on External Affairs and International Trade and the Canadian International Development Agency called upon the Progressive Conservative government of Brian Mulroney to link humanitarian aid more closely to the development of political, civil, and social rights.[80] Yet the government continued to prioritize geopolitical and economic interests in foreign policy. It did cancel several aid projects and banned high-level visits in the wake of the Tiananmen Square massacre in 1989. But this did not have a significant impact on Canada's relations with China. On the contrary. Bilateral aid to that country actually increased in 1991, and China was the leading recipient of Canadian aid by 1994.[81] In fact, as one historian has noted, "Canadian aid in this period was marginally more likely to flow to countries with poor human rights records than those with better records, making the aid–rights linkage almost entirely rhetorical."[82]

Still, Mulroney was quick to encourage intervention after the fall of governments in Yugoslavia and Haiti. This was a notable departure from the past policy of avoiding interfering in the internal politics of other nations. Canada participated in sanctions against Libya, Serbia, Montenegro, Haiti, Liberia, and Angola.[83] But by far the most visible human rights initiative in Canada's foreign policy involved participation in international sanctions against South Africa. The federal government implemented several new human rights policies. It linked developmental assistance to a state's human rights record; implemented a training program on human rights for personnel in the Department of External Affairs and the Canadian International Development Agency; established a human rights unit in the latter; produced a manual for reporting on human rights and distributed it to officials posted abroad; and published annual reports on the human rights records of countries receiving financial aid.[84] Aid to Indonesia was suspended in 1991 after reports of a massacre in East Timor.[85] Meanwhile, the Parliamentary subcommittee on international human rights, established in 1989, became a forum for advocacy groups and MPs to critique foreign policy. Parliament also created the International Centre for Human Rights and Democratic Development (Rights and Democracy) in 1988. This was one of the few state-sponsored human rights agencies in the world with a mandate to promote human rights through advocacy. The federal government was also a major funder of at least half a dozen international human rights organizations in the 1990s.[86]

Human rights had by now become an integral component of foreign policy discourse. Prime ministers routinely paid homage to this principle in speeches and lent rhetorical support to protecting human rights in other countries. In 1991, for instance, Prime Minister Mulroney declared before the Commonwealth Heads of Government meeting that "nothing in international relations is more important than respect for individual freedoms and human rights. For Canada, the future course is clear: we shall be increasingly channelling our development assistance to those countries that show respect for the fundamental rights and individual freedoms of their people."[87] By 1992, Canada had committed more than 4,400 military troops to fourteen peacekeeping missions abroad, most notably in Yugoslavia and Somalia. In 1993, two years after the Liberals defeated the Progessive Conservatives in a national election, the federal government reaffirmed its commitment to human rights in a White Paper that linked the promotion of human rights to security and good governance. Canada continued to bolster its credibility abroad as an advocate of human rights. In 1997, for example, it was the first country to initiate a bilateral human rights dialogue with Indonesia, which led others to soon do the same.[88] Canada also played a key role in establishing a landmark international treaty to ban land mines, and was later one of the first signatories to the 1998 Rome Statute that created the International Criminal Court to prosecute genocide, war crimes, and crimes against humanity.[89] The country has remained an active member of the UN Commission on Human Rights. Finally, it is worth pointing out that Canada has played a leading role in facilitating the diffusion of national human rights institutions around the world. This has taken the form of sending experts abroad to help train personnel, as well as providing financial assistance. Canada, for instance, has been one of the major financial backers of human rights commissions in South America, most notably the Inter-American Commission on Human Rights.[90]

Foreign policy has been both the weakest link in Canada's rights revolution and the least contested. Since 1986, export guidelines have banned the sale of arms to countries with a "persistent record of serious violations of the human rights of its citizens."[91] The policy did not, however, prevent the federal government from selling arms to Chile, Guatemala, Pakistan, the Philippines, South Korea, or Indonesia in the 1980s or to Saudi Arabia in 2005 and 2015.[92] And in relation to China, Mulroney and Jean Chrétien may have discussed human rights in private meetings with Chinese leaders, but they implicitly accepted that it was an internal matter.[93]

As long as the government's policies did not interfere with national security or economic interests, the human rights agenda did not generate controversy. It was, rather, around domestic policy that opponents of the rights revolution rallied their opposition.

The rights revolution at home was being increasingly contested by the 1990s. The Supreme Court of Canada's 1998 ruling on sexual orientation led to what one author described as "a venomous torrent of homophobic hatred," from attacks on radio shows to protests in front of the provincial legislature. Stockwell Day, the Alberta Treasurer, called on the provincial government to invoke the Charter's notwithstanding clause.[94] A decade after the Supreme Court's ruling, Albertans continue to struggle with discrimination based on sexual orientation. In 2008, Alberta resident Darren Lund successfully pursued a complaint before a provincial human rights tribunal against Reverend Stephen Boissoin of the Concerned Christian Coalition. Boissoin had written a letter, published in the *Red Deer Advocate*, condemning homosexuality as wicked and dangerous. The tribunal's decision was a victory for human rights, not only because it ruled in favour of homosexual rights but also because Lund had the support of both the commission and the provincial government. Unfortunately, the Court of Queen's Bench overturned the decision on the basis that Boissoin's hate speech constituted free speech. Lund's appeal to the Alberta Court of Appeal was dismissed in 2012, and he was ordered to pay Boissoin's legal costs.

Challenges to our rights culture usually involve the appropriation of rights discourse by disadvantaged peoples in order to secure recognition and equal rights. It is not, however, always a conflict between the marginalized and those with privilege. Kimberly Nixon's case in the late 1990s, for instance, highlighted divisions between the gay rights and women's rights movements. Egale Canada had adopted the position that sexual discrimination was a product of an intersection of rights violations based on gender, sexual orientation, race, and other factors. According to Egale, "social movements are never completely clearly-cut from each other. One doesn't end neatly before the next one begins." Kimberly Nixon was a male-to-female trans-identified person who had been victimized by a male domestic partner. After receiving support from Vancouver Rape Relief's Battered Women's Support Services, she decided to volunteer her time. When her trans status was discovered, she was asked to leave on the premise that only someone who had lived as a woman could understand rape. She responded by filing a human rights complaint. Egale endorsed Nixon's complaint, arguing that Vancouver Rape Relief's policy violated marginalized women's human rights. For its part, Vancouver Rape Relief argued that it had the right to maintain its own definition of who is a woman. It also insisted that a women's shelter had the right to assert its rights collectively, even if that came at the expense of an individual's rights. Moreover, it argued that the incident implied that a more interpretative and contextually relevant understanding of rights, and rights complaints, was needed. [95] The issue was ultimately resolved in 2003 when the Supreme Court of Canada ruled in favour of Vancouver Rape Relief.[96]

Far more concerning, however, is the way people with privilege have appropriated rights discourse for their own interests. This has been a trend in recent years. For instance, women have used human rights law to extend its protections to women who are pregnant, unmarried, single mothers, lesbians, or sexually harassed. Men, however, have twisted the *Charter of Rights and Freedoms'* equality section to their own benefit, using the Charter to mount challenges against laws regulating child support, social assistance for single mothers, affirmative action programs, sexual assault, and women's right to name their children or place them with adoptive parents.[97]

The fathers' rights movement has scored several victories. Most notably, in the 2003 *Trociuk* decision, the Supreme Court of Canada ruled that a law giving mothers the final authority on naming their children violated the biological father's rights.[98] The trend towards using comparator groups has led to decisions where, for instance, women on maternity leave have been denied benefits because they were compared with male workers who were also on leave. Such an analysis ignores the obvious reality that women alone carry the burden of bearing children.[99] The comparator approach focuses on universal (often male) standards rather than on the particular circumstances of each case, and in doing so often denies genuine equality.[100]

And then there is the *Gould* case. A woman in Whitehorse was refused membership in a private organization dedicated to promoting Yukon and preserving its heritage. The Yukon Human Rights Commission determined that the refusal constituted sex discrimination because the organization was offering a service normally available to the public. The Supreme Court of Yukon set aside the decision, and the appeal was dismissed in the Court of Appeal and the Supreme Court of Canada. The Court held that the refusal did not constitute discrimination because it was a social (rather than economic) organization that did not provide a public service.[101] It is ironic that, after securing one of the most important victories in the history of the women's movement, women will likely spend the next generation defending *existing* rights from men who are trying to exploit Section 15 of the Charter.

The conflict surrounding the appropriation of rights discourse by those who have privilege raises profound concerns for not only women but also for Aboriginal peoples and workers. For workers, one benefit of framing grievances as human rights was that their demands were less vulnerable to accusations that they were harming economic development. Workers' rights, like all human rights, should not depend on economic fluctuations. Workers have framed their grievances around principles such as freedom of association even though, until very recently, this approach has largely failed to secure legal victories in court. At the same time, employers have used rights discourse to undermine workers' rights, in much the same way that men have challenged women's rights. This has been more visible in the United States, where, in the 1990s and early 2000s, employers fought attempts to legislate workers' rights. Employers have appropriated rights discourse in several ways. They have claimed that limits on employers' ability to discourage employees from unionizing, and proposals to eliminate the secret ballot, violate employers' free speech. Another claim is that compulsory interest arbitration violates employers' collective bargaining rights by restricting their ability to reject an agreement. Appropriating rights discourse in this manner has been an effective tactic in resisting legislation protecting workers.[102]

A similar tension exists between Aboriginal rights and the principle of universal human rights. For some, the UN *Declaration on the Rights of Indigenous Peoples*, to which Canada acceded in 2010, is a milestone in advancing the rights of Aboriginal peoples. And in many ways it is. But a human rights approach to Aboriginal peoples' grievances, as exemplified in the UN treaty, may have the effect of overriding Aboriginal peoples' rights to their detriment. If human rights are those rights that everyone has by virtue of their humanity, then Aboriginal rights are rights specific to Aboriginal peoples. Aboriginal rights, like women's rights and workers' rights, are not universal.[103] This was most apparent in the debate over the 1969 White Paper when the federal government appealed to the principle of universal human rights to justify its recommendation to eliminate Indian status. There is a tendency to appropriate rights discourse as a way of homogenizing cultures for the purpose of trumping the claims of disadvantaged peoples. This was captured perfectly in 1974, when the former premier of British Columbia, as he struggled to explain why he refused to create a Ministry of Women's Rights, declared: "I believe in human rights, not women's rights."[104]

Today, we see the conflict in Aboriginal peoples' demands for self-government against the authority of the federal and provincial governments. We also see it in their demands for the exclusive right to fish, log, or hunt on Aboriginal lands that are claimed by non-Aboriginal Canadians. The contest between Aboriginal people's claims on the one hand and the Canadian state and private enterprise on the other has erupted in violent clashes, most famously at Kanesatake (Oka, Quebec) in 1990, but also in many similar confrontations since then from Gustavson Lake (British Columbia) to Caledonia (Ontario). The contested nature of Aboriginal rights claims has resulted in a seemingly never-ending cycle of violence. How we respond to these grievances, and the balance we strike in these competing rights claims, will define our rights culture as we move deeper into the twenty-first century.

Conclusion

CANADA'S RIGHTS CULTURE HAS CLEARLY changed since the days when Governors Prescott and Craig imprisoned journalists and detained people without due process. Before the twentieth century, our rights culture was defined exclusively in terms of restricting state action; today, human rights have become the dominant language we use to articulate almost any grievance in our community. Rights are no longer premised on citizenship and a relationship to the nation-state. Our modern conception of rights is that human rights are universal collective entitlements that supersede the state. Rights, however, derive from society, not from an abstract principle. While societies around the world might agree on a broad range of principles, for human rights to have social meaning they have to be interpreted and applied in ways that are specific to each society.[1] This process produces a distinct rights culture.

Rights are historically contingent. They change over time, and those changes depend on the societal preconditions that facilitate the emergence of new rights claims. Often, these preconditions are rooted in conflict, if not violence. The rebellions of the 1830s were, among other things, a demand for representative government and a repudiation of attempts to suppress French Canadians' religion and culture. Confederation did not include a bill of rights, but the new constitution did recognize the linguistic and religious rights of the French Catholic minority. This set the stage for battles over religious education in the late nineteenth and early twentieth centuries. Meanwhile, the state was obliterating any rights for Aboriginal peoples. Discrimination was rampant. But it was the state's blatant abuse of civil liberties in wartime, so reminiscent of the era that sparked the rebellions, that gave birth to a civil liberties movement. That movement produced only a minor victory—a weak federal bill of rights in 1960. That bill, however, set a powerful precedent that would lead to more tangible results in 1982. The principles on which that bill was based, though, were always highly contested. Aboriginal peoples rejected an attempt in 1969 to impose a rights-based legal regime that would have ignored their grievances. This was a critical moment in mobilizing the Aboriginal rights movement. And Aboriginal peoples were not alone. People organized in unprecedented numbers beginning in the 1960s to demand, among other things, legal recognition of the principle of non-discrimination. Once women and religious minorities had secured this basic right, it was inevitable that other marginalized groups, most notably sexual minorities, would frame their grievances in the same language. They would eventually succeed in securing these rights, but as has always been the case throughout history, only in the face of deep-rooted opposition. None of these victories were ever guaranteed. Even today, these victories are contested.

The process of translating abstract principles into social practice has been a slow one that builds on past rights claims. The first antidiscrimination laws may have been largely ineffective, but they established the foundation for further rights claims: Ontario's 1951 *Fair Employment Practices Act* recognized racial, religious, and ethnic discrimination; British Columbia's 1974 *Human Rights Code* further recognized discrimination on the basis of sex, marital status, and nationality; the 1977 federal *Human Rights Act* further recognized pardoned conviction, privacy, marital status, and physical disability, and expanded sex discrimination to include pregnancy, equal pay for work of equal value, and sexual harassment; the *Charter of Rights and Freedoms* further recognized language rights, education, Aboriginal peoples' rights, and multiculturalism. By the end of the twentieth century, Canadians' human rights vernacular included sexual orientation, family status, physical and mental disability, and concepts such as duty to accommodate. For many years after the Charter's equality section came into effect, Canada was the only country in the world with a constitutional equality provision for people with disabilities.[2] Public discourse surrounding human rights today, such as claims to clean water and genetic non-discrimination, has extended far beyond what was envisioned in even the recent past.

Social movements have been at the forefront of imagining new human rights and vigorously pursuing such claims. In the 1960s, women's groups initiated widespread campaigns against sexual harassment and for equal pay; in the 1990s, LGBT organizations successfully framed equal marriage as a right; today, Aboriginal peoples are seeking recognition of a human right to clean water and to education. Social movements have historically engaged in a wide range of activities—from education to political advocacy to changing social practices—that have facilitated new rights claims. Foreign policy is another indicator of how human rights have changed in this country. As Canada became increasingly active in the promotion of human rights abroad—from applying sanctions to ratifying treaties—these developments spurred action at home and armed activists with tools for making claims against the state. In turn, this prompted the state to become more active abroad. The Canadian government was opposed to the UDHR in 1948, but over time it has become a vocal advocate for international human rights law.[3]

Politics and law are two other barometers of our rights culture. Canada's political culture in the 1940s was deeply rooted in the British tradition of civil liberties and in the principle of Parliamentary supremacy. Constitutional debates facilitated the assertion of new rights claims, and human rights commissions and the courts have become forums for legitimizing such claims.

Citizens appropriate the language of rights and then make claims on the state through human rights agencies. For as long as human rights commissions exist, citizens will turn to them for redress when they believe they have been treated unfairly. When the first antidiscrimination laws were passed, there was no public debate surrounding gay rights. By the 1970s, federal and provincial governments found themselves having to rebuff demands to recognize sexual orientation in their respective human rights laws. Within a generation, discrimination on the basis of sexual orientation had been banned by law throughout Canada. Governments had been unable to resist the logic that sexual minorities were entitled to equal treatment.

The 1970s was an essential moment in the history of human rights. Historians Jan Eckel and Samuel Moyn have identified numerous factors to help explain why the idea of human rights gained such widespread popularity around the world beginning at this time: decolonization, détente, mass media, the transformation of the political left, and the transformation of churches.[4] Many of these factors, as we have seen, were present in Canada. After years of supporting overseas evangelical missionary work, many Canadian churches shifted their efforts to promoting humanitarianism and human rights abroad.[5] Similarly, the political left had fully embraced human rights by the 1970s, just at the time the worst excesses of the Cold War had dissipated in Canada.[6] However, the ways in which human rights came to have social meaning depended on the social context. Rights associations in Canada, for example, were divided among civil liberties and human rights organizations.[7] No similar philosophical distinctions divided rights associations in Australia or the United States (among others). At the same time, while Republicans in the United States largely eschewed human rights, conservatives in Canada embraced human rights in foreign policy. Likewise, conservative parties in Canada supported human rights law. In contrast, conservative governments in Australia rejected similar laws: it was the Australian Labor Party that introduced almost every human rights statute. Also, Canadians were ready to set aside Parliamentary supremacy to entrench a bill of rights in the constitution—an approach explicitly rejected in Australia.[8]

This book has sought to demonstrate how the idea of human rights has had a profound impact on Canada and that we have a unique rights culture. Our shared collective experience has produced the foundation for a dialogue to adjudicate our grievances using rights talk. Human rights, in this sense, are a product of our history. In seeking to understand the boundaries of our rights culture, and how we might challenge the limits of those boundaries, we should look to the past. For example, an integral aspect of Americans' rights culture entails debating the framers' original intent and the wording of the constitution; Canada's human rights history suggests no such predisposition. Rather, Canadians seem to be constantly reinventing their rights culture. The Fathers of Confederation debated civil liberties in 1867, and Canadians have collectively revisited these debates many times since. These debates have revealed an inherent conflict at the heart of Canada's rights culture. The conflict is a product of there being no unifying national myth and of struggles to reconcile within a single country multiple nations with their own distinct ideas about rights. A salient example of how history has shaped our rights culture is Canadians' recent commitment to the principle of self-determination, which encompasses Aboriginal self-government and a separatist movement in Quebec. Our approach to Aboriginal peoples may be flawed, but there is growing consensus around their collective rights. Moreover, we acknowledge the collective rights of French Canadians to protect their language and culture. Canada has gone so far as to legislate a formula for how a province can separate. It is a testament to how much our rights culture has changed—and how unique this country's rights culture is—that we have gone so far as to recognize a right to break up the country.

There is so much more to our rights culture. We do not believe in capital punishment. We accept a woman's right to choose. We are tolerant of religious diversity. Sexual minorities enjoy greater freedom in this country than in most others. We guarantee in law freedoms of speech, assembly, association, press, and religion as well as due process (with notable limits). The *Charter of Rights and Freedoms* is unique in the world in that, within this single document, we have recognized multiculturalism, minority language education rights, the equality of men and women, and Aboriginal rights as human rights. There may be no formally recognized human right to health care or education, but we have codified a right of equal access to such services.[9] There is a general right to request legal aid but no right to have legal aid. Citizens have the right to vote and to participate in the social, economic, and cultural life of the nation without discrimination. But we recognize no human right to material equality. Ours is a rights culture premised historically on the presumption that, in times of perceived emergency, we abrogate our rights temporarily to the state.

Our rights culture has been deeply informed by the British colonization of this region. At the same time, the presence of ethnic and religious minorities is the reason why Canada recognizes multiculturalism in its constitution. Liberalism and capitalism have also profoundly shaped Canada's rights culture. There has, for instance, never been a deep commitment to economic and social rights. Framing grievances using rights talk has not produced genuine material equality.[10] Our rights culture is largely premised on treating everyone the same and providing equal opportunity, and this has allowed systemic inequalities in wealth to flourish. In this way, Canada's rights revolution, rather than challenging the liberal order, has glorified its basic principles. Although women and minorities successfully appropriated rights discourse to secure formal legal equality, these reforms were never transformative. They never addressed the underlying causes of inequality in our society. Human rights law remains concerned with responding to individual complaints of discrimination even though some statutes have a mandate to address systemic discrimination (a mandate that is often ignored).

In its delineation of rights and in terms of those rights that are unrecognized, Canada's rights revolution symbolizes the success of the liberal order. It is within this framework that Canadians will continue to face new and unexpected rights claims. The right to private property might include control over natural resources, or preventing the state from creating a nature reserve, and pollution might be considered a violation of the right to equality.[11] Also, there has been a subtle shift in rights discourse over the past generation from universal (human) to particularistic rights claims. Feminists speak of women's rights in addition to (or rather than) human rights. Perhaps the greatest challenge to Canada's rights culture is emerging from Aboriginal peoples. Their appropriation of rights discourse to demand better living conditions, self-determination, and cultural rights puts us ill at ease because they do not easily fit within the liberal order.

The ability of rights talk to adapt over time as a frame for articulating grievances explains its popularity. Someone writing about our rights culture a generation from now may very well identify a completely different set of human rights. That is why articulating the boundaries of our rights culture is a difficult task. Our rights culture does not constitute an exhaustive list of rights. Human rights are, and always should be, a dialogue. In other words, understanding our rights culture is primarily an exercise in identifying those principles that underpin the foundation of the dialogue. Yet conversely, there is also a danger in failing to articulate a clear vision of our rights culture. How can we fairly promote human rights abroad—which includes providing material support for organizations and state institutions to protect human rights in other countries—if we have no clear sense of what human rights mean to us? Without an understanding of our rights culture, human rights become difficult to enforce and are subject to manipulation. Those who would make a mockery of our rights culture have already demonstrated how they can skilfully use rights discourse to undermine equality and liberty. It is perhaps most apparent in the way some individuals justify vicious attacks on homosexuals by appealing to the principle of free speech or religion. It is possible for human rights to become a tool of the powerful rather than, as it should be, a tool for challenging those in power. To save rights talk, we must reorient human rights within its long historical trajectory as a vernacular for resisting the arbitrary use of power. More importantly, any honest understanding of our rights culture must be premised, not only on those rights we recognize, but also on those rights we do not.

Notes

NOTES TO INTRODUCTION

1 Gloria Taylor died on 4 October 2012 while awaiting an appeal by the federal government to the British Columbia Court of Appeal. She died without the assistance of a doctor. *Carter v Canada (Attorney General)* [2015] SCC 5.

2 Hunt, *Inventing Human Rights*, 29.

3 Frager and Patrias, "'This Is Our Country,'" 1.

4 The resolution read as follows: "Fair Accommodation. WHEREAS there is concern caused by the practice of some proprietors, withholding service from groups or individuals because of race, colour, religion or national origin, and WHEREAS it is desirable that democratic nations make a concerted effort to remove every vestige of discrimination, and WHEREAS it is increasingly apparent that the law has a role in combating discrimination THEREFORE BE IT RESOLVED: That the Vancouver Council of Women request the Provincial Council of Women, to petition the British Columbia legislature to introduce appropriate legislation to prohibit discrimination in places supplying accommodation and services to the general public." British Columbia Archives, Provincial Council of Women, box 4, f. 3, Submission to Cabinet, 1959.

5 Moyn, *The Last Utopia*.

6 Stanley, *Contesting White Supremacy*, 167.

7 Mathieu, *North of the Color Line*, 100.

8 Lance Compa, "Framing Labor's New Human Rights Movement."

9 As Joseph McCartin explains, industrial democracy "was a direct challenge to the unaccountable power of employers to determine working conditions: democracy meant having a 'say' over those conditions." Some labour historians lament that the labour movement has abandoned the principles of industrial democracy in favour of advocating for human rights. According to Nelson Lichtenstein, industrial democracy was premised on the idea that "unionism would bring to the shop

and office floor those procedures and standards that had long been venerated in the courts, the legislatures, and at the ballot box." Rights discourse, however, is an individualist rather than a collective advancement of mutual interests. Human rights "are universal and individual, which means that employers and individual members of management enjoy them just as much as workers ... A discourse of rights has subverted the very idea and the institutional expression of union solidarity." Human rights-based activism "has had virtually no impact on the structure of industry or employment, in either the United States or abroad. A rights-based approach to the democratization of the workplace fails to confront capital with demands that cannot be defined as a judicially protected mandate." McCartin, "Democratizing the Demand for Workers' Rights"; Lichtenstein, "The Rights Revolution." See also McCartin, *Labor's Great War*.

10 "Gandhi generally disliked 'rightstalk' of all kinds, associating it with the self-indulgence of the modern age ... Gandhi preferred to frame his rhetoric in terms of 'duties' and kept his distance from 1940s human rights campaigns ... Gandhi expressed his distrust of rights-talk as early as 1910 in Hind Swaraj ... In the 1940s, he expressed his skepticism about human rights projects to both H.G. Wells and a UNESCO symposium that asked for his comments on the proposed Universal Declaration of Human Rights. In both cases, he urged people to think about their 'duties' instead of 'rights.'" Cmiel, "The Recent History of Human Rights," 119n8. See also Clément, "'I Believe in Human Rights.'"

11 They are the "highest moral rights, they regulate the fundamental structures and practices of political life, and in ordinary circumstances they take priority over other moral, legal, and political claims." Donnelly, *Universal Human Rights*, 1.

12 Hobsbawm, "Labour and Human Rights," 297.

13 Kallen, *Ethnicity and Human Rights in Canada*. Henry Shue makes a case for "basic rights" from which all other rights are derived or made possible; such rights include physical security and subsistence. Shue, *Basic Rights*.

14 Madsen and Verschraegen, "Making Human Rights Intelligible," 2.

15 Ibid., 8.

16 I am paraphrasing Madsen, who writes that human rights must "become institutionalised socially and become embedded in people's mindsets as well as in the day-to-day workings of societal institutions such as the judiciary, the schooling system, healthcare and the family." Ibid.

17 Arendt, *The Origins of Totalitarianism*, 376.

18 This idea is well developed in Goodhart, "Human Rights and the Politics of Contention."

19 For a discussion on Bentham, Burke, and Marx's debates on rights, see Jeremy Waldron, "*Nonesense Upon Stilts*."

20 Hobsbawm, "Labour and Human Rights," 309.

21 Habermas, *Religion and Rationality*, 153–54.

22 Minow, *Making All the Difference*, 307.

23 Kallen, *Ethnicity and Human Rights in Canada*, 1.

24 Sarah-Jane Mathieu observed a similar distinction between Canadians and Americans: "In the United States, African Americans marshaled the language of civil rights, whereas in Canada, a human rights movement defined the crusades spearheaded by African Canadians who worked with—or against when called for—Canada's leading trade unions and politicians." Mathieu, *North of the Color Line*, 189.

25 The right to self-determination in the ICCPR (1.1) requires some recognition of the economic, social, and cultural rights in the ICESCR; the right to family is enshrined in both the ICCPR (23.2) and the ICESCR (23.2); and the right to join a union in the ICCPR (10.1) is also entrenched in the ICESCR (8.1). Categorizing rights is therefore an artificial exercise at best, and we should appreciate that these boundaries "can obviously be blurred and quite arbitrary." Williams, *Human Rights under the Australian Constitution*, 7.

26 Cranston, *What Are Human Rights?*; Wellman, *The Proliferation of Rights*.

27 Henry Shue offers a compelling critique of the false dichotomy between negative and positive rights. He explores how basic rights to subsistence are no less viable than civil and political rights. Shue, *Basic Rights*, 35–51.

28 Berlin, *Four Essays on Liberty*, 124.

29 Ignatieff, *The Rights Revolution*, 89, 118.

30 As Todd Landman and Joe Foweraker explain, the "discourse of rights has no independent capacity for action, and cannot simply 'shower meanings on the society below' ... This discourse can only be effective when attached to social actors and organizations. Social movements, for their part, do not merely perceive or receive rights as symbols, but are active in discovering, shaping, and disseminating these rights." Foweraker and Landman, *Citizenship Rights and Social Movements*, 313–14.

31 Walker, *"Race," Rights, and the Law*, 320–21. "Human rights are of a juridical nature even if one can give a moral justification for them and even if their scope refers to all human beings." See also Jean L. Cohen, "Rethinking Human Rights," 599.

32 The former Soviet Union's 1977 constitution recognized a host of social rights such as health, education, housing, and rest and leisure. It also guaranteed a right to work and a maximum number of work hours per week. *Duties*, in the Soviet Union, unlike in Canada, were given equal consideration to rights for all citizens. China's current constitution prohibits discrimination on the basis of occupation and property status or length of residence. It also recognizes a right and a duty to work, as well as a right to rest. The Chinese constitution, however, also includes several rights that require citizens to protect and respect the State.

33 South Africa's Bill of Rights includes the right to "make decisions concerning reproduction" and the right to "security and control over their body."

34 On access-to-information legislation, see Larsen and Walby, *Brokering Access*.

35 On trade unions and the right to strike, see *Reference Re. Public Service Employee Relations Act [1987] 1 SCR 313*.

36 Bouchard and Taylor, *Building for the Future*.

37 Stammers, *Human Rights and Social Movements*, 1–3, 12–13. See also Allen Buchanan's critique of philosophers' failure to consider the critical role of history in grounding human rights theory: Buchanan, "The Egalitarianism of Human Rights," 688.

38 Ishay, *The History of Human Rights*; Lauren, *The Evolution of International Human Rights*.

39 For a discussion of religion and the history of human rights, see Joas, *The Sacredness of the Person*, Chapter 2.

40 "There is a strong tendency," as Neil Stammers points out, "to 'read history backwards'—that is to confuse outcomes with processes and assume that history 'is' what history 'became' ... [T]he significant involvement of historians in the field of human rights could sensitise scholars from other disciplines to the importance of such issues." Stammers, *Human Rights and Social Movements*, 14.

41 Ignatieff, *Human Rights as Politics and Idolatry*, 80.

42 Mckay, "The Liberal Order Framework," 624.

43 Stammers, *Human Rights and Social Movements*, 72–76.

44 On state formation and its impact on natural rights theory, see Vincent, *The Politics of Human Rights*, Chapter 3.

45 Moyn, *The Last Utopia*; Hunt, *Inventing Human Rights*.

46 Eckel, "The Rebirth of Politics," 13.

NOTES TO CHAPTER 1

1 Miller, "Human Rights for Some," 256–57.

2 Donnelly, *Universal Human Rights*, 57–61.

3 As one historian has aptly put it, by "contemporary British and even pre-revolutionary American standards, British North American governments interpreted and applied the law in a relentlessly repressive fashion." Greenwood and Wright, "Introduction: State Trials," 38.

4 Baehre, "Trying the Rebels," 56.

5 Ibid., 56–57.

6 One case in New France led to confiscation of a dead man's property and left his widow destitute. The judgment was later overturned, and the property was returned to the widow. Ibid., 58.

7 "In the period of the American revolution, civil liberties in Quebec were largely in abeyance, at least in the courts." Wright, "The Kingston and London Courts Martial," 148.

8 Upper Canada banned slavery in 1793. The last recorded slave sale in the colonies was in Halifax in 1820. Slavery was abolished throughout the British Empire in 1834.

9 "The system of generals," as one historian has described this period, "included hostility to the very notion of habeas corpus and to political dissent; secrecy in government, including the legislature; and determined opposition to an elected assembly which was being pressed for in these years by reformers." Moogk, "The Crime of Lèse-Majesté," 9.

10 Ibid., 25.

11 According to Ducharme, the only other journal in the colony was supportive of the government. Closing down the *Gazette* dampened public debate in the colony. Ducharme, *Le concept de liberté au Canada*, 48. Carleton also gave assent to New Brunswick's Tumults Bill in 1786, which banned all petitioning. Violators were to be fined and sent to jail for any petition with more than twenty signatures that did not have the consent of three justices of the peace or a grand jury. Wright, "Trying the Rebels," 232.

12 The British *Libel Act* of 1794 was supposed to prevent the arbitrary use of the charge of sedition to imprison citizens. The statute allowed juries, rather than judges, to determine whether libel was seditious. The Act severely restricted the right to bail for individuals charged with seditious offences, which were loosely defined in the statute. The statute "went beyond contemporary British restrictions on personal liberty. It was also far more authoritarian than the United States' Sedition Act of 1798 which required proof of malice, allowed truth as a defence, explicitly sanctioned the principle of Fox's act, did not suspend habeas corpus, and limited punishment to fines of $2,000 and imprisonment for two years." Moogk, "The Crime of Lèse-Majesté," 116–17.

13 During the War of 1812, the government of Upper Canada forced disloyal inhabitants to leave the country, expropriated their property as well as the property of people convicted of high treason or who had evaded prosecution, and suspended habeas corpus. The 1804 *Sedition Act*, which was passed out of fear that American or Irish inhabitants would support an invasion from the United States, "permitted the deportation of anyone who had not been an 'inhabitant' of the province for six months prior to the institution of proceedings against him, or who had not taken the oath of allegiance, if that person 'by words, actions or other behaviour or conduct' had 'given just cause to suspect that he [was] about to endeavour to alienate the minds of His Majesty's Subjects of this Province from his Person or Government, or in any wise with a seditious intent to disturb the tranquility of thereof.' The head of government, or any judge of the Court of King's Bench, or any executive or legislative councillor might order the arrest of such a person and require him to prove his innocence of the suspicions he had aroused. Should he fail to do so, the officer who had ordered his

arrest might direct him to leave the province. Disobedience to such an order was made a misdemeanor, the offender to be held without bail pending trial, and a second offence was made a capital felony." In addition, the legislature incorporated into the militia statute provisions that required militiamen to take an oath of allegiance (or be deemed an enemy alien); made desertion, mutiny, and sedition capital offences; and applied courts martial to lesser offences. It also included a provision for preventative detention (without bail) on suspicion of treasonable practices. "Since every male inhabitant between sixteen and sixty years of age was liable for service, the greater part of the adult male population was thereby rendered potentially subject to military justice or to the administrative measures directed against enemy aliens." Watt, "State Trial by Legislature," 380–81.

14 *An Act for the Better Preservation of His Majesty's Government, Lower Canada,* Provincial Statutes of Lower Canada, 1797, c.1; Greenwood and Wright, *Canadian State Trials,* 215; Greenwood and Wright, "Introduction: Rebellion."

15 Wright, "Trying the Rebels," 264. There was little in the way of judicial independence in Lower Canada. Judges held their positions at the pleasure of the Crown. Unlike in England, judges in the colony could also be members of the legislature.

16 Ajzenstat, *The Canadian Founding,* 128.

17 "The most typical sort of case involved an editor or printer publishing an anonymous article or letter to the editor that was highly critical of the government; he would then be summoned to court to respond to an action for libel initiated by a colony's attorney general or solicitor general on behalf of a member or members of the elite 'compacts' that dominated most of the colonies of British North America before the introduction of responsible government. The action might be for seditious libel, for criminal libel, occasionally for civil libel, and for contempt of a legislature. The number of prosecutions varied in the provinces; there appears to have been only two seditious libel cases in Nova Scotia between 1794 and 1835, while in Upper Canada there were well over thirty common-law sedition prosecutions between 1794 and 1829, in addition to summary deportations under the Sedition Act and parliamentary-privilege actions for contempt." Greenwood, "The Montreal Court Martial," 523.

18 Quoted in Moogk, "The Crime of Lèse-Majesté," 238. The grand jury refused to indict Bédard and the other editorialists.

19 Pitsula, *Keeping Canada British.*

20 High treason required allegiance to the Crown, but this legislation extended the crime to invaders from foreign countries at peace with Britain (rather than treating them as prisoners of war) and allowed them to be tried in military tribunals (without juries, which could not be trusted to convict). The Lawless Aggressions Act also dispensed

with the usual legal safeguards at the time for treasonable offences, including the requirement for at least two witnesses, and for allowing counsel to make a full defence and to have a copy of the indictment, lists of witnesses, and a pre-trial jury panel. The statute was repealed in 1838 and re-enacted in 1840 with even more provisions designed to facilitate prosecutions. Foreign invaders no longer had to have ties with British citizens. It was an offence simply to carry arms, and it was a capital offence for any foreigner to commit any act of hostility. Further amendments in 1866 extended its application to Lower Canada. The provisions for trying people in military courts when the country was not at war were especially controversial. Brown, "'Stars and Shamrocks Will Be Shown,'" 40–43. Greenwood and Wright, "Introduction: Rebellion, Invasion, and the Crisis of the Colonial State in the Canada, 1837–9," 39–40.

21 Another statute encouraged people to petition for pardons with the promise of leniency, although there was no guarantee of fair treatment and at least three men were later imprisoned after their petitions were used against them in court. Baehre, "Trying the Rebels," 44–48.

22 The courts ruled that many of the ordinances were unconstitutional. Watt, "State Trial by Legislature."

23 The use of courts martial had, as Barry Wright explains, serious consequences: "In effect, the rights of those under the protection of the crown were suspended by simply changing the name of the crime from reasonable levying of war to lawless aggression. Moreover, in general terms, the court martial of civilian British subjects in peacetime when ordinary courts could function clashed with prevailing British constitutional standards." Barry Wright, "The Kingston and London Courts Martial," 132. In addition, according to F. Murray Greenwood, "the prosecution [in Lower Canada] won about 90 percent of the motions on matters of procedure and evidence. The rights of the accused were often cavalierly ignored. None of the prisoners tried by this military tribunal ever received a list of witnesses or jurors (that is, the judges). Nor did any of them learn of the indictment more than four or five (rather than ten) days before the trial. In pleading before the court martial, counsel were not permitted to examine or cross-examine witnesses, although they could try to prepare their many clients in advance or pass them written suggestions. But often the accused were forced to react without adequate guidance and fared badly—particularly those who were illiterate and unilingual (French) ... Counsel could prepare written defence statements and read them to the court, but could not address it orally." Greenwood. "The General Court Martial at Montreal, 1838–9: Operation and the Irish Comparison," 290.

24 Most of the exiles were sent to Australia; however, several Patriote leaders were transported to Bermuda on pain of death if they returned to Lower Canada. Greenwood and Wright, "Introduction: Rebellion," 10.

25 Greenwood compares Canadian and British law to demonstrate that the former included far more draconian policies that restricted civil liberties. Greenwood, "The Drafting and Passage," 295-97.

26 Ajzenstat, *The Canadian Founding,* 125.

27 "Le menace que ces philosophes représentaient pour l'ordre d'Anci Régime ne provenait pas du fait qu'ils demandaient certaines réformes, mais plutôt qu'ils questionnaient la légitimité de l'ordre établi en lui refusant ses justifications traditionelles ... la liberté devait constituer le nouveau fondement de la légitimité de l'État et de l'ordre social." Ducharme, *Le concept de liberté au Canada,* 17.

28 The modernists were the true liberals because they believed in individual autonomy, although, as Elizabeth Heaman argues, rights talk in the nineteenth century was common among liberals and conservatives. For a fuller discussion on liberalism and rights in nineteenth-century Canada, see Dickinson and Dolmage, "Education, Religion, and the Courts in Ontario"; and Heaman, "Rights Talk and the Liberal Order Framework."

29 For a general history of human rights, see Hunt, *Inventing Human Rights;* Lauren, *The Evolution of International Human Rights;* and Ishay, *The History of Human Rights.* Ducharme identifies a similar series of rights when describing constitutional debates during this period. He also notes that "natural rights" rhetoric was sometimes replaced with reference to "birth-rights" or "absolute rights" but that the principles themselves remained consistent. Ducharme, *Le concept de liberté au Canada,* 169-78, 94-95.

30 "La liberté constituait certainement une des valeurs les plus importantes dans le monde atlantique à la fin du xviiie et au début du xixe siècle. Elle ne faisait alors pas uniquement référence à l'exercice de certains droits, mais elle était aussi vue comme le fondement de la légitimité de l'État." Liberty was a rallying cry for reformers and monarchists alike, but it was an abstract concept that often generated divisions and contradictions: "Premièrement, tous réclamaient une liberté qui était l'apanage des « individus » plutôt que de groupes sociaux particuliers ... Rien n'empêche que, dans les faits, bien peu d'« individus » pouvaient prétendre à cette liberté. La majorité des gens étaient, de facto, exclus de la jouissance de cette liberté. Les esclaves, les femmes, les pauvres et les étrangers ont dû attendre longtemps avant de pouvoir en jouir ... Deuxièmement, tous les promoteurs de la liberté assimilaient la liberté à la loi ... S'il ne fait aucun doute que tous ces penseurs partageaient une conception légaliste de la liberté, ils ne s'entendaient pas entre eux sur ce qu'était une loi légitime et encore moins sur des institutions législatives légitimes. En somme, même si tous ces promoteurs de la liberté associaient la liberté à la loi, ils ne défendaient par pour autant la même forme de liberté." Ducharme, *Le concept de liberté au Canada,* 25-26. Or, as Heaman suggests, "whereas property trumped liberty in

liberal discourse, democracy trumped liberty in republican discourse—leaving liberty itself something of an empty shell." Heaman, "Rights Talk and the Liberal Order Framework," 154.

31 This was consistent with the writings of William Blackstone, the famous British jurist of the late eighteenth century, who identified three fundamental liberties: personal security, personal liberty, and property.

32 The declaration called for abolishing imprisonment for debt as well as the death penalty except in murder cases. Curiously, the declaration also demanded equal rights for Aboriginal peoples—a rare claim during this period.

33 William Lyon Mackenzie. "Draft Constitution." *The Constitution*, 15 November 1837.

34 Papineau, *Journal d'un Fils de la liberté*.

35 The *Quebec Act* (1774) was a focal point for a debate over the concept of liberty. Monarchists saw the Act as an affirmation of British constitutional principles. Republicans argued that they obtained four rights through the Act: the right to participate in the Legislative Assembly; the right to petition the Assembly and seek redress in response to injustices; the right to criticize the law in public or private through speech or press; and the right to vote in determining representation in the Legislative Assembly. The *Quebec Act* also launched a bitter debate in the British House of Commons on the principle of the rights of man. Ducharme, *Le concept de liberté au Canada*, 17.

36 Hunt, *Inventing Human Rights*, 75–76.

37 For Burke, and for many colonists, rights were a product of history and derived from national traditions: "[The people of England] look upon the legal hereditary succession of the crown as among their rights, not as among their wrongs; as a benefit, not as a grievance; as a security for their liberty, not as a badge of servitude ... Government is not made in virtue of natural rights, which may and do exist in total independence of it." In his famous treatise *Reflections on the Revolution in France*, wherein he rejected the underlying principles of the French *Declaration of the Rights of Man and the Citizen*, Burke wrote: "The [English] Revolution was made to preserve our ancient, indisputable laws and liberties, and that ancient constitution of government which is our only security for law and liberty. If you are desirous of knowing the spirit of our constitution, and the policy which predominated in that great period which has secured it to this hour, pray look for both in our histories, in our records, in our acts of parliament, and journals of parliament, and not in the sermons of the Old Jewry, and the after-dinner toasts of the Revolution Society" (original author's emphasis). Burke feared that tyrannies would exploit the abstract nature of rights to advance their own interests. Turner, *Reflections on the Revolution in France*, 23, 27, 51.

38 Natural rights discourse flourished in the United States; however, by the mid-nineteenth century it was on the fringes of political thought in Canada and Britain. The conservative strand of rights discourse also pervaded the Catholic Church in the colonies. For many religious orders, the liberal notion of abstract universal rights threatened their privileged position and those protections guaranteed by the British Crown. Heaman, "Rights Talk and the Liberal Order Framework," 156.

39 Ibid., 159.

40 It is interesting to note that Patriote discourse was republican, not nationalist. Although they used their control of the Legislative Assembly to disenfranchise women, their rhetoric was culturally inclusive and was not racially or ethnically exclusive. Ducharme, *Le concept de liberté au Canada*, 157.

41 Ajzenstat, *The Canadian Founding*, Chapter 3.

42 Ibid., 58.

43 Although there is no reference to civil liberties or human rights in the British North America Act, Section 92 refers to property and civil rights (Section 92 delineates the jurisdiction of the provinces). However, the courts interpreted "civil rights" narrowly and limited the provinces' responsibilities under this section to contract and property law. Unlike the United States, therefore, the term "civil rights" has different connotations in Canada.

44 As Ajzenstat points out, "Canada's founding legislators describe good schools, high levels of employment, and material prosperity not as rights but as desirable political goals. The founders sought to secure the individuals against arbitrary and self-interested acts of autocratic rulers, bullies and demagogues." Ajzenstat, *The Canadian Founding*, 64.

45 "Racialized exclusions take many forms. They can be material: exclusions from particular territories, spaces, institutions; from access to social wealth, material goods, and services; or from life itself. They can be social: exclusions from particular social statuses, or networks or institutional roles; or from access to political rights. They can be symbolic: exclusion from being represented in particular ways or exclusion from having one's self-representations engaged or taken seriously." Stanley, *Contesting White Supremacy*, 10.

46 On state formation and race in British Columbia, see ibid., 10–12, 96–97, 230–31.

47 A survey conducted by the Toronto and District Committee for Human Rights in 1959 found that 60 percent of landlords were uncomfortable renting apartments to blacks. Similarly, black Winnipeggers reported that they were hassled when trying to rent an apartment or buy a home. Mathieu, *North of the Color Line*, 168–70, 210.

48 In some regions, blacks preferred to have their own schools. However, by the late nineteenth century, there were several political and legal battles over attempts by black parents to have their children admitted

to common schools. Black citizens paid taxes in Ontario and Nova Scotia for schools that their children were barred from attending if there existed a separate school for black children. Ontario's *Separate Schools Act* (1850), which allowed for the creation of separate schools, was designed to delay integration until local prejudices could be overcome, but white parents used the law to entrench segregation. Over time, separate schools in Nova Scotia and Ontario provided far worse education than white schools. Winks, "Negro School Segregation."

49 For a general history of racial discrimination in Canada, see Walker, *"Race," Rights, and the Law*; and Lambertson, *Repression and Resistance*. On segregation and education, see Stanley, *Contesting White Supremacy*.

50 André Picard, "Leprosy may be declining worldwide, but eradication is still elusive," *Globe and Mail*, 4 September 2013.

51 Lambertson, "Suppression and Subversion," 33. Saskatchewan's 1912 legislation was written as follows: "No person shall employ in any capacity any white woman or girl or permit any white person or girls to reside or lodge in or to work in or, save as bona fide customer in a public apartment thereof only, to frequent any restaurant, laundry or other place of business or amusement owner, kept or managed by any Japanese, Chinaman or other Oriental person." The law was extended in 1919 to include "lodging houses, boarding houses, public hotels, and cafés." Pitsula, *Keeping Canada British*, 118–19.

52 See, for example, Stanley, *Contesting White Supremacy*, 126–30.

53 Pitsula, *Keeping Canada British*.

54 Backhouse, *Colour-Coded*, Chapter 6.

55 Anderson, *Canadian Liberalism*, 47.

56 The initial bill included provisions to deport illiterate Chinese in Canada. The final version of the bill "required all those of 'Chinese race' living in Canada to register with the federal government and to obtain special residency permits, and it made those who failed to do so subject to fines, imprisonment, and deportation." The measure came into effect on Canada Day in 1923. Stanley, *Contesting White Supremacy*, 43. Canada implemented two policies to restrict immigration from Japan and India. In 1908, the federal government enacted an order-in-council that required immigrants to travel to Canada via continuous journey from their country of origin. In effect, banned immigration from India. The government also concluded a "gentlemen's agreement" with Japan in 1907 that limited the number of immigrants from that country.

57 Mathieu, *North of the Color Line*, 42.

58 Ibid., 57. See also Troper, "The Creek Negroes of Oklahoma."

59 On anti-Semitism in Canada, see Tulchinsky, *Branching Out*, Chapter 7; Davies, *Antisemitism in Canada*; and Patrias, "Race, Employment Discrimination, and State Complicity," 54.

60 Tulchinsky, *Branching Out*, 185.

61 Ibid., 173.

62 Pierre Berton, "No Jews Need Apply." *Maclean's Magazine*, 1 November 1948.

63 Ibid.

64 Anti-Catholic sentiment was not uncommon outside Quebec. For many British-born Protestants, Catholicism was inconsistent with British identity (the Ku Klux Klan in Canada was virulently anti-Catholic). Provincial governments restricted the spread of the French language and Catholic schools. Even Ivan Rand, considered one of the most progressive judges on the Supreme Court of Canada and the country's "greatest civil libertarian judge," had nothing but disdain for Catholics and French Canadians. Kaplan, *Canadian Maverick*, 111. On the KKK, see Pitsula, *Keeping Canada British*, Chapter 6.

65 In 1947 the *Land Sales Prohibition Act* was replaced with the *Communal Property Act* with the same intent of restricting land sales to Hutterites. The latter lasted until 1972. *Land Sales Prohibition Act*, S.A.1942, c.59; *Communal Property Act*, S.A. 1947, c.16.

66 Lambertson, "Domination and Dissent," 15.

67 Lambertson, "Suppression and Subversion," 33.

68 Lambertson, *Repression and Resistance*, 72.

69 Some versions of the law between 1920 and 1922, and 1933 to 1951, included involuntary enfranchisement. The 1876 Indian Act made enfranchisement a requirement for legal, medical, and religious professionals until it was made voluntary in 1880.

70 "Since 1857, when the Province of Canada (forerunner of Southern Ontario) passed the Gradual Civilization Act, adult First Nation males who applied and could convince a board of examiners that they were literate, debt-free, and of good moral character could surrender their status as 'Indians' and become full British Canadian citizens, with all attendant rights, including the vote, after a three-year probationary period in which they would demonstrate further their fitness to join the general citizenry ... The statute's reach was considerable: an enfranchised male's wife and children would also become enfranchised and lose Indian status, as would all their descendants forever." Miller, "Human Rights for Some," 235.

71 When they lost their status, Aboriginal women forfeited their right to live on Aboriginal lands, own band property, inherit land or a house on a reserve, and be buried on a reserve (yet, as one observer has noted, non-Aboriginals could bury dead dogs in a pet cemetery on a reserve). They could not regain their status, and thereby return to their home, if their marriage dissolved or they divorced. This provision remained in place until 1985. It was one among many forms of sex discrimination under the *Indian Act* that survived until the mid-1980s: women and their children were involuntarily enfranchised if their husband/father was enfranchised; married women's band membership was determined by their husband's band; illegitimate children of Aboriginal men or

non-Aboriginal women were denied status; and children lost status when they reached the age of twenty-one if their mother did not have status before she was married. The complete list of losses facing Aboriginal women who lost their status is described in detail in Sally Weaver, "First Nations Women and Government Policy," 93-94.

72 Miller, "Human Rights for Some," 242.

73 "If there was any denial of human rights greater than interference with cultural and spiritual observances it was the attempt to remake a community's children's identity and way of life ... Tens of thousands of them emerged from residential schooling damaged, confused, unattached to a community, and sometimes bitter and angry at what had happened." Hay, "Civilians Tried in Military Courts," 243-44.

74 Dicey, *Introduction to the Study*.

75 Quoted in Stanley, *Contesting White Supremacy*, 41.

76 Pitsula, *Keeping Canada British*, 1.

77 Ducharme, *Le concept de liberté au Canada*, 170. Similarly, in 1852, the British government banned public displays of Roman Catholic symbols. No such prohibitions existed in Canada. Radforth, "Collective Rights," 539.

78 An 1858 statute in the Canadas, the *Freedom of Worship Act*, reaffirmed the right to religious freedom: "Whereas the recognition of the legal equality among all Religious Denominations is an admitted principle of Colonial Legislation ... be it therefore declared ... that the free exercise and enjoyment of Religious Profession and Worship, without discrimination or preference, so as the same be not made an excuse of acts of licentiousness, or a justification of practices inconsistent with the peace and safety of the Provinces, is by the constitution and laws of this Province allowed to all Her Majesty's subjects." The 1841 legislation that unified Upper and Lower Canada also included provisions to protect religious diversity. Kaplan, *Canadian Maverick*, 127-28.

79 Ontario, Quebec, Saskatchewan, Alberta, and Newfoundland provided funding to Catholic (French) and Protestant (English) schools, whereas New Brunswick, Nova Scotia, Manitoba, and British Columbia provided no funding for denominational schools. The Manitoba Schools Question was the dominant issue in the 1896 federal election, which led to the downfall of the ruling Conservative Party. Miller, "D'Alton McCarthy."

80 The Judicial Committee of the Privy Council affirmed the validity of the *Public Schools Act* in separate cases in 1892 and 1895.

81 The regulation was amended in 1913 to also allow up to one hour of instruction in French after the first two years of school. In 1944, both Ontario and British Columbia allowed the recitation of the Lord's Prayer in public schools. On religion and human rights, see Berger, *Fragile Freedoms*.

82 House of Commons, *Hansard*, no. 1 (1893), 1792.

83 Pitsula, *Keeping Canada British,* 160.

84 Ian Radforth addresses a similar theme in this study of Catholic processions on the streets of Toronto. In at least two cases, the Corpus Christi celebrations of 1864 and the Jubilee Riots of 1875, the tensions between Protestants and Catholics erupted in violence. According to Radforth, Catholics appealed to their historical right as Catholics in Canada to practise their religion. Catholics framed their rights as minority or collective rights in the same way Protestants and Catholics framed the debate around denominational education. "Lynch, thus, made his case for the right of Catholics to practice their religion in a charged atmosphere where he expected his statements would be strongly opposed, but find resonance." Radforth, "Collective Rights," 534.

85 House of Commons, *Hansard,* no. 2 (1896), 2759.

86 Another rights debate ensued in the late nineteeth century and throughout the twentieth over immigration policies. Liberal internationalists in Parliament, who favoured open immigration, appealed to the principles of the "British constitution," whereas liberal nationalists sought to protect the nation by excluding non-whites. One MP, speaking in 1926 against the practice of deporting people accused of a crime, declared: "To what end do we owe it that we to-day enjoy the rights and privileges we have as British subjects under Magna Carta and under that other great protective charter of British liberty, the Habeas Corpus Act?" By the 1940s, immigration policies had become increasingly restrictive; these debates challenged the boundaries of a rights culture that discriminated against non-citizens. Anderson, *Canadian Liberalism,* 106.

87 *Re Mable French [1905]* 27 NBR 366.

88 For a history of the law and sex discrimination, see Clément, *Equality Deferred,* Chapter 1.

89 Kealey, "State Repression of Labour."

90 Mackenzie, "Section 98," 474.

91 There was almost no opposition to the legislation in Parliament: "This small amendment was a focal point for debates over control and the rights of non-citizens for almost ten years, bringing greater attention to due process rights within British liberalism and initiating a new round of rights-based politics in Canada." Anderson, *Canadian Liberalism,* 99–100, 96.

92 Petryshyn, "Class Conflict and Civil Liberties," 47.

93 Mackenzie, "Section 98," 478.

94 The government of Quebec, as we will see in Chapter 2, was especially prone to violations of freedom of assembly, association, and speech. The 1934 *Certain Meetings Advertising Act,* for instance, required individuals to seek permission from the local police chief before distributing flyers. This was a poorly disguised attempt to silence communists and trade unionists. Lambertson, *Repression and Resistance,* 34.

95 Whitaker, Kealey, and Parnaby, *Secret Service,* 122–26.

96 Quoted in Petryshyn, "Class Conflict and Civil Liberties," 43.

97 Ibid., 53.

98 Vipond, "Censorship in a Liberal State," 81–84. To discourage domestic support for the communists during the Spanish Civil War, the federal government amended the *Foreign Enlistment Act* in 1937 to prohibit individuals from participating in the war. Individuals who violated the law were liable for a fine of $2,000 and two years in jail. The government later used the legislation to ban all travel to Spain. Whitaker, Kealey, and Parnaby, *Secret Service*, 139.

99 Quoted in Mathieu, *North of the Color Line*, 122.

100 Anderson, *Canadian Liberalism*, 100.

101 Clément, *Canada's Rights Revolution*, 37.

102 Quoted in Petryshyn, "Class Conflict and Civil Liberties," 50. The House of Commons passed legislation to remove Section 98 in 1927, 1928, 1929, and 1930. In each case, the bill was defeated in the Senate. Mackenzie, "Section 98," 482.

103 *Alberta Press Bill*, Supreme Court Reports 100 (1938).

104 Ibid.

105 Historians of security policing in Canada have observed a similar trend. Throughout the Great Depression, state actors routinely justified repressive tactics against communists in order to protect British values or traditions. At the same time, non-state actors framed their grievances using a similar discourse: "strikers flew the Union Jack, 'vagrants' wore their medals from the Great War, and both argued that union recognition, abolition of relief camps, and unemployment insurance were precisely the ways to *restore* British values and traditions, which had been undermined by the calamity of the Great Depression, the government's heavy-handed application of the Criminal Code and Immigration Act, and the RCMP's persistent surveillance and harassment of putative subversives." Whitaker, Kealey, and Parnaby, *Secret Service*, 143.

NOTES TO CHAPTER 2

1 *Act Respecting Communistic Propaganda*, S.Q. 1937, c.11.

2 Lambertson, "Suppression and Subversion," 33.

3 In 1937, Duplessis's government passed *An Act Respecting Workmen's Wages* and the *Fair Wage Act*. The legislation allowed the government to intervene in the internal affairs of unions—including the collective bargaining process and the rights of workers to choose their own unions. This permitted Duplessis to destabilize non-Catholic unions. Lambertson, *Repression and Resistance*, 50.

4 No author. "Le premier ministre parle de sabotage et l'Opposition lui pose deux questions." *Le Devoir*, 1 February 1951.

5 As F. Murray Greenwood argues, legislators in Canada have historically "indulge[d] in drastic security legislation in times of crisis, real or

apprehended, without much concern for civil liberties and with almost no critical examination of the invariably elastic language used." Greenwood, "The Drafting and Passage," 292.

6 Whitaker, Kealey, and Parnaby, *Secret Service*, 29-30.

7 "All in all, the suspension of habeas corpus generated no public protests, no sense of panic, and no manifestation of popular anti-Fenianism; instead, it was treated as part of the humdrum business of Parliament." Wilson, "The D'Arcy McGee Affair," 87, 98.

8 Preceding the formation of Riel's Provisional Government in 1885, which precipitated the rebellion, in 1884 a committee of French and English representatives submitted a Petition of Rights to the federal government. This document is often referred to, erroneously, as the Riel or Métis Bill of Rights. The petition does not deal with civil liberties; rather, it lists a series of grievances involving property and the administration of the region (although it does demand responsible government for Manitoba). For a copy of the petition and some brief context, see Lewis H. Thomas, "Documents of Western History."

9 There were other, less notable, examples of legislative excess that were justified in the name of protecting public order. The more open-ended definition of sedition in Canada compared to Britain remained entrenched in law until 1951. The British Parliament removed the death penalty from a host of crimes in 1848; Canada did not follow suit until 1868. The British also accepted duress as a legitimate defence against the crime of levying war; Canadian policy-makers removed this defence in 1906. Greenwood, "The Drafting and Passage," 296-97.

10 The original bill included the following clause, which was later removed by Cabinet before the legislation was passed: "Every order and warrant made or issued by any minister ... shall be conclusive evidence of all statements and matters therein contained, and no court or judge shall inquire into or make any order in respect thereto." Quoted in Smith, "Emergency Government in Canada," 431.

11 The *Military Service Act* "made it an offence to resist or impede the conscription of men, either by word or in writing. Regulations which followed in its wake made it illegal to interrupt a recruiting speech, to refuse to aid a military officer making an arrest, or to attend a meeting where disloyal language was used. A month after the Act was passed, the Minister of Justice was empowered to proceed against persons whose 'designs were suspect.' To proceed against such persons, whoever they might be, meant to order them indoors, into court or into internment camps. Read literally, anyone who opposed conscription, even reputable politicians and newspapers, was in danger of being charged with sedition." Ibid., 441.

12 The minister could authorize the seizure of any telephone or telegraph company to control all transmissions, and the government gave itself the power to appoint a Chief Press Censor and a Chief Mail Censor.

All publications, including a simple leaflet, had to include the author's name. The regulations were extensive and included any communications with enemy agents or communicating information about the armed services or Cabinet. On censorship during the war, see Keshen, *Propaganda and Censorship*; and Steinhart, *Civil Censorship in Canada*.

13 Except for religious services, the order-in-council further banned meetings (and publishing any document) throughout the country in a language associated with an enemy, including Russian, Finish, or Ukrainian. These were severe restrictions on freedoms of assembly and press. The government suppressed the entire radical foreign press in Canada. The Chief Press Censor exercised his power with greater frequency as the war dragged on. He banned two publications in 1914, sixteen in 1915, fifty-two in 1916, fifty-eight in 1917, and fifty-nine in 1918. Whitaker, Kealey, and Parnaby, *Secret Service*, 63–68. Kealey, "State Repression of Labour," 288.

14 In April 1918, for instance, the federal government responded to a riot at a Military Service Registry office in Quebec City by declaring martial law, suspending habeas corpus, and threatening the rioters with conscription. Cook, *Warlords*, 129. More mundane powers included the authority to seize lands to settle veteran soldiers and to compensate the previous owners at whatever price the government deemed reasonable. For a detailed discussion of orders issued under the *War Measures Act* during the First World War, see Smith, "Emergency Government in Canada."

15 Greenwood, "The Drafting and Passage," 292.

16 For orders-in-council passed under the authority of the *War Measures Act*, see B. Chamberlin, *Acts of the Parliament of the Dominion of Canada, 1873–1951*, at http://eco.canadiana.ca.

17 Quoted in Kealey, "State Repression of Labour," 293.

18 Whitaker and Marcuse, *Cold War Canada*, 7–8.

19 Whitaker, Kealey, and Parnaby, *Secret Service*, 147, 57.

20 Lambertson, *Repression and Resistance*, 82.

21 Ibid., 85.

22 Ibid., 70–71.

23 Ibid., 82.

24 Eric Adams, "Building a Law of Human Rights," 445.

25 Bangarth, *Voices Raised in Protest*.

26 On the Gouzenko Affair, see Clément, "Spies, Lies and a Commission" and "The Royal Commission on Espionage." See also Lambertson, *Repression and Resistance*; and Knight, *How the Cold War Began*.

27 Adams, "The Idea of Constitutional Rights," 79.

28 Manitoba passed the country's first anti-hate legislation, in 1934, through an amendment to the *Libel Act* that prohibited "the publication of a libel against a race or creed likely to expose persons belonging to a race or professing the creed to hatred, contempt or ridicule, and

tending to raise unrest or disorder among the people." An Act to Amend the "Libel Act", S.M. 1934, c.23. The Racial Discrimination Act, S.O. 1944, c.51.

29 Tulchinsky, *Canada's Jews*, 172; Lambertson, "Suppression and Subversion," 33.

30 The statute also made reference to creed and colour. *An Act to Protect Certain Civil Rights*, S.S. 1947, c.35.

31 According to F.P. Varcoe, a future federal justice minister: "A right connotes a corresponding duty in some other person or the state toward the person holding the right; for example, if a person has a right to education, there is a corresponding duty on the state to provide it. A freedom, on the other hand, is a benefit or advantage which a person derives from the absence of legal duties imposed upon him." Canada, *Special Joint Committee [...] on Human Rights and Fundamental Freedoms*, 132.

32 Canada, *Special Committee on Human Rights and Fundamental Freedoms*, 89.

33 Ibid., 174.

34 Palmer, *Working Class Experience*, 266.

35 Mathieu, *North of the Color Line*, 62, 133. The union's racialized organizational structure remained in place until the mid-1960s, despite a substantial black membership.

36 Over two million immigrants entered the country between 1946 and 1961. Many of these new Canadians filled the ranks of unions. Lambertson, "The Dresden Story," 48–49.

37 "The party's opposition to discrimination was a product of several factors, including its members' dedication to secular humanism, social gospel and economic and social equality ... Responding to both Canadian and international developments, CCF members grew increasingly concerned about safeguarding civil liberties and human rights during the later 1930s and the 1940s. Domestically, they were reacting to the intensification of anti-Semitism in the late 1930s, Duplessis's 1937 anti-Communist Padlock Law, the detention of Communists and the seizure of Ukrainian Labour and Farmer Temple Federation halls at the outbreak of the Second World War, the expulsion of Japanese Canadians from the West Coast in 1942 and the deportation of many of them to Japan at war's end, and the arrest and detention of suspected Communists without trial following Soviet embassy clerk Igor Gouzenko's defection in 1945." Patrias, "Socialists, Jews, and the 1947 Saskatchewan Bill of Rights," 268, 71.

38 Bangarth, "'We Are Not Asking You."

39 On the history of the first civil liberties groups in Canada, see Lambertson, *Repression and Resistance*.

40 Walker, *"Race," Rights and the Law*, Chapter 3.

41 Ibid., 177–78.

42 Scott, *Essays on the Constitution*, 353.

NOTES TO CHAPTER 2
171

43 For background on these cases, see Kaplan, *Canadian Maverick*, Chapter 4; and Berger, *Fragile Freedoms*, Chapter 6.
44 Quoted in Kaplan, *Canadian Maverick*, 135.
45 Ibid., 136.
46 *Boucher v The King* (1949) 95 CCC 119; *Saumur v City of Quebec* (1953) SCR 265; *Switzman v Elbling and Attorney-General of Quebec* (1957) SCR 285; *Roncarelli v Duplessis* (1959) SCR 121.
47 In his analysis of the *Roncarelli* case, Adams concludes that "Justice Rand's rule of law was premised on judicial enforcement of administrative rationality, not human rights." Adams, "Building a Law of Human Rights," 449.
48 *Noble et al. v Alley* [1951] SCR 64.
49 Quote in Walker, "The 'Jewish Phase.'"
50 University of British Columbia Rare Books and Special Collections (UBC RBSC), Vancouver Labour Committee for Human Rights, Report on Activities, box 1, 1959.
51 Norman, "Saskatchewan's One Bright Shinning Moment."
52 *The Fair Employment Practices Act*, S.O. 1951, c.24; *The Fair Accommodation Practice Act*, S.O. 1954, c.28; *The Female Employees Fair Remuneration Act*, S.O. 1951, c.26.
53 Ernest Manning to Michel Gouault (United Council for Human Rights), 8 June 1964, LAC, Jewish Labour Committee (JLC), MG 28 V75, vol. 36, file 14. Maureen Riddell, *The Evolution of Human Rights Legislation in Alberta*, 6.
54 *Fair Employment Practices Act*, S.B.C. 1956, c.16.
55 "Discrimination and the Law," *Toronto Star*, 3 August 1961.
56 Clément, "'I Believe in Human Rights'"; Tarnopolsky, *Discrimination and the Law in Canada*, Chapter 2.
57 Frager and Patrias, "'This Is Our Country,'" 4.
58 Frager and Patrias, *Discounted Labour*, 82–83. Phil Girard makes a similar argument regarding the National Council of Women's position on the law regulating women, marriage, and nationality. Girard, "'If Two Ride a Horse,'" 44.
59 Knopff and Morton, *The Charter Revolution*, 14.
60 Gwyn, *Smallwood*, 239; Gillespie, "A History of the Newfoundland Federation of Labour," 27–29.
61 Several studies on the history of human rights have concluded that, until the 1970s, the Cold War had a dampening effect on human rights progress. Sellars, *The Rise and Rise of Human Rights*, 139; Mazower, "The Strange Triumph of Human Rights," 395; Gordon and Wood, "Canada and the Reshaping of the United Nations," 499; Lambertson, *Repression and Resistance*; Clément, *Canada's Rights Revolution*; Watson, *Brian Fitzpatrick*; Clément, "'It Is Not the Beliefs'"; Clarke, "Debilitating Divisions," 182.
62 Walker, "The 'Jewish Phase.'"

63 Quoted in Schabas, "Canada and the Adoption," 424. Schabas also states: "A 112-paragraph document entitled 'Views of Canada on Matters Before the United Nations' prepared by External Affairs bureaucrats for the Assembly did not even mention the Declaration."

64 Canada, *Special Committee on Human Rights and Fundamental Freedoms* [1950]; Hobbins, "Eleanor Roosevelt."

65 Mazower, "The Strange Triumph of Human Rights," 394–95. On Australia's opposition to interference in domestic affairs, see Devereux, *Australia and the Birth*, 204–15.

66 "Human rights were not so much a casualty of the San Francisco conference as a simple non-event. The United Nations was a coalition of sovereign states, consulting and combining for specific and limited purposes. Interference in domestic affairs from a notional world body was not welcomed by anyone, and Canada was no exception. The United Nations' job was to prevent war, not meddle in its members' affairs, a point Mackenzie King explicitly made to his delegation. Subjects such as human rights, immigration, and education in Canada were nobody's business outside the country. Not all members of the delegation agreed with the prime minister, but they knew better than to contradict him." Bothwell, *Alliance and Illusion*, 21.

67 Schabas, "Canada and the Adoption," 427.

68 Nossal, "Cabin'd, Cribb'd, Confin'd," 50.

69 Nolan, "Reluctant Liberal," 287–88.

70 "For the most part, however, foreign policy reflected a commitment to state sovereignty and a willingness to accept, if not respect different values and traditions, and different state practices. It also supported the view that interventions for whatever reasons constituted violations of international order and should not be condoned." Gecelovsky and Keating, "Liberal Internationalism for Conservatives," 1–2.

71 Nolan, "Reluctant Liberal," 294.

72 Some commentators used the terms "civil rights" and "civil liberties" interchangeably. On the Gouzenko Affair, including media coverage, Parliamentary debates, and the contribution of civil liberties associations, see: Clément, "The Royal Commission" and "Spies, Lies and a Commission."

73 "Topics of the Day," *Dalhousie Review* 26 (1946–47): 96–98.

74 In contrast, the constitution of the Canadian Labour Defence League (a communist-affiliated Canadian civil liberties group) incorporated social and economic rights, including the right to work and to a fair wage. Similarly, the Association for Civil Liberties in Toronto did not campaign for antidiscrimination legislation until the 1950s. Frank Scott, who was deeply involved in the early movement and helped create several civil liberties organizations, explained to a colleague in 1933 that "to my mind, a civil liberties association should concern itself

solely with the preservation of the right to freedom of speech and association." Petryshyn, "A.E. Smith," 42; Lambertson, "The Dresden Story," 29.

75 Lambertson, *Repression and Resistance*, 34.

76 Moyn, *The Last Utopia*; Quataert, *Advocating Dignity*; Korey, *NGOs*.

77 Moravcsik, "The Paradox."

78 Maul, "The International Labour Organization," 305.

79 Moyn, *The Last Utopia*, 225. On international law, see also Pendas, "Toward World Law?"

80 A Gallup poll taken in 1949 asked respondents if they believed in complete freedom of speech and if people should be allowed to say anything at any time about government and the country. Of the 2,019 respondents, 36.2 percent said no and another 15 percent had no opinion or had a qualified answer. Four years later, a new poll found that 62 percent of respondents favoured limiting the speech of communists and only 26 percent considered it a fundamental democratic right. Opinion polls were still in their infancy at this time and were a crude measurement of overall opinion, yet these few examples demonstrate, at the very least, an undercurrent of opinion sympathetic to state-imposed limitations on individual rights. Canadian Institute of Public Opinion/Gallup (1949), *Canadian Gallup Poll 191*. Poll retrieved 1 November 2011 from Carleton Data Centre/Roper Center for Public Opinion Research. See also Axelrod, *Scholars and Dollars*.

81 Clarke, "Debilitating Divisions," 182.

82 Bagnall, "The Ontario Conservatives," 122.

83 Marshall, "The Cold War."

84 Margaret Hillyard Little argues that mothers' pensions (as they were called in that province) were framed as statutory rights and that rights discourse pervaded public debate around pensions. However, as Little explains, this use of rights talk was linked to citizenship and excluded racial minorities (among others). Little, "Claiming a Unique Place." See also Marshall, "The Language of Childen's Rights."

NOTES TO CHAPTER 3

1 On human rights violations during the October Crisis, see Clément, "The October Crisis of 1970."

2 Claude Ryan, "Les retombées de la crise d'octobre au Canada Anglais," *Le Devoir*, 1 February 1971 (translated by author).

3 Lauren, *The Evolution of International Human Rights*.

4 These were among the most prominent human rights organizations in the world, but certainly not the only ones. Regional organizations such as the Asian Coalition of Human Rights Organizations and the Inter-African Network for Human Rights also reported on human rights abuses. Human Rights Watch was founded in 1978.

5 By 1996 there were no less than 295 registered human rights groups worldwide, almost half of which had been formed since the 1970s. Today, an estimated 35,000 organizations worldwide are concerned with human rights enforcement.

6 On human rights and the early Cold War period, see Forsythe, *Human Rights in International Relations*, 41, 43; Devereux, *Australia and the Birth*; Sellars, *The Rise and Rise*; Olzak, *The Global Dynamics*; Donnelly, "Genocide and Humanitarian Intervention" and *International Human Rights*, 7; Soohoo, "Human Rights and the Transformation,"; and Eckel, "The International League."

7 On the Cold War and human rights, see MacLennan, *Toward the Charter*, 75. Kristen Sellars suggests that the Ford Foundation, which has become a major funding source for transnational human rights activism since the 1970s, only turned to human rights work as the Cold War eased. Sellars, *The Rise and Rise*, 139; Donnelly, "Genocide and Humanitarian Intervention," 94, 97; Risse, Ropp, and Sikkink, *The Power of Human Rights*; Keck and Sikkink, *Activists Beyond Borders*; Olzak, *The Global Dynamics*.

8 The worst excesses of domestic Cold War politics had dissipated by the 1970s. Anticommunist purges in trade unions and within the civil service had exhausted themselves; several of the more outrageous laws restricting basic rights had been eliminated; and political debates no longer drew as heavily on Cold War rhetoric. The communist movement in Canada was a shell of its former self, and rights associations were no longer riddled with internal ideological conflicts.

9 Historian Samuel Moyn contends that human rights only came to the fore in international politics in the 1970s because other utopian ideals, such as communism, had become discredited: "It was, instead, only in the 1970s that a genuine social movement around human rights made its appearance, seizing the foreground by transcending official government institutions, especially international ones." Moyn, *The Last Utopia*, 8.

10 Risse, Ropp, and Sikkink, *The Power of Human Rights*, 266. Risse and colleagues' study demonstrates how a process of "normalization" or "socialization" occurred wherein human rights principles became an integral part of international politics. They offer a series of case studies to demonstrate how violators can deny or reject rights claims but over time must accept and engage in dialogue surrounding their human rights record (or risk isolation and sanctions). Over time, this dialogue became a basis for addressing rights abuses within states.

11 *The Ontario Human Rights Code*, S.O. 1961-62, c.93. The Human Rights Commission was, in fact, created in 1961 to enforce antidiscrimination legislation before the code was passed into law.

12 James St.G. Walker, in "The 'Jewish Phase,'" offers an insightful analysis of the evolution of human rights law in Canada.

13 "A substantive equality approach asks whether the same treatment in practice produces equal or unequal results ... Substantive equality requires taking into account the underlying differences between individuals in society and accommodating those differences in order to ensure equality of impact and outcome." Cornish, Faraday, and Pickel, *Enforcing Human Rights in Ontario*, 39.

14 Ontario, *Report of the Royal Commission*; Quebec, Commission of Enquiry.

15 *Official Languages Act*, S.C. 1969, c.54.

16 *Criminal Law Amendment Act*, S.C. 1968-69, c.38.

17 "Under s. 318 of the Criminal Code, everyone who advocates or promotes genocide is guilty of an offence punishable by five years' imprisonment ... Under s. 319(1) of the Criminal Code, anyone who communicates statements in a public place and thereby incites hatred against an identifiable group where such incitement leads to a breach of the peace is guilty of an indictable offence punishable by two years' imprisonment or a summary conviction offence." Rosen, "Hate Propaganda."

18 Canada, *Statement of the Government of Canada on Indian Policy*, 5.

19 Ibid., 6-8.

20 "Full and equal access for *individuals* of aboriginal descent to the democratic rights and economic opportunities of the mainstream society—the integrationist approach—was not something to be spurned. This approach, however, held the promise of being part of a postcolonial relationship only if it could be combined with an autonomist approach recognizing the *collective* right of Aboriginal peoples to survive and develop as distinct, self-governing communities on or in connection with traditional lands and waters ... The inadequacy of the liberal, civil-rights approach as the basis for reaching a consensual accommodation with Aboriginal peoples became crystal clear in Canada in 1969." Russell, "Colonization of Indigenous Peoples," 76.

21 The Indian Chiefs of Alberta published a provocative critique in 1970 titled *Citizens Plus* (the "Red Paper"). They argued that the White Paper "offers despair instead of hope," and would condemn future generations of Aboriginal peoples "to the despair and ugly specter of urban poverty in ghettos." Harold Cardinal's 1970 bestselling book *Unjust Society* further articulated Aboriginal peoples' grievances and offered a vision for the future. The White Paper, he wrote, was a tool for "cultural genocide." Cardinal decried Aboriginal peoples' poor living conditions, lack of educational opportunities, and systemic unemployment. Indian Chiefs of Alberta, 1970. *Citizens Plus*; Cardinal, *The Unjust Society*, 5.

22 Four national Aboriginal peoples' associations and thirty-three separate provincial organizations emerged in the aftermath of the White Paper. Many of these groups were pioneers in organizing Aboriginal peoples beyond the local level. In Alberta, for instance, the Alberta Native Federation, Alberta Native Youth Society, Treaty Voice of Alberta, and the Native Human Rights Association were formed between 1968 and 1972.

Indian Friendship Centres multiplied across the country. Whiteside, "Historical Development"; Ramos, "What Causes Canadian Aboriginal Protest?" and "Aboriginal Protest." On the Aboriginal rights movement and the White Paper, see Ramos, "Divergent Paths."

23 Long, "Culture, Ideology, and Militancy," 121.

24 *Statute Law (Status of Women) Amendment Act,* S.C. 1974-76, c.66.

25 British Columbia Archives, Department of Labour, Memorandum from D.H. Cameron to W. Mitchell. G85 168, Acc. 880057-3714, box 4, f. H-5-L, 1981; British Columbia Archives, Status of Women Action Group, Report on discrimination in the retail trades. v. 3, f. 32, 1972; LAC, Dan Hill, Victoria Human Rights Council Brief to the Human Rights Commission, MG 31 H155, vol.16, file 17, 1979; UBC RBSC, Vancouver Status of Women, Day of mourning for the human rights code. v. 6, f. 15, 1976.

26 For a history of Canada's human rights movement, see Clément, *Canada's Rights Revolution*.

27 A similar divide emerged in the United States, although in this case it was a conceptual divide between "civil rights" and "human rights" (rather than civil liberties and human rights). See Soohoo, Albisa, and Davis, *Bringing Human Rights Home*.

28 For a complete history of the debates surrounding the federal Bill of Rights, see Clément, *Canada's Rights Revolution*, Chapter 1; and MacLennan, *Toward the Charter*.

29 Frank Scott to Gordon Dowding, 20 September 1964, LAC, Frank Scott Papers, MG 30, D211, vol. 47.

30 Canada, *Special Joint Committee [...] Final Report*, 18-19.

31 There was a new emphasis placed on language rights, which was addressed by each province before the committee. Ibid., 3-68 to 3-133.

32 "The government of Manitoba believes that the constitution would be incomplete if it did not recognize the duty of governments to ensure humane standards of social welfare and other important social and economic benefits for all Canadians. The need for such benefits and the ability of governments to meet them will vary considerably from time to time, of course, but the constitution ought, in it preamble, to state that the fulfilment of this duty is one of the objectives of Canadian federalism." Canada, *Special Joint Committee [...] Minutes of Proceedings and Evidence*, 3:112, 3:33.

33 The NDP members of the committee, Andrew Brewin and Douglas Rowland, challenged the proposed protections for private property out of concern that it could be used to undermine workers' rights. Two MPs from Quebec, Pierre DeBané and Martial Asselin, produced a minority report with a recommendation to recognize the right to self-determination. LAC, RG 14, Acc. 1991-92/138, box 49', Special Joint Committee on the Constitution of Canada, Statement by Andrew Brewin and Douglas Rowland on the Report of that Committee, 16 March 1972; A

Minority Report by Me Pierre DeBané and Me Martial Asselin, 7 March 1972.

34 Canada, *Special Joint Committee [...] Minutes of Proceedings and Evidence,* 74:33–87.

35 Ibid., 88:6–35.

36 Ibid., 62:29–34.

37 Ibid., 62:33.

38 Behiels, "Canada and the Implementation."

39 Canada, Department of External Affairs, *Foreign Policy for Canadians,* 3:26–27.

40 Black, "The Long and Winding Road," 84.

41 According to James Struthers, much "of the unit's work involved monitoring the lives of the women left behind, rather than the men who fled. Since most husbands, in fact, could not be found, local resentment against the increased welfare costs produced by family fragmentation was directed against mothers seeking assistance." Struthers, *The Limits of Affluence,* 198.

42 No author, "Appeal court upholds decision that woman should get welfare because man not spouse," *Globe and Mail,* 2 April 1975; Mary Gooderham, "Ontario drops 'spouse' welfare rule," *Globe and Mail,* 26 June 1987; No author, "Ontario drops 'spouse in the house' appeal," *CBC News,* 2 September 2004.

43 British Columbia was an exception. See Chapter 2.

44 Leslie Pal argues that the federal government played a critical role in facilitating the emergence of rights-based social movement organizations in the 1970s through various funding programs. The government encouraged movements to frame their grievances in the language of rights and privileged such organizations by providing them with state funding. Pal, *Interests of State,* 252.

45 A survey of English-speaking university students in Canada in 1970 found overwhelming support for communists' right to free speech and opposition to the banning of organizations that were critical of the government. They poll also suggested strong support for due process and laws prohibiting hate speech. W.B. Devall, "Support for Civil Liberties Among English-speaking Canadian University Students.," *Canadian Journal of Political Science/ Revue canadienne de science politique* 3, no. 3 (1970): 434-51.

46 Canadian Institute of Public Opinion/Gallup [hereafter CIPO/G] (1955), *Canadian Gallup Poll 243,* retrieved 1 November 2011 from Carleton Data Centre/Roper Center for Public Opinion Research [hereafter CDC].

47 CIPO/G (1960), *Canadian Gallup Poll 281,* retrieved 1 November 2011 from CDC.

48 CIPO/G (1968), *Canadian Gallup Poll 331,* retrieved 2 November 2011 from from CDC.

49 CIPO/G (1962), *Canadian Gallup Poll 298*, retrieved 2 November 2011 from CDC; CIPO/G (1965), *Canadian Gallup Poll 312, Elections/Life,* retrieved 2 November 2011 from CDC; CIPO/G (1972), *Canadian Gallup Poll 355,* retrieved 2 November 2011 from CDC.

50 Bylaw 3926 was ironically titled "bylaw relating to the exceptional measures to safeguard the free exercise of civil liberties, to regulate the use of the public domain and to prevent riots and other violations of order, peace and public safety." The bylaw prohibited assemblies that endangered the public order, required individuals participating in demonstrations to refrain from hindering others, made it illegal to "jostle" others, and banned any assembly that endangered the peace. Since the bylaw did not define an illegal assembly, any group of two or more people would fall under the scope of the law. For a detailed analysis of Bylaw 3926, see Marx, "Notes and Comments."

51 *Dupond v City of Montreal et al.* [1978] SCR 770.

NOTES TO CHAPTER 4

1 Doris Anderson, *Rebel Daughter*, 124.

2 Ibid., 173.

3 Backhouse and Cohen, *The Secret Oppression*. For further details on how sexual harassment evolved as a human rights issue, see Epp, *Making Rights Real*, Chapter 8.

4 British Columbia Human Rights Commission, *I'm Okay*, 43.

5 Ibid.

6 Anderson, *Rebel Daughter*, 89.

7 *Julie Webb v Cyprus Pizza* [1985] 6 CHRR 444 (BC BOI).

8 Rabinovitch, "Teaching the Personal Is Political," 284.

9 Full-Time University Enrolment, by Sex, Canada and Provinces, Selected Years, 1920 to 1975 (Table W340-438), in Statistics Canada, *Historical Statistics of Canada*, Cat. no. 11-516-XWE (Ottawa: Statistics Canada, 1983).

10 Graydon, "I Was a Slow Learner," 160.

11 Frager and Patrias, *Discounted Labour*, 153; Cohen, "Paid Work," 85.

12 Quoted in ibid., 83.

13 Brockman, *Gender in the Legal Profession*, 8–9.

14 Burt, "The Changing Patterns of Public Policy," 228.

15 Men with only a high school degree could anticipate earning as much as female university graduates. Prentice et al., *Canadian Women*, 379; Cohen, "Paid Work," 86–87.

16 Canada, Status of Women, *The Royal Commission*, 312, 19.

17 *Human Rights Code of British Columbia Act*, S.B.C. 1973, c.119.

18 The one exception to the clause was tenants: it did not apply to renters. British Columbia, *Debates of the Legislative Assembly* (5 November 1973), 1260.

19 Howard Ramos argues that the 1960s was a watershed for the Aboriginal peoples' rights movement. State funding, new political opportunities, and the emergence of a Pan-Aboriginal identity facilitated Aboriginal mobilization. Moreover, "formally organized contention, representing a broad range of Aboriginal interests, was the exception rather than the norm during the 1950s." Ramos, "What Causes Canadian Aboriginal Protest?"; Ramos, "Aboriginal Protest," 59.

20 Pal, *Interests of State*, 14.

21 Brouwer, "When Missions Became Development."

22 These ideological divisions were quite real for Canadian activists: for many years the leading national rights association in the country was an umbrella group awkwardly called the Canadian Federation of Civil Liberties and Human Rights Associations. It was a uniquely Canadian organization.

23 Ligue des droits de l'homme, *Les Droits de l'Homme dans la Société Actuelle*, 27 September 1972 (published report).

24 On social movements and human rights in Canada, see Ramos, "What Causes Canadian Aboriginal Protest?" and "Aboriginal Protest," 59. Clément, *Equality Deferred*.

25 These organizations included the Vancouver Island Multicultural Association, Women Against Violence Against Women, Canadian Council of Christians and Jews, Associated Disabled Persons of B.C., Survey Delta Immigrant Services Society, Committee for Racial Justice, Vancouver Native Police Liaison Program, and the Vancouver Gay Community Centre Society. Clément, *Equality Deferred*.

26 *Women Unite! An Anthology of the Canadian Women's Movement* (Toronto: Canadian Women's Educational Press, 1972), 9.

27 Warner, *Never Going Back*, Chapter 3.

28 Pam Blackstone to Nina Lopez-Jones, 30 November 1984, University of Victoria Archives [UVA], Women Against Pornography, v. 1, f. 9.

29 Except for a few articles about equal pay, the Vancouver Women's Caucus's newsletter (*The Pedestal*) was silent on human rights legislation. In fact, one of the articles explored how the Vancouver General Hospital had succeeded in circumventing an equal pay ruling in 1971, and the author concluded that equal pay could only be achieved, not through human rights legislation, but with "strikes, working to rule, or demonstrations outside and inside Commission hearings." Rape Relief occasionally added its voice to various coalitions calling for changes to the existing human rights legislation, but the issue remained, at best, marginal to its activities. For a detailed discussion on social movements and human rights advocacy, see Clément, "'I Believe in Human Rights.'"

30 Eckel, "The Rebirth of Politics," 233.

31 Eckel, "The International League."

32 Eckel, "The Rebirth of Politics," 229–31.

33 Eckel, "The International Human Rights Campaign Against Chile."

34 "One of the two sources of Amnesty's political effectiveness was the new kind of information politics that the Secretariat took great pains to forge and to steadily improve. Amnesty started to systematically gather information about human rights violations, innovating NGO work in a way that in hindsight seems as simple as it was momentous at the time. Not only did the International Secretariat regularly monitor violations (as defined by Amnesty's "mandate") in a great number of countries and, by the mid-1980s, in virtually all countries of the world. Amnesty also set out to produce facts by building up channels of information, carrying out investigations, and verifying allegations. High-quality research was an essential part of Amnesty's political capital, providing credibility as well as informational advantage." Eckel, "The International League," 194–95. On transnational human rights activism, including case studies, see Risse, Ropp, and Sikkink, *The Power of Human Rights*.

35 Nossal, Roussel, and Paquin, *International Policy and Politics in Canada*.

36 The federal government spent several years developing a consultation mechanism with the provinces. Canada became a party to conventions on racial discrimination and women's rights. Over the years, Canada routinely demonstrated its commitments to promoting human rights with interventions in sessions of the Commission on Human Rights and other international forums. Nolan, "Human Rights in Canadian Foreign Policy," 109.

37 Ibid.

38 Foster, "UN Commission on Human Rights," 83.

39 Canadian governments also had to respond to complaints at the UN's Human Rights Commission, such as Sandra Lovelace's successful complaint surrounding the *Indian Act*'s requirement that Aboriginal women who married non-Aboriginal men had to surrender their status. Berry and McChesney, "Human Rights and Foreign Policy-Making," 60.

40 Donnelly, "Genocide and Humanitarian Intervention," 98. On the Helsinki Accords and the emergence of a transnational human rights network, see Snyder, *Human Rights Activism*.

41 Nolan, "The Influence of Parliament," 387–88.

42 Ibid., 380, 87.

43 A private members' bill was introduced in 1975 to prohibit foreign aid to countries with poor human rights records. The bill drew attention to the human rights component of Canadian foreign policy and forced the government to defend and elaborate its aid policies in public. "The point of main interest here is that even though the government opposed this private member's bill its presence on the agenda compelled a public elaboration of policy, and thus contributed to the progressive expansion of a definition of a human rights component in Canada's aid programs. In this way, parliamentary prerogatives were used to assist in the development and promulgation of a general principle of human rights limits to development assistance, a principle which

would later be defined in more explicit form in a House committee report." Ibid., 382.

44 Clément, "Human Rights," 765.

45 British Columbia, *Debates of the Legislative Assembly* (4 December 1980), 4219.

46 MATCH International Centre, *History*, available at http://matchinter national.org/about/history.html.

47 Brouwer, "When Missions Became Development."

48 Gecelovsky and Keating, "Liberal Internationalism," 203.

49 For a detailed study of the impact of Canadian churches on foreign policy in the 1970s, see Gardiner, "Building a Counter-Consensus," 63, 65.

50 For a detailed comparison of foreign aid and human rights among these three countries in the 1980s, see Gillies, *Between Principle and Practice*, 119. On the United States, see Donnelly, *International Human Rights*, 108.

51 Keenleyside and Taylor, *The Impact of Human Rights Violations*.

52 Nolan, "The Influence of Parliament," 383.

53 Brysk, *Global Good Samaritans*, 73.

54 Blanchette, *Canadian Foreign Policy, 1945–2000* and *Canadian Foreign Policy, 1977–1992*.

55 Pries, "Repression, Freedom, and Minimal Geography."

56 For a critique of Canadian foreign policy (with regard to human rights), see Nossal, "Cabin'd, Cribb'd, Confin'd"; and Gillies, *Between Principle and Practice*.

57 Black, "The Long and Winding Road."

58 "This is the first case in Canada to deal with employment discrimination against a pregnant woman and the B.C. human rights legislation is singularly able to provide protection to pregnant women because Section 8 prohibits discrimination without reasonable cause." Shelagh Day, "Recent Developments in Human Rights," *Labour Research Bulletin* (June 1977): 21. See also British Columbia, "Human Rights Boards of Inquiry: Rights of Pregnant Women," *Labour Research Bulletin* (July 1976): 69–71; British Columbia, "Human Rights Boards of Inquiry: *Warren v Becket, Nadon & Creditel of Canada Limited*," Labour Research Bulletin (January 1977): 62–63; Peter Comparelli and Glen Schaefer, "Two Women Sexually Harassed, Inquiries Rule," *Vancouver Sun*, 28 July 1984; and Julie Webb v. Cyprus Pizza, [1985] 6 C.H.R.R. D/2794.

59 For a review of decisions arising from the reasonable cause section, see Howe, "Incrementalism and Human Rights Reform," 35–36. The decision on sexual orientation was later overturned in court, albeit not on the basis that sexual orientation was not a reasonable cause.

60 The Alberta *Bill of Rights* dealt with fundamental freedoms whereas the *Individual Rights Protection Act* prohibited discrimination.

61 Quebec's *Charter of Human Rights and Fundamental Freedoms* was the most expansive human rights legislation in Canada. Clément, *Canada's Rights*

Revolution, 121–23; Morel, "Le Charte québécoise"; Sheppard, "The Promise and Practice."

62 University of British Columbia, Rare Books and Special Collections, Renate Shearer, v. 2, f. 7, *Trudy Ann Holloway v Claire McDonald and Shop Easy*, 1982.

63 In his report to the Human Rights Branch, Alan Andison insisted that the case was "a clear example of how a pregnant employee has been denied her rightful choice of working while pregnant. This denial of equal opportunity is a contravention of Section 8 of the B.C. Human Rights Code. Continuation of such practices will detrimentally affect women's rights and needs to carry children and continue working." British Columbia Archives, G 85 168, box 4, f. case summaries, Alan Andison Final Report Trudy Ann Holloway case, 7 August 1981.

64 British Columbia Archives, G 85 168, box 4, f. case summaries, memorandum Hanne Jensen to Jack Heinrich, 17 March 1982.

65 *Canadian Human Rights Act*, S.C. 1977, c.33.

66 On the history of human rights law in Canada, as well as the role of social movements, see Clément, *Equality Deferred*.

67 According to the former chairman of the Canadian Human Rights Commission and representative to the UN Human Rights Committee, the Canadian model had few peers: "It should be noted that it is a particular type of commission that has similar, sister agencies in countries like Australia and New Zealand. But nothing of the sort exists, for example, in France or other European countries, where the model calls for broad-ranging commission with widely representative (and usually numerous) membership that issue comments and criticisms of government activities or failure to act but do not deal with individual complaints as do several Canadian commissions." Yalden, *Transforming Rights*, 143.

68 Pegram, "Diffusion Across Political Systems," 731–32. "The survey of the diffusion of 124 [National Human Rights Institutions] strongly suggests such a contagion effect, especially at the regional level with a wave phenomenon of varying intensity across regions. Europe provides the most constant curve, while all regions show a marked increased in the mid-1970s, with Africa and the Americas experiencing rapid acceleration from 1990 onwards. Interestingly, an incipient NHRI presence can also be found in Arab Group countries with human rights commissions established in Morocco (1990), Palestine (1993), Qatar (2002), Egypt (2003), Jordan (2006) and Saudi Arabia (2006)." Ibid., 737.

69 "In my view, all of the following factors contribute to the effectiveness of national human rights institutions: the democratic governance structure of the state; the degree of independence of the institution from government; the extent of the institution's jurisdiction; the adequacy of the powers given to the institution, including the power to investigate; the accessibility of the institution to members of the public;

the level of cooperation of the institution with other bodies; the operational efficiency of the institution; the accountability of the institution, the personal character of the person(s) appointed to head the institution; the behavior of government in not politicizing the institution and in having a receptive attitude toward its activities; and the credibility of the office in the eyes of the populace." Reif, "Building Democratic Institutions," 24. See also Mertus, *Human Rights Matters*; International Council on Human Rights, "Performance and Legitimacy."

70 There was disagreement among stakeholders in Ontario over the definition of "disability." These divisions became apparent during the public consultations led by the Human Rights Commission in the mid-1970s. Whereas there was a broad consensus around prohibiting discrimination on the basis of physical disability, it was less clear that the prohibition should include mental disability. "Debates such as these revealed that the public remained divided not only on the details of which rights should be included in a revised Human Rights Code, but also on the understanding of the term 'human rights' itself." Tunnicliffe, "'Life Together,'" 455.

71 Canada, Standing Committee on Justice and Legal Affairs, 1977, Appendix JLA-1, Statement by the Minister of Justice to Justice and Legal Affairs Committee, 6A:1.

72 Most of the debate in Parliament and within the committee revolved around the lack of an explicit appeal mechanism to the Federal Court. Another issue was the exemptions under the privacy provisions for access to information. Several of the organizations that made representations were also critical of the wording of the equal pay section, which was ultimately amended before third reading. Six organizations made representations before the Standing Committee on Justice and Legal Affairs: the Canadian Labour Congress, the Canadian Bar Association, the Advisory Council on the Status of Women, the National Action Committee on the Status of Women, the Canadian Civil Liberties Association, and the Canadian Federation of Human Rights and Civil Liberties Association. Among parliamentarians it was Gordon Fairweather, the future chairman of the commission, who was the most vocal, especially on the need to ban discrimination on the basis of sexual orientation. House of Commons, *Hansard*, nos. 3 and 6 (1976/7), 2975-3412, 6143-6226; *Canada, Standing Committee on Justice and Legal Affairs*, 1977, 6A to 13A.

73 For instance, as Sarah-Jane Mathieu has observed, many politicians insisted that there was no segregation in Canada or discrimination in immigration policies. Mathieu, *North of the Color Line*, 74–75.

74 "In retrospect, it is striking how limited the support for parliamentary supremacy, the symbol of our former Britishness, turned out to be in the final debates leading up to the Charter ... With hindsight, as the support for the Charter suggests, it now appears that the backing for

parliamentary supremacy derived from the imperial connections and lack indigenous roots." Cairns, "The Past and Future," 334.

75 LAC, RG 14, session 1, box 68, wallet 26, Special Joint Committee on the Constitution.

76 LAC, RG 14, session 1, box 62, wallet 10; box 60, wallet 5; box 62, wallet 10, Special Joint Committee on the Constitution.

77 The Canadian Consultative Council on Multiculturalism insisted that its members did not want to challenge the status of official languages, but merely complement them by promoting freedom and equality for all cultures as a human right. LAC, RG 14, session 1, box 62, wallet 9, Special Joint Committee on the Constitution.

78 The Canadian Catholic School Trustees, for example, sought to ensure their schools' right to expect a Catholic lifestyle from employees. LAC, RG 14, session 1, box 62, wallet 9, Special Joint Committee on the Constitution.

79 The British Columbia Federation of Labour suggested that prohibiting age discrimination made sense in some cases, but acknowledged that mandatory retirement had a legitimate social function. LAC, RG 14, session 1, box 60, wallet 6, Special Joint Committee on the Constitution.

80 LAC, RG 14, session 1, box 61, wallet 7; box 62, wallet 9; box 62, wallet 10, Special Joint Committee on the Constitution.

81 As quoted in Rebick, *Ten Thousand Roses*, 148.

82 LAC, RG 14, session 1, box 62, wallet 9, Special Joint Committee on the Constitution.

83 The demand to recognize a right to learning and training was a response to the feminization of poverty and women's unequal socio-economic status. LAC, RG 14, session 1, box 68, wallet 26; box 68, wallet 26; box 73, wallet 37, Special Joint Committee on the Constitution.

84 LAC, RG 14, session 1, box 62, wallet 10, Special Joint Committee on the Constitution.

85 LAC, RG 14, session 1, box 62, wallet 10, Special Joint Committee on the Constitution. The Canadian Human Rights Commission, the Canadian Teachers' Federation, and the United Church of Canada echoed many of these demands. LAC, RG 14, session 1, box 62, wallet 10; box 72, wallet 35, Special Joint Committee on the Constitution.

86 LAC, RG 14, session 1, box 62, wallet 10; box 72, wallet 35, Special Joint Committee on the Constitution.

87 LAC, RG 14, session 1, box 68, wallet 26, Special Joint Committee on the Constitution.

88 LAC, RG 14, session 1, box 61, wallet 8, Special Joint Committee on the Constitution.

89 LAC, RG 14, session 1, box 62, wallet 10, Special Joint Committee on the Constitution.

90 LAC, RG 14, session 1, box 62, wallet 10, Special Joint Committee on the Constitution.

91 New Brunswick's Human Rights Commission established a "Native Desk" in 1982. However, the commission received fewer than seventy complaints from Aboriginal peoples between 1967 and 1997. S. Williams, "Human Rights in Theory and Practice," 63. Based on a series of interviews with human rights officials, Allan McChesney offers some potential explanations for why Aboriginal peoples have rarely used anti-discrimination laws: McChesney, "Aboriginal Communities," 224–26. Peter Kulchinsky argues that human rights are, in some cases, inconsistent with Aboriginal rights: Kulchinsky, *Aboriginal Rights*.

92 Tunnicliffe, "'Life Together,'" 454.

93 This was not limited to Indigenous peoples in Canada. See Vincent, *The Politics of Human Rights*, 139–46; and Freeman, *Human Rights*, Chapter 6.

94 Williams, "Human Rights in Theory and Practice"; McChesney, "Aboriginal Communities."

95 LAC, RG 14, session 1, box 60, wallet 4, Special Joint Committee on the Constitution.

96 LAC, RG 14, session 1, box 68, wallet 26, Special Joint Committee on the Constitution.

97 Aboriginal rights also featured prominently in the briefs submitted by other organizations, such as the Anglican Church of Canada, the British Columbia Civil Liberties Association, and women's rights groups. LAC, RG 14, session 1, box 60, wallet 4; box 60, wallet 6, Special Joint Committee on the Constitution.

98 As Sally Chivers suggests, "constitutional politics provided an unparalleled political opportunity to assert the political and social rights of those who had traditionally been marginalized in Canadian society." Chivers, "Barrier by Barrier," 314. See also M. Smith, "Identity and Opportunity," 189.

99 Even sex discrimination was rarely discussed in Parliamentary or legislative hearings surrounding the first antidiscrimination laws in the 1950s. Most of the leading SMOs of the period did not advocate for banning sex discrimination. Clément, Silver, and Trottier, "The Evolution of Human Rights in Canada"; Frager and Patrias, "'This Is Our Country'"; Clément, *Canada's Rights Revolution*, 158–60; Fudge, "The Effect of Entrenching a Bill of Rights," 445–48; James, *Misrecognized Materialists*, Chapter 6; Kelly, *Governing with the Charter*, 63–73.

100 CROP Inc./Canadian Human Rights Commission, *Selected Tables from a Survey of Public Opinion on Human Rights* (Ottawa: Canadian Human Rights Commission, 1981).

101 In another poll, 65 percent of Canadians insisted that the best strategy to protect human rights was to promote public awareness, while only 22 percent thought that the government should ban specific acts of discrimination. Ibid.

102 Canadian Bar Association, *Towards a New Canada*, 16–17.

103 *Youth Protection Act*, S.Q. 1977, c.20; *An Act to revise The Child Welfare Act*, S.O. 1978, c.85.

104 *Access to Information Act*, S.C. 1980–83, c.111.

105 Eckel, "The International League," 204.

106 Ibid., 202–3.

107 Ibid., 119.

108 The issues are explored in greater detail in Clément, *Canada's Rights Revolution*.

109 Canada, *Security and Information*, vol. 1; Canada, *Freedom and Security under the Law*, vol. 2; Canada, *Certain RCMP Activities*, vol. 3.

110 Comités d'Organisation des Jeux Olympiques, *Montréal 1976: Official Report*, vol. 1, 566.

111 *Temporary Immigration Security Act*, S.C. 1976, c.91. "Recent acts of terrorism world-wide which, in one form or another become associated with airports and/or aircraft, call for manpower to act quickly in containing and stabilizing a terrorist act at major airports. Other airports in Canada, including Ottawa and Vancouver, will receive special attention and security will be increased on an as required basis in line with local conditions and security survey recommendations." LAC, RG 146, vol. 4358, f. Wallet, RCMP, National Security Plan, 1976.

112 Comités d'Organisation des Jeux Olympiques, *Montréal 1976: Official Report*, vol. 1, 572.

113 York University (1977), *Social Change in Canada*, poll retrieved 5 November 2011 from the Canadian Opinion Research Archive/Queen's University [hereafter CORA/QU].

114 Decima Research (1981), *Decima Quarterly 8*, December 1981, poll retrieved 10 November 2011 from CORA/QU.

115 Ipsos-Reid (1991), *National Angus Reid Poll, July 1991* [Canada], poll retrieved 5 November 2011 from CORA/QU.

116 Canada, *Report of the Committee [...] Abortion Law*, 17.

117 Warner, *Never Going Back*, 148-49.

118 Korinek, "'The Most Openly Gay Person,'" 589.

119 No author, "Heavy Hand of the Law," *Globe and Mail*, 9 February 1981.

120 Ontario Human Rights Commission, *Life Together*, 81–82.

121 Quebec, *Quebec–Canada*.

122 Once again, the Ligue is an ideal case study on Canadians' evolving ideas of rights. In the 1970s the Ligue became a fervent advocate of Quebeckers' right to self-determination and to make French the predominant language in the province. But these were not among the group's founding principles. See Clément, *Canada's Rights Revolution*, Chapter 4; and Clément, "Generations and the Transformation." See also Igartua, *The Other Quiet Revolution*; Ignatieff, *The Rights Revolution*, Chapter 3; Mandel, *The Charter of Rights*, Chapter 3; and Berger, *Fragile Freedoms*, Chapter 7.

123 Jean Chartier. "Décès tragique de l'artisan de la Charte québécoise des droits de la personne," *Le Devoir*, 12 November 1998.

124 Doug Collins, "Big Sister Ruff Is Watching You," *Vancouver Sun*, 1 October 1977.
125 Doug Collins, "The Ruff Penalty for Being Innocent," *Vancouver Sun*, 17 December 1977.
126 In reference to a case where an East Indian Man was refused employment with a major lumber company because English was not his first language, Collins insisted that "I don't care whether he was discriminated against or not. But we have to be out of our skulls to award a guy a hundred thousand bucks simply because someone didn't want to hire him." In truth, the inquiry only awarded costs and loss of wages. Collins routinely attacked Kathleen Ruff, the director of the Human Rights Branch. He eventually left the *Vancouver Sun* for a small community paper called the *North Shore News*. In 1984, Collins was forced to appear before a hearing of the BC Press Council on charges that his columns were racist. Collins, "Human Wrongs Bunch? Good Riddance!," *Vancouver Sun*, 28 July 1983. See also Collins, "Come On and Kiss Me, Kate," *Vancouver Sun*, 21 October 1977; Collins, "Aye, Aye, M'am: Ruff Strikes Again," *Vancouver Sun*, 15 October 1977.
127 Hunter, "Liberty and Equality."
128 Howe and Johnson, *Restraining Equality*, 23.
129 For a more detailed discussion of the honest belief defence, see Knopff, *Human Rights and Social Technology*, 111–14; and 1989 Tarnopolsky, *Discrimination and the Law in Canada*, 387–89.
130 *Vancouver Sun v Gay Alliance* [1977] 77 *Dominion Law Reports* (BCCA) 487.
131 Block and Walker, *Discrimination, Affirmative Action and Equal Opportunity*, 107.
132 "There is no support for the contention that in the absence of discrimination the various racial groupings (and sexes) would be alike in their income, wealth and job selection or indeed, in any other economic or sociological variable. Accordingly, the existence of inequality in wages, disproportionate representation in professional and managerial positions, and other numerical inequalities, do not necessarily provide evidence of discrimination ... Discrimination is morally neutral." Ibid., xv.
133 "Critics Rap Socreds over Rights Record," *Vancouver Sun*, 22 September 1984; "B.C. Rights Move Rapped in Ottawa," *The Province*, 9 September 1983.
134 Ken Norman to William Bennett, 2 July 1983, UBC RBSC, Solidarity Coalition Papers, v. 19, f. 1.
135 UBC RBSC, Solidarity Coalition Papers, v. 19. f. 1, Press Release, CASHRA, 14 July 1983.
136 For further information on the reforms in British Columbia, see Clément, *Equality Deferred*.

NOTES TO CHAPTER 5

1 *Gilles Fontaine v Canadian Pacific Limited and Canadian Human Rights Commission* [1989] 11 CHRR D/288 (CHRT).

2 In addition to the Fontaine case, AIDS as a disability under human rights legislation was confirmed in: *Biggs v. Hudson* [1988] 9 C.H.R.R. D/5391 (British Columbia Human Rights Commission) and *E. (S.T.) v. Bertelsen* [1989] 10 C.H.R.R. D/6294 (Alberta Board of Inquiry).

3 The exception was Ontario and Nova Scotia, where complaints on the basis of race still predominated, although sex represented the second-largest number of complaints in both provinces.

4 Nova Scotia and the federal government had already banned discrimination on the basis of physical disability by this time.

5 There was also "considerable public support" for the inclusion of disability as an enumerated ground in the *Ontario Human Rights Code* when the commission made the recommendation in 1977. Tunnicliffe, "'Life Together,'" 458.

6 During International Year of Disabled Persons, most governments in Canada invited disability rights organizations to participate in a review of public services. Vanhala, *Making Rights a Reality?*, 54–57; Neufeldt, "Growth and Evolution."

7 The idea that Canadians had a right to a basic standard of living informed the justification for the welfare state. Raymond Blake captures this sentiment in his book on the history of the Family Allowance. According to Blake, it was only in the 1980s that Canadians began to associate the Family Allowance with financial need. From the 1930s to the 1970s, this program, which was integral to the welfare state, was seen as a basic right (or entitlement) for citizens. Blake, *From Rights to Needs*.

8 Canada, *Report of the Commission*.

9 Andiappan, Reavley, and Silver, "Discrimination Against Pregnant Employees," 8.

10 Ibid., 9.

11 Abella's recommendations addressed issues such as training, child care, equal pay for work of equal value, creating educational institutions and programs aimed at minorities, programs to help integrate new immigrants (e.g., language training), and monitoring hiring practices and trends.

12 Howe and Johnson, *Restraining Equality*, 25.

13 *Employment Equity Act*, S.C. 1986, c.31.

14 Réaume, "Of Pigeonholes and Principles."

15 As Martha Minow explains, "each person is alone at the unique crossroad of each intersecting group. Each of us is a unique member of the sets of endless groupings that touch us, whether called racial, gender, disability, family, ethnicity, or nationality." Minow, *Not Only for Myself*, 39.

16 Diane Pothier offers a personal narrative to more fully explain this point. Pothier, "Connecting Grounds of Discrimination," 64. As Nitya Duclos notes, "it is not hard to see that stereotypes arising from particular combinations of race and gender are often the source of the discriminatory treatment that gives rise to the complaint ... Stereotypes which combine race and gender are common to everyday experience. Race and gender are equally apparent and, together with other visible characteristics, are likely to form part of our initial generalizations about people. It is only when one becomes immersed in the world of law that race and gender are extracted from the whole person and become mutually exclusive categories of discrimination." Duclos, "Disappearing Women," 33.

17 "This notion [intersectionality] refers to the way in which any particular individual stands at the crossroads of multiple groups. All women also have a race; all whites also have a gender. The individuals stand in different places as gender and racial politics converge and diverge. Moreover, the meanings of gender are inflected and informed by race, and the meanings of racial identity are similarly influenced by images of gender." Minow, *Not Only for Myself*, 38.

18 "In essence, the categorical structure of equality rights requires those injured through relations of inequality to caricaturize both themselves and their experiences of inequality, in order to succeed with a legal claim." Iyer, "Categorical Denials," 181. Iyer uses the *Mossop* case to demonstrate her argument. Mossop was a public servant working for the federal government who was denied bereavement leave to attend his partner's father's funeral because his partner was male. According to Iyer, Mossop failed in his appeal to the Supreme Court of Canada because the judges defined family status in terms of variations on heterosexual families, and insisted that Mossop's case fell under the category of sexual orientation, which at the time was not recognized in the *Canadian Human Rights Act*. In other words, by thinking in terms of categories of discrimination, and defining each category in terms of how they differed from an assumed norm, the court was blind to how Mossop experienced discrimination. Ibid., 194–97.

19 Duclos offers at least four reasons why racial minority women were underrepresented in federal human rights cases: distrust of the law, negative experiences with the immigration system, observing police mistreatment against racial minorities (especially family and friends), and a complaints system that failed to respond to the realities of their lives. Duclos, "Disappearing Women," 38. Colleen Sheppard has also found that women of colour are underrepresented in human rights complaints in Quebec. Sheppard, "The Promise and Practice."

20 Duclos, "Disappearing Women," 34–35.

21 Ibid., 44–45.

22 "No matter how long or inclusive the list of protected grounds or characteristics, the mechanical, categorical, or category-based, approach to equality embedded in such a structure obscures the complexity of social identity in ways that are damaging both to particular rights claimants, and to the larger goal of redressing relations of inequality. The categorical approach to equality fails to comprehend complex social identities. It therefore cannot accurately describe relationships of inequality, which is a precondition both for redressing particular rights violations, and for succeeding with the larger project of social reform. In essence, the categorical structure of equality rights requires those injured through relations of inequality to caricaturize both themselves and their experiences of inequality, in order to succeed with a legal claim. Because law perceives and accepts this caricature of social identity and social relations, it cannot properly address inequality." Iyer, "Categorical Denials," 181.

23 Duclos, "Disappearing Women," 36.

24 As Nitya Iyer explains, "claimants who are discriminated against in complex ways will fail if they cannot simplify the story of who they are and of their unequal treatment, so that it resonates with the dominant group's narrower understanding of the category grounding their claim." Iyer, "Categorical Denials," 179.

25 Women's rights activists used the intersectional analysis to attack the spouse-in-the-house policy and, in 1986, convinced the Ontario government to dispense with the regulation. Later attempts by governments in Nova Scotia and Ontario to reintroduce the policy were rebuffed by the courts. These were significant victories that emerged from the recognition of the intersectionality of gender and poverty. The legal cases involving the man in the house policy represented "important litigation successes recognizing the intersectionality of poverty and sex discrimination in a manner that was emphasized by women's groups in 1985 ... The exclusion of public housing tenants from security of tenure provisions constitutes discrimination because of race, sex and poverty." *Falkiner v Ontario* [2002] 212 DLR (4th) 633. See also Porter, "Twenty Years of Equality Rights," 174. In 1998, the *Canadian Human Rights Act* was amended to recognize that "a discriminatory practice includes a practice based on ... the effect of a combination of prohibited grounds."

26 For surveys on Charter jurisprudence in Canada discussed in this section, see Kelly, *Governing with the Charter*; Knopff and Morton, *The Charter Revolution*; Mandel, *The Charter of Rights*; and Manfredi, *Feminist Activism in the Supreme Court*. There is also a special issue of the Osgoode Hall Law Journal (50, no. 3, 2013) with several articles that address the legacy of the Charter.

27 The *Charter of Rights and Freedoms* contains an override clause that allows governments to pass legislation notwithstanding (s.33) the Charter. Several sections are immune from this section, including democratic

rights such as the right to vote and hold office, as well as mobility and language rights.

28 Clément, *Equality Deferred*, Chapter 1.

29 As Miriam Smith explains, "many issues that were previously defined as moral have come to be defined as questions of rights ... The impact of the court decision and the political mobilization of the lesbian and gay movement have been successful in putting forth an alternative conception of lesbian and gay issues, one that defines these as a matter of rights, rather than a matter of individual conscience or religious belief." M. Smith, *A Civil Society?*, 85.

30 *R. v Sparrow* [1990] 1 SCR 1075.

31 For an overview of key Charter decisions, see Mandel, *The Charter of Rights*; Manfredi, *Feminist Activism in the Supreme Court*; Knopff and Morton, "Canada's Court Party"; Sharpe and Roach, *Brian Dickson*; Kelly, *Governing with the Charter*; and James, *Misrecognized Materialists*.

32 French nationalists were furious that the Charter included education. After all, one of the founding principles of the original compact in 1867 was provincial jurisdiction over education, and Quebec had refused to approve the new constitution. In 1984, the court determined that the Charter now guaranteed the right to education in English or French throughout Canada. The exception to the education provisions in Bill 101 included students who were in English-speaking schools *in Quebec*. In other words, Canadians from other provinces would be forced to place their children in French schools. Attorney General of Quebec v. Quebec Association of Protestant School Boards et al., [1984] 2 S.C.R. 66; *Ford v. Quebec* (Attorney General) [1988] 2 SCR 712.

33 *Mahe v Alberta* [1990] 1 SCR 342.

34 *Re Manitoba Language Rights* [1985] 1 SCR 72. Language rights, though, did have limits. The court, for instance, dismissed claims that judges should be bilingual or that the constitution guaranteed French-language school boards as well as schools.

35 Kelly, *Governing with the Charter*, 111

36 There is no right to free legal aid; however, the court determined that separating a child from its parents constituted a violation of the right to physical security because it harmed the mental and physical security of parent and child. In these cases, the state is obligated to provide parents with legal aid.

37 The court was concerned that the law did not allow for the possibility that the accused was unaware that the girl was under fourteen years old. Parliament amended the law to require individuals accused of sexual assault to demonstrate that they had attempted to determine the victim's age. The law was also revised to reaffirm that intoxication was not a defence in sexual assault cases, and a revised rape-shield law allowed for judicial discretion on admissibility of evidence (but narrowed the definition of consent). In addition, lower courts ruled in separate cases

that the Criminal Code sections on incest and sex with a minor were unconstitutional because they only applied to females and, therefore, violated the equality section. These decisions were later overturned. Fudge, "The Effect of Entrenching."

38 Other due process cases touched on excluding blood sample evidence that was illegally obtained by a medical professional or evidence that entailed searching the outside of an individual's home for evidence of marijuana crops. In one case involving a confession, the police asked the friend of a man they were interrogating to use a wiretap while speaking to him in private (the court excluded the evidence). The Supreme Court has also decided that children testifying in assault cases can provide testimony via video or with a physical barrier separating them from their accused. Finally, according to the court, it is a violation of the principles of fundamental justice to extradite an individual to a jurisdiction that has the death penalty without securing a guarantee that they death penalty will not apply. Kelly, *Governing with the Charter*, Chapter 4.

39 The court has also resisted numerous attempts to challenges procedures in prisons as violating the Charter. Mandel, *The Charter of Rights*, 219.

40 The court also found that the criteria for approving abortions were arbitrary and unfair. In addition, the availability of abortion services varied from province to province, and the service was not equally available to all citizens. *R. v. Morgentaler* [1988] 1 SCR 30.

41 Video surveillance in a private dwelling without a warrant is also a violation of the right to privacy. In some situations, such as border crossings, people have a lower expectation of privacy.

42 Mandel, *The Charter of Rights*, Chapter 4; Kelly, *Governing with the Charter*, Chapter 4.

43 In summarizing the impact of the Charter, Chief Justice Beverley McLachlin identified a similar list of priorities: "The rights of those detained by the state are better protected because of the *Charter*. We have a fairer criminal justice system because of the *Charter*. The *Charter* has strengthened the protection of minority-language rights and the mechanisms and attitudes that help our nation of diverse groups to live together. The *Charter* has brought the promise of a modest measure of accountability in the provision of medical and hospital services, under the rubrics of equality and security of the person." McLachlin, "The Charter 25 Years Later," 366.

44 The court determined in several cases, such as the ban on advertising to children under thirteen years old, secondary picketing, and the hate speech provisions of the Criminal Code, that the law violated free speech but was legal under Section 1 of the Charter (which allows for limits on rights in certain circumstances).

45 *Multani v. Commission scolaire Marguerite-Bourgeoys* [2006] 1 SCR 256. On religion and the law in Canada, see Waldron, *Free to Believe*.

46 The court also nullified legislation that allowed for the indeterminate detention of individuals found not guilty for a crime by reason of insanity; a Criminal Code provision banning convicted sex offenders from loitering in public places; and a requirement that political parties field at least fifty candidates to participate in federal elections (the latter on the basis that the law violated democratic rights).

47 Dixon, "The Supreme Court of Canada."

48 Reference *Re. Public Service Employee Relations Act* (Alta.), [1987] 1 S.C.R. 313.

49 Michael Mandel argues that "the whole idea of the Charter can be seen as a legitimation of the basic inequalities of Canadian society, of which the subordination of labour to business is one of the most basic." Mandel, *The Charter of Rights*, 260.

50 *Health Services and Support-Facilities Subsector Bargaining Assn. v. British Columbia* [2007] 2 SCR 391. The court also ruled in 2011 that the Ontario government violated farm workers' freedom of association when it attempted to ban them from organizing. The court forced the government to introduce legislation specifying classes of farm workers. *Ontario (Attorney General) v. Fraser* [2011] 2 SCR 3. See also Tucker, "The Constitutional Right to Bargain Collectively."

51 *Saskatchewan Federation of Labour v Saskatchewan* [2015] SCC 4. In a similar ruling, the Supreme Court of Canada ruled that the federal government's restrictions on RCMP members' right to organize and strike violated their freedom of association. The court delayed the decision for a year to give the government an opportunity to revise its procedures. *Mounted Police Association of Ontario v Canada (Attorney General)* [2015] SCC 1.

52 Songer, Johnson, and Bowie, "Do Bills of Rights Matter?," 313-14.

53 Kelly, *Governing with the Charter*, 144.

54 Songer, Johnson, and Bowie, "Do Bills of Rights Matter?," 315-16.

55 *Carter v Canada (Attorney General)* [2015] SCR 5; *Canada (Attorney General) v Bedford* [2013] 3 SCR 1101.

56 Epp, *The Rights Revolution*, 182. See also Court Challenges Program of Canada, *Annual Report, 2005–2006* (Winnipeg: 2006).

57 James Kelly argues that we should be wary of focusing too much on judicial activism. According to him, the rights revolution has produced a culture of rights within the federal government, most notably the Department of Justice. The bureaucracy has become adept at vetting legislation for potential rights violations before bills become law. Kelly, *Governing with the Charter*, Chapter 7

58 Although every jurisdiction in Canada banned discrimination on the basis of sex, only a handful explicitly listed sexual harassment as one of the enumerated grounds in the legislation. However, the Supreme Court of Canada extended protections against sexual harassment to all jurisdictions in 1989 when it ruled that sexual harassment should be

considered a form of sex discrimination. *Janzen v Platy Enterprises Ltd.* (1989) 1 SCR 1252.

59 British Columbia's reasonable cause provision led to the first successful human rights board of inquiry decision on sexual orientation. The decision, however, was overturned in the Supreme Court of Canada. On the history of the British Columbia Human Rights Code and sexual orientation, including the *GATE v Vancouver Sun* case, see Anderson, "The Development of Human Rights Protections in British Columbia," Chapter 5; and Clément, *Equality Deferred.*

60 Tunnicliffe, "'Life Together,'" 57–58.

61 On the history of sexual orientation and human rights law in Ontario, see Herman, *Rights of Passage*; and Warner, *Never Going Back*. The Ontario Human Rights Commission recommended adding sexual orientation to the Code as early as 1977. Ontario Human Rights Commission, *Life Together.*

62 Iyer, "Categorical Denials," 198.

63 The former Minister of Justice and Attorney General for Newfoundland, Lynn Verge, when confronted during a committee hearing in 1990 on the government's decision to not include sexual orientation in 1988, argued that the failure was "because I couldn't get the Cabinet to go along with what I wanted. Basically, the Cabinet as a whole got hung up on a couple of recommendations about extending protection, significantly on extension of protection to gays, and I decided as a matter of political strategy to take a two-step approach, step one, which I accomplished, which was amending the code to change the procedures." Newfoundland House of Assembly [hereafter NHA], *Hansard*, no. 8 (1990), 30; NHA, *Hansard*, vol. 16, no. 88 (1990), 22–24. See also NHA, *Hansard*, vol. 1, no. 75 (1983), 9577; NHA, *Hansard*, no. 8 (1990), 30.

64 NHA, *Hansard*, vol. 16, no. 88 (1990), 22–23. Examples of discrimination on the basis of sexual orientation in St. John's in 1990 included one case of a man who was told to vacate an apartment because the landlord did not want a homosexual living in the building, and another case of a box-boy at a local supermarket who was fired when the owner discovered he was gay. NHA, *Hansard*, no. 8 (1990), 4–7. In 1993, the Newfoundland Human Rights Commission announced, based on a recent ruling in the Supreme Court of Canada *(Haig v Canada)*, that it would begin investigating cases involving sexual orientation.

65 Several provinces made similar amendments between 1987 and 1993. Newfoundland amended its statute in 1997, and Prince Edward Island introduced amendments in 1998. Alberta did not formally amend its legislation until 2010, although the Supreme Court forced the province to apply the law to sexual orientation beginning in 1998.

66 Warner, *Never Going Back*, 309.

67 Ibid., 86–87.

68 Ibid., 181.

69 Ibid., 309.

70 "The minister in charge of the commission defended the appointment with the claim that sexual orientation is voluntarily chosen, and therefore less deserving of protection from discrimination than involuntary characteristics such as race. Persons disclosing their sexual orientation, he contended, should expect discrimination because by flaunting their sexuality they may violate the rights of others." Ibid., 153.

71 Ibid., 209.

72 Ibid., 241.

73 Ibid., 335.

74 Ibid., 339.

75 Fletcher and Howe, "Public Opinion and Canada's Courts," 275.

76 Warner, *Never Going Back*, 209.

77 Eckel, "The Rebirth of Politics," 231–32.

78 For context on human rights in Canadian foreign policy, see Gecelovsky and Keating, "Liberal Internationalism for Conservatives"; Clément, Silver, and Trottier, "The Evolution of Human Rights in Canada"; and Lui, *Why Canada Cares*.

79 Keenleyside and Taylor, *The Impact of Human Rights Violations*.

80 Bonser, "Human Rights in Canadian Foreign Policy," 84–85.

81 Paltiel, "Negotiating Human Rights with China."

82 Webster, "Canada and Bilateral Human Rights Dialogues," 45.

83 Bonser, "Human Rights in Canadian Foreign Policy."

84 Keenleyside and Taylor, *The Impact of Human Rights Violations*, 3–4.

85 Wood, *Direct Action, Deliberation, and Diffusion*; Schmitz, "Human Rights, Democratization, and International Conflict."

86 Brysk, *Global Good Samaritans*, 73.

87 As quoted in Scharfe, "Blood on Their Hands," 20.

88 Webster, "Canada and Bilateral Human Rights Dialogues," 52.

89 Lui, *Why Canada Cares*, 78–80.

90 Cardenas, *Chains of Justice*, 45; Hillebrecht, "The Domestic Mechanisms of Compliance." Canada was also the first country to establish formal ties with Indonesia's human rights commission, beginning with a $500,000 grant in 1997. It has also provided funding to assist India's human rights commission to develop education programs. Bonser, "Human Rights in Canadian Foreign Policy," 92–93; Brysk, *Global Good Samaritans*, 74.

91 Quoted in Brysk, *Global Good Samaritans*, 75.

92 On Indonesia, see Scharfe, "Blood on Their Hands"; and Webster, *Fire and the Full Moon*.

93 "From this perspective it becomes almost impossible to pursue human rights as claims across national boundaries. At most, therefore, Canada could engage in explaining what human rights means in a Canadian context, without touching on what human rights entail with respect to the behaviour of the Chinese regime on its own soil. This kind of diplomacy denies the universality of human rights and its ineffectiveness is

compounded by the policy decision of Chrétien to commit Canada to vigorously pursue human rights only where Canada can claim influence." Paltiel, "Negotiating Human Rights with China," 179.

94 Warner, *Never Going Back*, 211.

95 "Women of the world, unite ... with LGBT people" (2006), Egale Canada, http://www.egale.ca/index.asp?lang=E&menu=1&item =1300; "Background on *Nixon v Vancouver Rape Relief*" (2005), Egale Canada, http://www.egale.ca/index.asp?lang=E&menu =1&item=1147; "B.C. Rights Case Asks: What Is a Woman?" (2001), Vancouver Rape Relief & Women's Shelter, from http://raperelief shelter.bc.ca/learn/news/bc-rights-case-asks-what-woman; "Duelling Rights" (2005), Vancouver Rape Relief & Women's Shelter, http://rape reliefshelter.bc.ca/learn/resources/duelling-rights. Retrieved 18 April 2013.

96 *Vancouver Rape Relief Society v Nixon et al.* [2003] BCSC (B.C. Supreme Court) 1936. The British Columbia Court of Appeal sustained the lower court's decision, and the Supreme Court of Canada refused in 2007 to consider Nixon's appeal.

97 There is an extensive literature on how men have exploited the equality provisions of the *Charter of Rights and Freedoms*. In many cases, litigation has put feminists on the defensive rather than advancing women's equality. See, for instance, Wiegers, "Gender, Biology, and Third Part Custody Disputes"; Chambers, "'In the Name of the Father'" and "Newborn Adoption"; Boyd, "Is Equality Enough?"; Brodsky, *Canadian Charter Equality Rights for Women*; and Lessard, "Mothers, Fathers, and Naming."

98 Lessard, "Mothers, Fathers, and Naming."

99 See, for instance, A. Wright, "Formulaic Comparisons." For an example of a successful challenge to standards based on male performance in the workplace, see Fudge and Lessard, "Challenging Norms and Creating Precedents."

100 As Andrea Wright explains, "the comparator group approach is an artificial, formalist search for a comparable 'other,' which leads to unpredictable results, in part because there are myriad ways to reasonably articulate a basis of comparison, and in part because the approach often neglects the gravamen of the complaint and the objective of substantive equality. Put simply, it is easy to get the choice of comparator group wrong, it is easy to reasonably justify several different comparator group choices, and it is easy to lose sight of the objective of substantive equality when searching for comparisons based on formalistic assessments of sameness and difference." A. Wright, "Formulaic Comparisons," 417.

101 *Gould v Yukon Order of Pioneers* [1996] 1 SCR 571.

102 Compa, "Framing Labor's New Human Rights Movement."

103 For a polemical discussion on Aboriginal rights and human rights, see Kulchinsky, *Aboriginal Rights Are Not Human Rights*.

104 Brown, *Being Brown*, 131. See also UBC RBSC, VSW, v. 2, f. 1, male chauvinist pig awards, 1972. In 1991, however, the NDP created Canada's first stand-alone Ministry of Women's Equality.

NOTES TO CONCLUSION

1   In the context of international human rights law, Daniel M. Goldstein describes this process as vernacularization: "Vernacularization instead describes a process of reception and transformation, a dialectic in which transnational conceptions are made meaningful within—or rejected on the basis of—local realities, themselves already conditioned by their broader inclusion within transnational frameworks of economics, politics, and culture." Goldstein, "Whose Vernacular?," 112.

2   Vanhala, *Making Rights a Reality?*, 57.

3   In retrospect, Lester B. Pearson's warning to the federal Cabinet in 1948 appears prescient: "If we vote for the declaration, some private member might introduce a resolution incorporating the text or expressing approval of the declaration which might put every Member of Parliament in the position of having to take a stand on every Article in the declaration." Quoted in MacLennan, *Toward the Charter*, 78–79.

4   Eckel, "The Rebirth of Politics"; Moyn, *The Last Utopia*.

5   See also Brouwer, "When Missions Became Development."

6   See also Clément, *Canada's Rights Revolution*.

7   Ibid.

8   Clément, "The Rights Revolution in Canada and Australia."

9   Gearty offers a useful distinction between rights as recognized in law, and human rights law: "These legal rights can come onto and go from the statute books without embarrassment because, whatever about the early human rights claims that got them enacted, there is no question now but that they are offshoots of the political, expressions of the passing wishes of the community. They might not even call themselves human rights. Indeed in such a political system, whether or not they are human rights to start with, they become (mere) legal rights the moment they are turned into legislation, their moral ambitions trimmed in the name of successful and practical enforceability. General human rights laws are different. Taking their cue from the international, these measures seek to capture the power of the human rights ideal in legislation but in an abstract way." Gearty, *Can Human Rights Survive?*, 68–69.

10 As Irwin Cotler noted in 1993: "At present a disproportionate number of NGO's deal with matters pertaining to political and civil rights, while the cause of economic, social and cultural rights appears to be under-represented among the NGO's." Cotler, "Human Rights as the Modern Tool of Revolution," 19.

11 Shelton, "The Environmental Jurisprudence."

Works Cited

Adams, Eric. "Building a Law of Human Rights: *Roncarelli v Duplessis* in Canadian Constitutional Culture." *McGill Law Journal* 55, no. 3 (2010): 437–60.
——. "The Idea of Constitutional Rights and the Transformation of Canadian Constitutional Law, 1930–1960." University of Toronto, 2009.
Ajzenstat, Janet. *The Canadian Founding: John Locke and Parliament*. Montreal: McGill–Queen's University Press, 2007.
Alberta Press Bill, Supreme Court Reports 100 (1938).
Anderson, Christopher G. *Canadian Liberalism and the Politics of Border Control, 1867–1967*. Vancouver: UBC Press, 2013.
Anderson, Donald. "The Development of Human Rights Protections in British Columbia." MA thesis, University of Victoria, 1986.
Anderson, Doris. *Rebel Daughter: An Autobiography*. Toronto: Key Porter Books, 1996.
Andiappan, P., M. Reavley, and S. Silver. "Discrimination against Pregnant Employees: An Analysis of Arbitration and Human Rights Tribunal Decisions in Canada." *Journal of Business Ethics* 9, no. 2 (1990): 143–51.
Arendt, Hannah. *The Origins of Totalitarianism*. New York: Schocken Books, 2004.
Axelrod, Paul. *Scholars and Dollars: Politics, Economics, and the Universities of Ontario, 1945–1980*. Toronto: University of Toronto Press, 1982.
Backhouse, Constance. *Colour-Coded: A Legal History of Racism in Canada, 1900–1950*. Toronto: University of Toronto Press, 1999.
Backhouse, Constance, and Leah Cohen. *The Secret Oppression: Sexual Harassment of Working Women*. Toronto: Macmillan, 1978.
Baehre, Rainer. "Trying the Rebels: Emergency Legislation and the Colonial Executive's Overall Legal Strategy in the Upper Canadian Rebellion." In *Canadian State Trials: Rebellion and Invasion in*

the Canadas, 1837–1839, edited by F. Murray Greenwood and Barry Wright. 41–61. Toronto: University of Toronto Press, 2002.

Bagnall, John C. "The Ontario Conservatives and the Development of Anti-Discrimination Policy." MA thesis, Queen's University, 1984.

Bangarth, Stephanie. *Voices Raised in Protest: Defending North American Citizens of Japanese Ancestry, 1942–49.* Vancouver: UBC Press, 2007.

Bangarth, Stephanie D. "'We Are Not Asking You to Open Wide the Gates for Chinese Immigration': The Committee for the Repeal of the Chinese Immigration Act and Early Human Rights Activism in Canada." *Canadian Historical Review* 84, no. 3 (2003): 395–422.

Behiels, Michael. "Canada and the Implementation of International Instruments of Human Rights: A Federalist Conundrum, 1919–1982." In *Framing Canadian Federalism: Historical Essays in Honour of John T. Saywell*, edited by Dimitry Anastakis and P.E. Bryden. 151–84. Toronto: University of Toronto Press, 2009.

Berger, Thomas. *Fragile Freedoms: Human Rights and Dissent in Canada.* Toronto: Clarke Irwin, 1981.

Berlin, Isaiah. *Four Essays on Liberty.* London: Oxford University Press, 1969.

Berry, Victoria, and Allan McChesney. "Human Rights and Foreign Policy-Making." In *Human Rights in Canadian Foreign Policy*, edited by Robert O. Matthews and Cranford Pratt. 59–76. Montreal and Kingston: McGill-Queen's University Press, 1988.

Black, David. "The Long and Winding Road: International Norms and Domestic Political Change in South Africa." In *The Power of Human Rights: International Norms and Domestic Change*, edited by Thomas Risse, Stephen C. Ropp, and Kathryn Sikkink. 78–108. Cambridge: Cambridge University Press, 1999.

Blake, Raymond. *From Rights to Needs: A History of Family Allowances in Canada, 1929–92.* Vancouver: UBC Press, 2008.

Blanchette, Arthur E. *Canadian Foreign Policy, 1945–2000: Major Documents and Speeches.* Kemptville: Golden Dog Press, 2000.

——. *Canadian Foreign Policy, 1977–1992: Selected Speeches and Documents.* Ottawa: Carleton University Press, 1994.

Block, W.E., and M.A. Walker, eds. *Discrimination, Affirmative Action, and Equal Opportunity: An Economic and Social Perspective.* Vancouver: Fraser Institute, 1982.

Bonser, Michael J. "Human Rights in Canadian Foreign Policy: From Principle to Practice." MA thesis, Acadia University, 1999.

Bothwell, Robert. *Alliance and Illusion: Canada and the World, 1945–1984.* Vancouver: UBC Press, 2007.

Bouchard, Gérard, and Charles Taylor. *Building for the Future: A Time for Reconciliation.* Quebec: Government of Quebec, 2008.

Boyd, Susan. "Is Equality Enough? Fathers' Rights and Women's Rights Advocacy." In *Rethinking Equality Projects in Law: Feminist Challenges*, edited by Rosemary Hunter. 59–79. Oxford: Hart Publishing, 2008.

British Columbia Human Rights Commission. *I'm Okay; We're Not So Sure about You: A Report of the BC Human Rights Commission on Extensions to the Code*. Victoria: 1983.

Brockman, Joan. *Gender in the Legal Profession: Fitting in or Breaking the Mould*. Vancouver: UBC Press, 2006.

Brodsky, Gwen. *Canadian Charter Equality Rights for Women: One Step Forward or Two Steps Back?* Ottawa: Canadian Advisory Council on the Status of Women, 1989.

Brouwer, Ruth Compton. "When Missions Became Development: Ironies of 'Ngoization' in Mainstream Canadian Churches in the 1960s." *Canadian Historical Review* 91, no. 4 (2010): 661–93.

Brown, R. Blake. "'Stars and Shamrocks Will Be Shown': The Fenian State Trials, 1866–7." In *Canadian State Trials: Political Trials and Security Measures*, edited by Barry Wright and Susan Binnie. 35–84. Toronto: University of Toronto Press, 2009.

Brown, Rosemary. *Being Brown: A Very Public Life*. Toronto: Random House, 1989.

Brysk, Alison. *Global Good Samaritans: Human Rights as Foreign Policy*. New York: Oxford University Press, 2009.

Buchanan, Allen. "The Egalitarianism of Human Rights." *Ethics* 120, no. 4 (2010): 679–710.

Burt, Sandra. "The Changing Patterns of Public Policy." In *Changing Patterns: Women in Canada*, edited by Sandra Burt, Lorraine Code, and Lindsay Dorney. 212–41. Toronto: McClelland and Stewart, 1993.

Cairns, Alan C. "The Past and Future of the Canadian Administrative State." *University of Toronto Law Journal* 40, no. 1 (1990): 319–63.

Canada. *Certain RCMP Activities and the Question of Governmental Knowledge*. Vol. 3. Ottawa: Queen's Printer, 1981.

———. *Freedom and Security under the Law: Commission of Inquiry Concerning Certain Activities of the Royal Canadian Mounted Police*. Vol. 2. Ottawa: Queen's Printer, 1981.

———. *Report of the Commission on Equality in Employment*. Ottawa: Queen's Printer, 1984.

———. *Report of the Committee on the Operation of the Abortion Law*. Ottawa: Minister of Supply and Services Canada, 1977.

———. *Security and Information*. Vol. 1. Ottawa: Queen's Printer, 1979.

———. *Special Committee on Human Rights and Fundamental Freedoms*. Ottawa: Queen's Printer, 1960.

———. *Special Committee on Human Rights and Fundamental Freedoms*. Ottawa: Queen's Printer, 1950.

———. *Special Joint Committee of the Senate and House of Commons on the Constitution of Canada: Final Report*. Ottawa: Queen's Printer, 1972.

———. *Special Joint Committee of the Senate and House of Commons on the Constitution of Canada: Minutes of Proceedings and Evidence*. Ottawa: Queen's Printer, 1970.

———. *Special Joint Committee of the Senate and the House of Commons on Human Rights and Fundamental Freedoms*. Ottawa: King's Printer, 1947.

———. *Statement of the Government of Canada on Indian Policy*. Ottawa: Queen's Printer, 1969.

Canada, Status of Women. *The Royal Commission on the Status of Women: An Overview 25 Years Later*. Ottawa: 1995.

Canada, Department of External Affairs. *Foreign Policy for Canadians*. Vol. 3. Ottawa: Queen's Printer, 1970.

Canadian Bar Association, Committee on the Constitution. *Towards a New Canada*. Ottawa: 1978.

Cardenas, Sonia. *Chains of Justice: The Global Rise of State Institutions for Human Rights*. Philadelphia: University of Pennsylvania Press, 2014.

Cardinal, Harold. *The Unjust Society*. Vancouver: Douglas & McIntyre, 1999.

Chambers, Lori. "'In the Name of the Father': Children, Naming Practices, and the Law in Canada." *UBC Law Review* 43, no. 1 (2010–11): 1–45.

———. "Newborn Adoption: Birth Mothers, Genetic Fathers, and Reproductive Autonomy." *Canadian Journal of Family Law* 26, no. 1 (2010): 339–93.

Chivers, Sally. "Barrier by Barrier: The Canadian Disability Movement and the Fight for Equal Rights." In *Group Politics and Social Movements in Canada*, edited by Miriam Smith. 159–80. Peterborough: Broadview Press, 2007.

Clarke, Frank K. "Debilitating Divisions: The Civil Liberties Movement in Early Cold War Canada, 1946–8." In *Whose National Security? Surveillance and the Creation of Enemies in Canada*, edited by Gary Kinsman. 171–87. Toronto: Between the Lines, 2000.

Clément, Dominique. *Canada's Rights Revolution: Social Movements and Social Change, 1937–1982*. Vancouver: UBC Press, 2008.

———. *Equality Deferred: Sex Discrimination and British Columbia's Human Rights State, 1953–1984*. Vancouver: UBC Press and the Osgoode Society for Canadian Legal History, 2014.

———. "Generations and the Transformation of Social Movements in Post-War Canada." *Histoire Sociale/Social History* 42, no. 84 (2009): 361–88.

——. "Human Rights in Canadian Domestic and Foreign Politics: From 'Nigardly Acceptance' to Enthusiastic Embrace." *Human Rights Quarterly* 34, no. 3 (2012): 751–78.

——. "'I Believe in Human Rights, Not Women's Rights': Women and the Human Rights State, 1969–1984." *Radical History Review* 101 (2008): 107–29.

——. "'It Is Not the Beliefs but the Crime That Matters:' Post-War Civil Liberties Debates in Canada and Australia." *Labour History (Australia)* 86 (May 2004): 1–32.

——. "The October Crisis of 1970: Human Rights Abuses under the War Measures Act." *Journal of Canadian Studies* 42, no. 2 (2008): 160–86.

——. "The Rights Revolution in Canada and Australia: International Politics, Social Movements, and Domestic Law." In *Taking Liberties: A History of Human Rights in Canada*, edited by Stephen Heathorn and David Goutor. 88–113. Toronto: Oxford University Press, 2013.

——. "The Royal Commission on Espionage and the Spy Trials of 1946–9: A Case Study in Parliamentary Supremacy." *Journal of the Canadian Historical Association* 11, no. 1 (2000): 151–72.

——. "Spies, Lies and a Commission, 1946–8: A Case Study in the Mobilization of the Canadian Civil Liberties Movement." *Left History* 7, no. 2 (2001): 53–79.

Clément, Dominique, Will Silver, and Dan Trottier. "The Evolution of Human Rights in Canada." Ottawa: Canadian Human Rights Commission, 2012.

Cmiel, Kenneth. "The Recent History of Human Rights." *American Historical Review* 109, no. 1 (2004): 117–35.

Cohen, Jean L. "Rethinking Human Rights, Democracy, and Sovereignty in the Age of Globalization." *Political Theory* 36, no. 4 (2008): 578–606.

Cohen, Marjorie Griffin. "Paid Work." In *Canadian Women's Issues*, Vol. 2: *Bold Visions*. 83–116. Toronto: James Lorimer, 1995.

Comités d'Organisation des Jeux Olympiques. *Montréal 1976: Official Report*, edited by COJO. Vol. 1. Montreal: 1976.

Compa, Lance. "Framing Labor's New Human Rights Movement." In *The Diffusion of Social Movements: Actors, Mechanisms, and Political Effects*. New York: Cambridge University Press, 2010.

Cook, Tim. *Warlords: Borden, Mackenzie King, and Canada's World Wars*. Toronto: Allen Lane, 2012.

Cornish, Mary, Fay Faraday, and Jo-Anne Pickel. *Enforcing Human Rights in Ontario*. Aurora: Canada Law Books, 2009.

Cotler, Irwin. "Human Rights as the Modern Tool of Revolution." In *Human Rights in the Twenty-First Century: A Global Challenge*, edited by Kathleen E. Mahoney and Paul Mahoney. London: Martinus Nijhoff Publishers, 1993.

Cranston, Maurice. *What Are Human Rights?* New York: Basic Books, 1973.

Davies, Alan, ed. *Antisemitism in Canada: History and Interpretation*. Waterloo: Wilfrid Laurier University Press, 1992.

Devall, W.B. "Support for Civil Liberties among English-Speaking Canadian University Students." *Canadian Journal of Political Science / Revue canadienne de science politique* 3, no. 3 (1970): 434–51.

Devereux, Annemarie. *Australia and the Birth of the International Bill of Human Rights, 1946–1966*. Sydney: Federation Press, 2005.

Dicey, A.V. *Introduction to the Study of the Law of the Constitution*. London: St. Martin's Press, 1962.

Dickinson, Greg M., and W. Rod Dolmage. "Education, Religion, and the Courts in Ontario." *Canadian Journal of Education* 21, no. 4 (1996): 363–83.

Dixon, Rosalind. "The Supreme Court of Canada and Constitutional (Equality) Baselines." *Osgoode Hall Law Journal* 50, no. 3 (2013): 637–69.

Donnelly, Jack. "Genocide and Humanitarian Intervention." *Journal of Human Rights* 1, no. 1 (2002): 93–109.

———. *International Human Rights*. Boulder: Westview Press, 1998.

———. *Universal Human Rights in Theory and Practice*. New York: Cornell University Press, 2003.

Ducharme, Michel. *Le Concept de liberté au Canada* à l'époque des révolutions Atlantiques 1776–1838. Montreal and Kingston: McGill-Queen's University Press, 2010.

Duclos, Nitya. "Disappearing Women: Racial Minority Women in Human Rights Cases." *Canadian Journal of Women and the Law* 6, no. 1 (1993): 25–51.

Eckel, Jan. "The International Human Rights Campaign Against Chile." In *Human Rights in the Twentieth Century*, edited by Stefan-Ludwig Hoffman. Cambridge: Cambridge University Press, 2011.

———. "The International League for the Rights of Man, Amnesty International, and the Changing Fate of Human Rights Activism from the 1940s through the 1970s." *Humanity* 4, no. 2 (2013): 183–214.

———. "The Rebirth of Politics from the Spirit of Morality: Explaining the Human Rights Revolution of the 1970s." In *The Breakthrough: Human Rights in the 1970s*, edited by Jan Eckel and Samuel Moyn. 226–59. Philadelphia: University of Pennsylvania Press, 2014.

Epp, Charles. *Making Rights Real: Activists, Bureaucrats, and the Creation of the Legalistic State*. Chicago: University of Chicago Press, 2009.

Epp, Charles R. *The Rights Revolution: Lawyers, Activists, and Supreme Courts in Comparative Perspective.* Chicago: University of Chicago Press, 1998.

Fletcher, Joseph F., and Paul Howe. "Public Opinion and Canada's Courts." In *Judicial Power and Canadian Democracy,* edited by Paul Howe and Peter H. Russell. 255–96. Montreal and Kingston: McGill–Queen's University Press, 2001.

Forsythe, David. *Human Rights in International Relations.* Cambridge: Cambridge University Press, 2006.

Foster, John W. "UN Commission on Human Rights." In *Human Rights in Canadian Foreign Policy,* edited by Robert O. Matthews and Cranford Pratt. 77–100. Montreal and Kingston: McGill–Queen's University Press, 1988.

Foweraker, Joe, and Todd Landman. *Citizenship Rights and Social Movements: A Comparative and Statistical Analysis.* Oxford: Oxford University Press, 1997.

Frager, Ruth A., and Carmela Patrias. *Discounted Labour: Women Workers in Canada, 1870–1939.* Toronto: University of Toronto Press, 2005.

Frager, Ruth, and Carmela Patrias. "'This Is Our Country, These Are Our Rights': Minorities and the Origins of Ontario's Human Rights Campaigns." *Canadian Historical Review* 82, no. 1 (2001): 1–35.

Freeman, Michael. *Human Rights: An Interdisciplinary Approach.* Cambridge: Polity Press, 2011.

Fudge, Judy. "The Effect of Entrenching a Bill of Rights upon Political Discourse: Feminist Demands and Sexual Violence in Canada." *International Journal of the Sociology of Law* 17, no. 4 (1989): 445–63.

Fudge, Judy, and Hester Lessard. "Challenging Norms and Creating Precedents: The Tale of a Woman Firefighter in the Forests of British Columbia." In *Challenging Norms and Creating Precedents,* edited by Judy Fudge and Eric Tucker. 315–54. Toronto: University of Toronto Press, 2010.

Gardiner, Robert. "Building a Counter-Consensus in Canada." In *Canadian Churches and Foreign Policy,* edited by Bonnie Greene. Toronto: James Lorimer, 1990.

Gearty, Conor. *Can Human Rights Survive?* Cambridge: Cambridge University Press, 2006.

Gecelovsky, Paul, and Tom Keating. "Liberal Internationalism for Conservatives: The Good Governance Initiative." In *Diplomatic Departures: The Conservative Era in Canadian Foreign Policy, 1984–1993,* edited by Kim Richard Nossal and Nelson Michaud. 194–207. Vancouver: UBC Press, 2001.

Gillespie, William A. "A History of the Newfoundland Federation of Labour, 1936–1963." MA thesis, Memorial University of Newfoundland, 1980.

Gillies, David. *Between Principle and Practice: Human Rights in North South Relations*. Montreal and Kingston: McGill-Queen's University Press, 1996.

Girard, Philip. "'If Two Ride a Horse, One Must Ride in Front': Married Women's Nationality and the Law in Canada 1880–1950." *Canadian Historical Review* 94, no. 1 (2013): 28–55.

Goldstein, Daniel M. "Whose Vernacular? Translating Human Rights in Local Contexts." In *Human Rights at the Crossroads*, edited by Mark Goodale. 111–21. New York: Oxford University Press, 2013.

Goodhart, Michael. "Human Rights and the Politics of Contention." In *Human Rights at the Crossroads*, edited by Mark Goodale. 31–44. New York: Oxford University Press, 2013.

Gordon, Nancy, and Bernard Wood. "Canada and the Reshaping of the United Nations." *International Journal* 47, no. 3 (1991): 479–503.

Graydon, Shari. "I Was a Slow Learner." In *Feminist Journeys*, edited by Marguerite Andersen. 157–62. Ottawa: Feminist History Society, 2010.

Greenwood, F. Murray. "The Drafting and Passage of the War Measures Act in 1914 and 1927: Object Lessons in the Need for Vigilance." In *Canadian Perspectives on Law and Society: Issues in Legal History*, edited by W. Wesley Pue and Barry Wright. 291–327. Ottawa: Carleton University Press, 1988.

——. "The Montreal Court Martial, 1838–9: Legal and Constitutional Reflections." In *Canadian State Trials: Rebellion and Invasion in the Canadas, 1837–1839*, edited by F. Murray Greenwood and Barry Wright. 325–52. Toronto: University of Toronto, 2002.

Greenwood, F. Murray, and Barry Wright, eds. *Canadian State Trials: Law, Politics, and Security Measures, 1608–1837*. Vol. 1. Toronto: University of Toronto Press, 1996.

——. "Introduction: Rebellion, Invasion, and the Crisis of the Colonial State in the Canadas, 1837–9." In *Canadian State Trials: Rebellion and Invasion in the Canadas, 1837–1839*, edited by F. Murray Greenwood and Barry Wright. 3–40. Toronto: University of Toronto Press, 2002.

——. "Introduction: State Trials, the Rule of Law, and Executive Powers in Early Canada." In *Canadian State Trials: Law, Politics, and Security Measures, 1608–1837*, edited by F. Murray Greenwood and Barry Wright. 3–54. Toronto: University of Toronto Press, 1996.

Gwynn, Richard. *Smallwood: The Unlikely Revolutionary*. Toronto: McClelland and Stewart, 1999.

Habermas, Jurgen. *Religion and Rationality: Essays on Reason, God, and Modernity*. Cambridge, MA: MIT Press, 2002.

Hay, Douglas. "Civilians Tried in Military Courts: Quebec, 1759–1764." In *Canadian State Trials: Law, Politics, and Security Measures, 1608–1837*, edited by F. Murray Greenwood and Barry Wright. 114–28. Toronto: University of Toronto Press, 1996.

Heaman, E.A. "Rights Talk and the Liberal Order Framework." In *Liberalism and Hegemony: Debating the Canadian Revolution*, edited by Jean-François Constant and Michel Ducharme. 147–75. Toronto: University of Toronto Press, 2009.

Herman, Didi. *Rights of Passage: Struggles for Lesbian and Gay Legal Equality*. Toronto: University of Toronto Press, 1994.

Hillebrecht, Courtney. "The Domestic Mechanisms of Compliance with International Human Rights Law: Case Studies from the Inter-American Human Rights System." *Human Rights Quarterly* 34, no. 2 (2012): 959–85.

Hobbins, A.J. "Eleanor Roosevelt, John Humphrey, and Canadian Opposition to the Universal Declaration of Human Rights: Looking Back on the 50th Anniversary of the UDHR." *International Journal* 53, no. 2 (1998): 325–42.

Hobsbawm, E.J. "Labour and Human Rights." In *Worlds of Labour: Further Studies in the History of Labour*, edited by E.J. Hobsbawm. 297–316. London: Weidenfeld and Nicolson, 1984.

Howe, R. Brian. "Incrementalism and Human Rights Reform." *Journal of Canadian Studies* 28, no. 3 (1993): 29–44.

Howe, R. Brian, and David Johnson. *Restraining Equality: Human Rights Commissions in Canada*. Toronto: University of Toronto Press, 2000.

Hunt, Lynn. *Inventing Human Rights: A History*. New York: W.W. Norton, 2007.

Hunter, Ian A. "Liberty and Equality: A Tale of Two Cities." *McGill Law Journal* 29, no. 1 (1983): 1–24.

Igartua, José. *The Other Quiet Revolution: National Identities in English Canada, 1945–1971*. Vancouver: UBC Press, 2008.

Ignatieff, Michael. *Human Rights as Politics and Idolatry*. Princeton: Princeton University Press, 2001.

——. *The Rights Revolution*. Toronto: House of Anansi, 2000.

International Council on Human Rights. "Performance and Legitimacy: National Human Rights Institutions." Geneva, Switzerland: 1999.

Ishay, Micheline R. *The History of Human Rights: From Ancient Times to the Globalization Era*. Berkeley: University of California Press, 2008.

Iyer, Nitya. "Categorical Denials: Equality Rights and the Shaping of Social Identity." *Queen's Law Journal* 19, no. 1 (1993): 179–207.

James, Matt. *Misrecognized Materialists: Social Movements in Canadian Constitutional Politics*. Vancouver: UBC Press, 2006.

Joas, Hans. *The Sacredness of the Person: A New Genealogy of Human Rights*. Washington: Georgetown University Press, 2013.

Kallen, Evelyn. *Ethnicity and Human Rights in Canada*. Don Mills: Oxford University Press, 2010.

———. *Ethnicity and Human Rights in Canada: A Human Rights Perspective on Ethnicity, Racism, and Systemic Inequality*. Toronto: Oxford University Press, 2003.

Kaplan, William. *Canadian Maverick: The Life and Times of Ivan C. Rand*. Toronto: University of Toronto Press, 2009.

Kealey, Gregory S. "State Repression of Labour and the Left in Canada, 1914–1920: The Impact of the First World War." *Canadian Historical Review* 73, no. 3 (1992): 281–315.

Keck, Margaret E., and Kathryn Sikkink. *Activists Beyond Borders: Advocacy Networks in International Politics*. Ithaca: Cornell University Press, 1998.

Keenleyside, T.A., and Patricia Taylor. *The Impact of Human Rights Violations on the Conduct of Canadian Bilateral Relations: A Contemporary Dilemma*. Toronto: Canadian Institute of International Affairs, 1984.

Kelly, James B. *Governing with the Charter: Legislative and Judicial Activism and Framers' Intent*. Vancouver: UBC Press, 2005.

Keshen, Jeffrey A. *Propoganda and Censorship during Canada's Great War*. Edmonton: University of Alberta Press, 1996.

Knight, Amy. *How the Cold War Began: The Gouzenko Affair and the Hunt for Soviet Spies*. Toronto: McClelland and Stewart, 2005.

Knopff, Rainer. *Human Rights and Social Technology: The New War on Discrimination*. Ottawa: Carleton University Press, 1989.

Knopff, Rainer, and F.L. Morton. *The Charter Revolution and the Court Party*. Peterborough: Broadview Press, 2000.

———. "Canada's Court Party." In *Perspectives on Canadian Constitutional Reform, Interpretation, and Theory*, edited by Anthony A. Peacock. 63–87. Toronto: Oxford University Press, 1996.

Korey, William. *NGOs and the Universal Declaration of Human Rights: "A Curious Grapevine."* New York: Palgrave, 1998.

Korinek, Valerie. "'The Most Openly Gay Person for at Least a Thousand Miles': Doug Wilson and the Politicization of a Province." *Canadian Historical Review* 84, no. 4 (2003): 516–51.

Kulchinsky, Peter. *Aboriginal Rights Are Not Human Rights*. Winnipeg: ARP Books, 2013.

Lambertson, Ross. "Domination and Dissent." In *A History of Human Rights in Canada*, edited by Janet Miron. 1–26. Toronto: Canadian Scholars' Press, 2009.

———. "The Dresden Story: Racism, Human Rights, and the Jewish Labour Committee of Canada." *Labour/Le Travail* 47 (2001): 43–82.

———. *Repression and Resistance: Canadian Human Rights Activists, 1930–1960.* Toronto: University of Toronto Press, 2005.

———. "Suppression and Subversion." In *A History of Human Rights in Canada*, edited by Janet Miron. 27–42. Toronto: Canadian Scholars' Press, 2009.

Larsen, Mike, and Kevin Walby, eds. *Brokering Access: Power, Politics, and Freedom of Information Process in Canada.* Vancouver: UBC Press, 2012.

Lauren, Paul Gordon. *The Evolution of International Human Rights: Visions Seen.* Philadelphia: University of Pennsylvania Press, 2011.

Lessard, Hester. "Mothers, Fathers, and Naming: Reflections on the Law Equality Framework and *Trociuk v. British Columbia (Attorney General).*" *Canadian Journal of Women and the Law* 16, no. 1 (2004): 165–211.

Lichtenstein, Nelson. "The Rights Revolution." *New Labor Forum* 12, no. 1 (2003): 61–73.

Little, Margaret Hillyard. "Claiming a Unique Place: The Introduction of Mothers' Pensions in British Columbia." *BC Studies* 105–6 (Spring-Summer 1995): 80–102.

Long, David. "Culture, Ideology, and Militancy: The Movement of Native Indians in Canada, 1969–91." In *Organizing Dissent: Contemporary Social Movements in Theory and in Practice*, edited by William K. Carroll. 151–70. Toronto: Garamond Press, 1997.

Lui, Andrew. *Why Canada Cares: Human Rights and Foreign Policy in Theory and Practice.* Montreal and Kingston: McGill-Queen's University Press, 2012.

Mackenzie, J.B. "Section 98, Criminal Code, and Freedom of Expression in Canada." *Queen's Quarterly* 1, no. 1 (1971–2): 469–85.

MacLennan, Christopher. *Toward the Charter: Canadians and the Demand for a National Bill of Rights, 1929–1960.* Montreal and Kingston: McGill-Queen's University Press, 2003.

Madsen, Mikael Rask, and Gert Verschraegen. "Making Human Rights Intelligible: An Introduction to a Sociology of Human Rights." In *Making Human Rights Intelligible*, edited by Mikael Rask Madsen and Gert Verschraegen. 1–24. Portland: Hart Publishing, 2013.

Mandel, Michael. *The Charter of Rights and the Legislation of Politics in Canada.* Toronto: Thompson Educational Publishing, 1994.

Manfredi, Christopher. *Feminist Activism in the Supreme Court: Legal Mobilization and the Women's Legal Education and Action Fund.* Vancouver: UBC Press, 2004.

Marshall, Dominique. "The Cold War, Canada, and the United Nations Declaration of the Rights of the Child." In *Canada and the Early Cold War, 1943–1957,* edited by Greg Donaghy. 183–214. Ottawa: Department of Foreign Affairs and International Trade, 1998.

———. "The Language of Childen's Rights, the Formation of the Welfare State, and the Democratic Experience of Poor Families in Quebec, 1940–55." *Canadian Historical Review* 78, no. 3 (1997): 409–43.

Marx, Herbert. "Notes and Comments: The Montreal Anti-Demonstration Bylaw—'Bed Everywhere.'" *Manitoba Law Journal* 4, no. 1 (1970–1): 347–56.

Mathieu, Sarah-Jane. *North of the Color Line: Migration and Black Resistance in Canada, 1870–1955.* Chapel Hill: University of North Carolina Press, 2010.

Maul, Daniel Roger. "The International Labour Organization and the Globalization of Rights, 1944–1970." In *Human Rights in the Twentieth Century,* edited by Stefan-Ludwig Hoffman. 301–20. Cambridge: Cambridge University Press, 2011.

Mazower, Mark. "The Strange Triumph of Human Rights, 1933–1950." *Historical Journal* 47, no. 2 (2004): 379–98.

McCartin, Joseph A. "Democratizing the Demand for Workers' Rights." *Dissent* 1 (2005): 61–8.

———. *Labor's Great War: The Struggle for Industrial Democracy and the Origins of Modern American Labor Relations, 1912–1921.* Chapel Hill: University of North Carolina Press, 1997.

McChesney, Allan. "Aboriginal Communities, Aboriginal Rights, and the Human Rights System." In *Human Rights in Cross-Cultural Perspectives: A Quest for Consensus,* edited by Abdullahi Ahmed An-Na'im. 221–52. Philadelphia: University of Pennsylvania Press, 1992.

Mckay, Ian. "The Liberal Order Framework: A Prospectus for a Reconnaissance of Canadian History." *Canadian Historical Review* 81, no. 4 (2000): 617–51.

McLachlin, Beverley. "The Charter 25 Years Later: The Good, the Bad, and the Challenges." *Osgoode Hall Law Journal* 45, no. 2 (2007): 365–77.

Mertus, Julie A. *Human Rights Matters: Local Politics and National Human Rights Institutions.* Stanford: Stanford University Press, 2008.

Miller, J.R. "D'alton Mccarthy, Equal Rights, and the Origins of the Manitoba Schools Question." *Canadian Historical Review* 54, no. 4 (1973): 369–92.

———. "Human Rights for Some: First Nations Rights in Twentieth-Century Canada." In *Taking Liberties: A History of Human Rights in Canada*, edited by Stephen Heathorn and David Goutor. 233–60. Toronto: Oxford University Press, 2013.

Minow, Martha. *Making All the Difference: Inclusion, Exclusion, and American Law*. Ithaca: Cornell University Press, 1990.

———. *Not Only for Myself: Identity, Politics, and the Law*. New York: New Press, 1997.

Moogk, Peter N. "The Crime of Lèse-Majesté in New France: Defence of the Secular and Religious Order." In *Canadian State Trials: Law, Politics, and Security Measures, 1608–1837*, edited by F. Murray Greenwood and Barry Wright. 55–71. Toronto: University of Toronto Press, 1996.

Moravcsik, Andrew. "The Paradox of U.S. Human Rights Policy." In *American Exceptionalism and Human Rights*, edited by Michael Ignatieff. 147–96. Princeton: Princeton University Press, 2005.

Morel, André. "Le Charte Québécoise: Un Document unique dans l'histoire législative canadienne." *Revue juridique themis* 21, no. 1 (1987): 1–23.

Moyn, Samual. *The Last Utopia: Human Rights in History*. Boston: Belknap Press of Harvard University Press, 2010.

Neufeldt, Aldred H. "Growth and Evolution of Disability Advocacy in Canada." In *Making Equality: History of Advocacy and Persons with Disabilities in Canada*, edited by Deborah Stienstra and Ailee Wight-Felske. 11–32. Concord: Captus Press, 2003.

Nolan, Cathal J. "Human Rights in Canadian Foreign Policy." In *Human Rights in Canadian Foreign Policy*, edited by Robert O. Matthews and Cranford Pratt. 101–14. Montreal and Kingston: McGill-Queen's University Press, 1988.

———. "The Influence of Parliament on Human Rights in Canadian Foreign Policy." *Human Rights Quarterly* 7, no. 3 (1985): 373–90.

———. "Reluctant Liberal: Canada, Human Rights, and the United Nations." *Diplomacy and Statecraft* 2, no. 3 (1990): 281–305.

Norman, Ken. "Saskatchewan's One Bright Shining Moment, at Least It Seemed So at the Time." In *14 Arguments in Favour of Human Rights Institutions*, edited by Shelagh Day, Lucie Lamarche, and Ken Norman. 87–110. Toronto: Irwin Law, 2014.

Nossal, Kim Richard. "Cabin'd, Cribb'd, Confin'd: Canada's Interests in Human Rights." In *Human Rights in Canadian Foreign Policy*, edited by Robert O. Matthews and Cranford Pratt. 23–45. Montreal and Kingston: McGill-Queen's University Press, 1988.

Nossal, Kim Richard, Stéphane Roussel, and Stéphane Paquin. *International Policy and Politics in Canada*. Toronto: Pearson Canada, 2011.

Olzak, Susan. *The Global Dynamics of Racial and Ethnic Mobilization*. Stanford: Stanford University Press, 2006.

Ontario. *Report of the Royal Commission Inquiry into Civil Rights*. Toronto: Queen's Printer, 1968.

Ontario Human Rights Commission. *Life Together: A Report on Human Rights in Ontario*. Toronto: 1977.

Pal, Leslie. *Interests of State: The Politics of Language, Multiculturalism, and Feminism in Canada*. Montreal and Kingston: McGill-Queen's University Press, 1993.

Palmer, Bryan. *Working Class Experience: Rethinking the History of Canadian Labour, 1800–1991*. Toronto: McClelland & Stewart, 1992.

Paltiel, Jeremy T. "Negotiating Human Rights with China." In *Canada Among Nations 1995: Democracy and Foreign Policy*, edited by Maxwell A. Cameron and Mauree Appel Molot. 165–86. Ottawa: Carleton University Press, 1995.

Papineau, Louis-Joseph. *Journal d'un fils de la liberté, réfugié aux États-Unis, par suite de l'insurrection canadienne, en 1837*. Montreal: Réédition-Québec, 1972.

Patrias, Carmela. "Race, Employment Discrimination, and State Complicity in Wartime Canada, 1939–1945." *Labour/Le Travail* 59 (2007): 9–42.

———. "Socialists, Jews, and the 1947 Saskatchewan Bill of Rights." *Canadian Historical Review* 87, no. 2 (2006): 265–92.

Pegram, Thomas. "Diffusion Across Political Systems: The Global Spread of National Human Rights Institutions." *Human Rights Quarterly* 32, no. 3 (2010): 729–60.

Pendas, Devin O. "Toward World Law? Human Rights and the Failure of the Legalist Paradigm of War." In *Human Rights in the Twentieth Century*, edited by Stefan-Ludwig Hoffman. 215–36. Cambridge: Cambridge University Press, 2011.

Petryshyn, J. "A.E. Smith and the Canadian Labour Defence League." PhD diss., University of Western Ontario, 1977.

———. "Class Conflict and Civil Liberties: The Origins and Activities of the Canadian Labour Defense League, 1925–1940." *Labour/Le Travail* 10 (1982): 39–63.

Pitsula, James M. *Keeping Canada British: The Ku Klux Klan in 1920s Saskatchewan*. Vancouver: UBC Press, 2013.

Porter, Bruce. "Twenty Years of Equality Rights: Reclaiming Expectations." *Windsor Y.B. Access Justice* 23, no. 1 (2005): 145–92.

Pothier, Diane. "Connecting Grounds of Discrimination to Real People's Real Experiences." *Canadian Journal of Women and the Law* 13, no. 1 (2001): 37–73.

Prentice, Allison, Paula Bourne, Gail Cuthbert Brandt, Beth Light, Wendy Mitchenson, and Naomi Black. *Canadian Women: A History.* Toronto: Harcourt Brace, 1996.

Pries, Kari Mariska. "Repression, Freedom, and Minimal Geography: Human Rights, Humanitarian Law, and Canadian Involvement in El Salvador, 1977–1984." MA thesis, Queen's University, 2007.

Quataert, Jean H. *Advocating Dignity.* Philadelphia: University of Pennsylvania Press, 2009.

Quebec. *Quebec-Canada: A New Deal.* Quebec City: 1979.

Quebec. Commission of Inquiry into the Administration of Justice on Criminal and Penal Matters in Quebec. *Crime, Justice, and Society.* Quebec City: 1969.

Rabinovitch, Shelley Tsivia. "Teaching the Personal Is Political." In *Feminist Journeys,* edited by Marguerite Andersen. 283–86. Ottawa: Feminist History Society, 2010.

Radforth, Ian. "Collective Rights, Liberal Discourse, and Public Order: The Clash over Catholic Processions in Mid-Victorian Toronto." *Canadian Historical Review* 95, no. 4 (2014): 511–45.

Ramos, Howard. "Aboriginal Protest." In *Social Movements,* edited by Suzanne Staggenborg. 55–70. Toronto: Oxford University Press, 2007.

———. "Divergent Paths: Aboriginal Mobilization in Canada, 1951–2000." PhD diss., McGill University, 2004.

———. "What Causes Canadian Aboriginal Protest? Examining Resources, Opportunities, and Identity, 1951–2000." *Canadian Journal of Sociology* 31, no. 2 (2006): 211–35.

Réaume, Denise G. "Of Pigeonholes and Principles: A Reconsideration of Discrimination Law." *Osgoode Hall Law Journal* 40, no. 1 (2002): 113–44.

Rebick, Judy. *Ten Thousand Roses: The Making of a Feminist Revolution.* Toronto: Penguin Canada, 2005.

Reif, Linda. "Building Democratic Institutions: The Role of National Human Rights Institutions in Good Governance and Human Rights Protection." *Harvard Human Rights Journal* 13 (2000): 1–69.

Riddell, Maureen. *The Evolution of Human Rights Legislation in Alberta, 1945–1979.* Edmonton: Government of Alberta, 1978–79.

Risse, Thomas, Stephen C. Ropp, and Kathryn Sikkink, eds. *The Power of Human Rights: International Norms and Domestic Change.* Cambridge: Cambridge University Press, 1999.

Rosen, Philip. "Hate Propoganda." Edited by Parliamentary Research Branch. Ottawa: Library of Parliament, 2000.

Russell, Peter. "Colonization of Indigenous Peoples: The Movement Toward New Relationships." In *Parties Long Estranged: Canada and Australia in the Twentieth Century*, edited by Margaret MacMillan and Francie McKenzie. 62–95. Vancouver: UBC Press, 2003.

Schabas, William A. "Canada and the Adoption of the Universal Declaration of Human Rights." *McGill Law Journal* 43, no. 2 (1998): 403–44.

Scharfe, Sharon. "Blood on Their Hands: Human Rights in Canadian Foreign Policy? A Case Study of the Canada–Indonesia Relationship." MA thesis, Carleton University, 1994.

Schmitz, Gerald J. "Human Rights, Democratization, and International Conflict." In *Canada Among Nations, 1992–1993: A New World Order?*, edited by Fen Osler Hampson and Christopher J. Maule. 235–55. Ottawa: Carleton University Press, 1992.

Scott, Frank. *Essays on the Constitution: Aspects of Canadian Law and Politics.* Toronto: University of Toronto Press, 1977.

Sellars, Kirsten. *The Rise and Rise of Human Rights.* Phoenix Mill: Sutton Publishing, 2002.

Sharpe, Robert J., and Kent Roach. *Brian Dickson: A Judge's Journey.* Toronto: University of Toronto Press, 2003.

Shelton, Dinah. "The Environmental Jurisprudence of International Human Rights Tribunals." In *Linking Human Rights and the Environment*, edited by Romina Picolotti and Jorge Daniel Taillant. 1–30. Tucson: University of Arizona Press, 2003.

Sheppard, Colleen. "The Promise and Practice of Protecting Human Rights: Reflections on the Quebec *Charter of Human Rights and Freedoms*." In *Mélanges*, edited by Paul-André Crépeau. 641–78. Cowanville: Les Éditions Yvon Blais, 1997.

Shue, Henry. *Basic Rights: Subsistence, Affluence, and U.S. Foreign Policy.* Princeton: Princeton University Press, 1996.

Smith, David Edward. "Emergency Government in Canada." *Canadian Historical Review* 50, no. 4 (1969): 429–49.

Smith, Miriam. *A Civil Society? Collective Actors in Canadian Political Life.* Peterborough: Broadview Press, 2005.

——. "Identity and Opportunity: The Lesbian and Gay Rights Movement." In *Group Politics and Social Movements in Canada*, edited by Miriam Smith. 159–80. Peterborough: Broadview Press, 2007.

Snyder, Sarah. *Human Rights Activism and the End of the Cold War: A Transnational History of the Helsinki Network.* Cambridge: Cambridge University Press, 2011.

Songer, Donald R., Susan W. Johnson, and Jennifer Barnes Bowie. "Do Bills of Rights Matter? An Examination of Court Change, Judicial Ideology, and the Support Structure for Rights in Canada." *Osgoode Hall Law Journal* 51, no. 1 (2013): 297–329.

Soohoo, Cynthia. "Human Rights and the Transformation of the 'Civil Rights' and 'Civil Liberties' Lawyer." In *Bringing Human Rights Home: A History of Human Rights in the United States*, edited by Cynthia Soohoo, Catherine Albisa, and Martha F. Davis. 71–104. Westport: Praeger, 2008.

Soohoo, Cynthia, Catherine Albisa, and Martha F. Davis, eds. *Bringing Human Rights Home: A History of Human Rights in the United States*. Westport: Praeger, 2008.

Stammers, Neil. *Human Rights and Social Movements*. London: Pluto Press, 2009.

Stanley, Timothy J. *Contesting White Supremacy: School Segregation, Anti-Racism, and the Making of Chinese Canadians*. Vancouver: UBC Press, 2011.

Steinhart, Allan L. *Civil Censorship in Canada during World War I*. Toronto: Unitrade Press, 1986.

Struthers, James. *The Limits of Affluence: Welfare in Ontario, 1920–1970*. Toronto: University of Toronto Press, 1994.

Tarnopolsky, Walter Surma. *Discrimination and the Law in Canada*. Toronto: De Boo, 1982.

Thomas, Lewis H. "Documents of Western History: Louis Riel's Petition of Rights, 1884." *Saskatchewan History* 23, no. 3 (1970): 16–26.

Troper, Harold. "The Creek Negroes of Oklahoma and Canadian Immigration, 1909–11." *Canadian Historical Review* 53, no. 3 (1972): 272–99.

Tucker, Erik. "The Constitutional Right to Bargain Collectively: The Ironies of Labour History in the Supreme Court of Canada." *Labour/Le Travail* 61, no. 1 (2008): 151–82.

Tulchinsky, Gerald. *Branching Out: The Transformation of the Canadian Jewish Community*. Toronto: Stoddart, 1998.

——. *Canada's Jews: A People's Journey*. Toronto: University of Toronto Press, 2008.

Tunnicliffe, Jennifer. "'Life Together': Public Debates over Human Rights Legislation in Ontario, 1975–1981." *Histoire Sociale/Social History* 46, no. 92 (2013): 443–70.

Turner, Frank M., ed. *Reflections on the Revolution in France*. New Haven: Yale University Press, 2003.

Vanhala, Lisa. *Making Rights a Reality?: Disability Rights Activists and Legal Mobilization*. Cambridge: Cambridge University Press, 2010.

Vincent, Andrew. *The Politics of Human Rights*. Oxford: Oxford University Press, 2010.

Vipond, Mary. "Censorship in a Liberal State: Regulating Talk on Canadian Radio in the Early 1990s." *Historical Journal of Film, Radio, and Television* 30, no. 1 (2010): 75–94.

Waldron, Jeremy, ed. *'Nonsense upon Stilts': Bentham, Burke, and Marx on the Rights of Man*. London and New York: Methuen, 1987.

Waldron, Mary Anne. *Free to Believe: Rethinking Freedom of Conscience and Religion in Canada*. Toronto: University of Toronto Press, 2013.

Walker, James St.G. "The 'Jewish Phase' in the Movement for Racial Equality in Canada." *Canadian Ethnic Studies* 34, no. 1 (2002): 1–29.

——. *"Race," Rights, and the Law in the Supreme Court of Canada: Historical Case Studies*. Waterloo: Wilfrid Laurier University Press, 1997.

Warner, Tom. *Never Going Back: A History of Queer Activism in Canada*. Toronto: University of Toronto Press, 2002.

Watson, Don. *Brian Fitzpatrick: A Radical Life*. Sydney: Hale & Iremonger, 1979.

Watt, Steven. "State Trial by Legislature: The Special Council of Lower Canada, 1838–41." In *Canadian State Trials: Rebellion and Invasion in the Canadas, 1837–1839*, F. Murray Greenwood and Barry Wright. 248–78. Toronto: University of Toronto Press, 2002.

Weaver, Sally. "First Nations Women and Government Policy, 1970–92: Discrimination and Conflict." In *Changing Patterns: Women in Canada*, edited by Sandra Burt, Lorraine Code, and Lindsay Dorney. 92–147. Toronto: McClelland and Stewart, 1988.

Webster, David. "Canada and Bilateral Human Rights Dialogues." *Canadian Foreign Policy Journal* 16, no. 3 (2010): 43–63.

——. *Fire and the Full Moon: Canada and Indonesia in the Decolonizing World*. Vancouver: UBC Press, 2009.

Wellman, Carl. *The Proliferation of Rights: Moral Progress or Empty Rhetoric?* Boulder: Westview Press, 1999.

Whitaker, Reg, Gregory S. Kealey, and Andrew Parnaby. *Secret Service: Political Policing in Canada from the Fenians to Fortress America*. Toronto: University of Toronto Press, 2012.

Whitaker, Reg, and Gary Marcuse. *Cold War Canada: The Making of a National Insecurity State, 1945–1957*. Toronto: University of Toronto Press, 1994.

Whiteside, Don. "Historical Development of Aboriginal Political Associations in Canada." Ottawa: National Indian Brotherhood, 1973.

Wiegers, Wanda. "Gender, Biology, and Third Part Custody Disputes." *Alberta Law Review* 47, no. 1 (2009): 1–37.

Williams, George. *Human Rights Under the Australian Constitution*. Melbourne: Oxford University Press, 1999.

Williams, Shannon. "Human Rights in Theory and Practice: A Sociological Study of Aboriginal Peoples and the New Brunswick Human Rights Commission, 1967–1997." MA thesis, University of New Brunswick, 1998.

Wilson, David A. "The D'arcy McGee Affair and the Suspension of Habeas Corpus." In *Canadian State Trials: Political Trials and Security Measures, 1840–1914*, edited by Barry Wright and Susan Binnie. 85–122. Toronto: University of Toronto Press, 2009.

Winks, Robin W. "Negro School Segregation in Ontario and Nova Scotia." *Canadian Historical Review* 50, no. 2 (1969): 164–92.

Women Unite! An Anthology of the Canadian Women's Movement. Toronto: Canadian Women's Educational Press, 1972.

Wood, Lesley J. *Direct Action, Deliberation, and Diffusion: Collective Action after the WTO Protests in Seattle.* Cambridge: Cambridge University Press, 2012.

Wright, Andrea. "Formulaic Comparisons: Stopping the Charter at the Statutory Human Rights Gate." In *Making Equality Rights Real: Securing Substantive Equality Under the Charter*, edited by Fay Faraday, Margaret Denike, and M. Kate Stephenson. 409–41. Toronto: Irwin Law, 2006.

Wright, Barry. "The Kingston and London Courts Martial." In *Canadian State Trials: Rebellion and Invasion in the Canadas, 1837–1839*, edited by F. Murray Greenwood and Barry Wright. 130–59. Toronto: University of Toronto Press, 2002.

Yalden, Maxwell. *Transforming Rights: Reflections from the Front Lines.* Toronto: University of Toronto Press, 2009.

Index

Abella, Rosalie, 123

Aboriginal peoples: access to democratic rights, 175n20; associations of, 175n22; complaints about, 185n91; demands for self-government, 144; discrimination of, 38–39, 118, 175n21, 187n126; engagement in human rights policy, 111–12; government policy toward, 79; human rights claims, 144; marginalization of, 38–39, 164n69, 164n70; residential schools, 39, 165n73; rights traditions of, 24; segregation of, 35–36

Aboriginal rights: *vs.* universal human rights, 143

Aboriginal rights movement, 78–79, 179n19

Aboriginal women, 164–65n71

abortion, 1, 33, 42, 44, 110, 111, 192n40; and *Charter of Rights and Freedoms*, 14; federal inquiry (1977), 116; partly legalized (1969), 78; Supreme Court decision (1988), 129; polling results on, 86. *See also* Morgentaler, Henry

Action League for the Physically Handicapped Advancement (ALPHA), 81–82

African Americans: civil rights activism of, 155n24

African Canadians: forced relocation of, 86; human rights activism of, 155n24; social movement organizations, 94

Africville (N.S.), 86

Ajzenstat, Janet, 33

Alberta: *Act to Ensure the Publication of Accurate News and Information*, 46; *Bill of Rights*, 103; discrimination based on sexual orientation in, 135–36, 140; employment practices, 124, 188n11; *Land Sales Prohibition Act*, 38; press censorship in, 46; restriction of common law marriages, 135; sexual minorities in, 133–34, 134–35

Alberta Human Rights Association, 80

Alberta Human Rights Commission, 134

Alberta Lesbian and Gay Rights Association, 134

Alexander v British Columbia, 125–26

Alien Act, 27

Allende, Salvador, 97

American Declaration of the Rights of Man, 75

Amnesty International (AI): campaign against Pinochet's dictatorship, 97; effectiveness of, 180n34; engagement in human rights politics, 98, 114; foundation of, 75

Laurier Studies in Political Philosophy Series
Published by Wilfrid Laurier University Press